Tim Wallace-Murphy studied medicine at University College, Dublin and then qualified as a psychologist. He is now an author, lecturer and historian, and has spent over 30 years following his personal spiritual path. He has written several bestsellers: *The Mark of the Beast* (with Trevor Ravenscroft), *Rex Deus, The True Mystery of Rennes-Le-Château* and *Rosslyn: Guardian of the Secrets of the Holy Grail* (with Marilyn Hopkins), used by Dan Brown as source material for his best-selling novel, *The Da Vinci Code*, and more recently, *Cracking the Symbol Code*. He lives in Devon.

BY THE SAME AUTHOR

The Mark of the Beast – with Trevor Ravenscroft

An Illustrated Guidebook to Rosslyn Chapel

The Templar Legacy and the Masonic Inheritance within Rosslyn Chapel

Rosslyn – Guardian of the Secrets of the Holy Grail –
  with Marilyn Hopkins

*Rex Deus, The True Mystery of Rennes-le-Château and the Dynasty
  of Jesus* – with Marilyn Hopkins & Graham Simmans

Templars in America – with Marilyn Hopkins

Custodians of Truth – with Marilyn Hopkins

Cracking the Symbol Code

What Islam Did for Us

The Enigma of the Freemasons

THE KNIGHTS *of* THE HOLY GRAIL

THE SECRET HISTORY OF THE KNIGHTS TEMPLAR

TIM WALLACE-MURPHY

WATKINS PUBLISHING

LONDON

Distributed in the United States and Canada by
Sterling Publishing Co., Inc.
387 Park Avenue South, New York, NY 10016-8810

This edition published in the UK 2007 by
Watkins Publishing, Sixth Floor, Castle House,
75–76 Wells Street, London W1T 3QH

1 3 5 7 9 10 8 6 4 2

Designed and typeset by Jerry Goldie Graphic Design

Printed and bound in Great Britain

Library of Congress Cataloging-in-Publication data available

ISBN-10: 1-905857-33-0
ISBN-13: 978-1-905857-33-3

For information about custom editions, special sales, premium and
corporate purchases, please contact Sterling Special Sales
Department at 800-805-5489 or specialsales@sterlingpub.com

www.watkinspublishing.com

For my spiritual brother,
Niven Sinclair of London,
the best friend a man could
wish for.

ACKNOWLEDGEMENTS

No work such as this is ever produced without the help, encouragement and support of a large number of people. And while responsibility for this book rests entirely with the author, I gratefully acknowledge the assistance received from: Paul Amorus of the Moulin de Soleils, Provence; Stuart Beattie of the Rosslyn Chapel Trust; Richard Beaumont of Staverton, Devon; Laurence Bloom of London; Robert Brydon of Edinburgh; Richard Buades of Marseilles; Mike Cooke of Nice; Nicole Dawe of Okehampton; Baroness Edni di Pauli of London; David Fayle of Taunton; Jean-Michel Garnier of Chartres; Thierry Garnier of Marseilles; Antonia Goodland-Clark of Cannes; Michael Halsey of Auchterarder; Marilyn Hopkins of Harberton; the late Guy Jourdan of Bargemon, Provence; Georges Keiss of the Centre d'Études et de Recherches Templière, Campagne-sur-Aude; the late Michael Monkton of Buckingham; James Mackay Munro of Edinburgh; Andrew Pattison of Edinburgh; Alan Pearson of Rennes-les-Bains; David Pykett of Burton-on-Trent; Amy Ralston of Staverton, Devon; Victor Rosati of Totnes; Pat Sibille of Aberdeen; Niven Sinclair of London; Anne Young of Antibes; Prince Michael of Albany; my editorial consultant John Baldock and, last, but certainly not least, Michael Mann and Penny Stopa of Watkins Publishing.

CONTENTS

SECTION 1
GNOSTICISM, JUDAISM, CHRISTIANITY & ISLAM

SECTION 2
THE KNIGHTS TEMPLAR

SECTION 3

THE WORLDWIDE PROPAGATION OF REX DEUS
& TEMPLAR BELIEFS

LIST OF PLATES

AREAS OF REX DEUS INFLUENCE IN EUROPE: 11TH–15TH CENTURIES

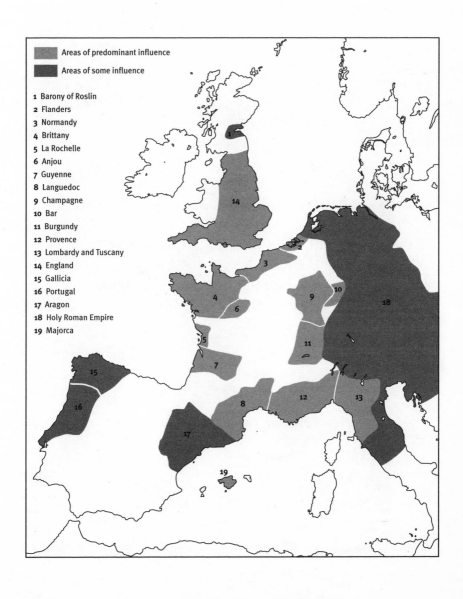

Areas of predominant influence

Areas of some influence

1 Barony of Roslin
2 Flanders
3 Normandy
4 Brittany
5 La Rochelle
6 Anjou
7 Guyenne
8 Languedoc
9 Champagne
10 Bar
11 Burgundy
12 Provence
13 Lombardy and Tuscany
14 England
15 Gallicia
16 Portugal
17 Aragon
18 Holy Roman Empire
19 Majorca

PRINCIPAL TEMPLAR PROPERTIES FROM THE ORDER'S FOUNDATION PRIOR TO 1150

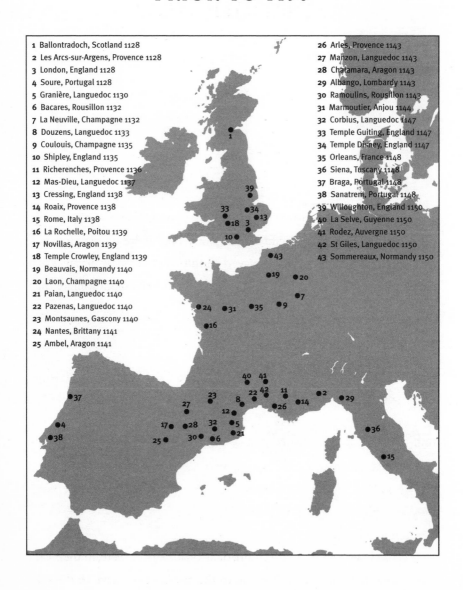

1 Ballontradoch, Scotland 1128
2 Les Arcs-sur-Argens, Provence 1128
3 London, England 1128
4 Soure, Portugal 1128
5 Granière, Languedoc 1130
6 Bacares, Rousillon 1132
7 La Neuville, Champagne 1132
8 Douzens, Languedoc 1133
9 Coulouis, Champagne 1135
10 Shipley, England 1135
11 Richerenches, Provence 1136
12 Mas-Dieu, Languedoc 1137
13 Cressing, England 1138
14 Roaix, Provence 1138
15 Rome, Italy 1138
16 La Rochelle, Poitou 1139
17 Novillas, Aragon 1139
18 Temple Crowley, England 1139
19 Beauvais, Normandy 1140
20 Laon, Champagne 1140
21 Paian, Languedoc 1140
22 Pazenas, Languedoc 1140
23 Montsaunes, Gascony 1140
24 Nantes, Brittany 1141
25 Ambel, Aragon 1141

26 Arles, Provence 1143
27 Manzon, Languedoc 1143
28 Chalamara, Aragon 1143
29 Albango, Lombardy 1143
30 Ramoulins, Rousillon 1143
31 Marmoutier, Anjou 1144
32 Corbius, Languedoc 1147
33 Temple Guiting, England 1147
34 Temple Disney, England 1147
35 Orleans, France 1148
36 Siena, Tuscany 1148
37 Braga, Portugal 1148
38 Sanatrem, Portugal 1148
39 Willoughton, England 1150
40 La Selve, Guyenne 1150
41 Rodez, Auvergne 1150
42 St Giles, Languedoc 1150
43 Sommereaux, Normandy 1150

Introduction

The origins of the Order of the Knights Templar are shrouded in mystery and a matter of dispute that is under active investigation, yet the order grew in size, power and influence with amazing speed and attained an apparently unassailable position within Christian Europe with bewildering rapidity. Rightly renowned for their bravery in battle, they soon displayed a multifaceted *modus operandi* that had more in common with a modern multinational conglomerate than with a medieval monastic order.

Warriors of immense skill and commitment, they displayed an astounding commercial genius and, in many respects, laid the foundations of the modern commercial world. Fighters and farmers; they raised sheep; modernized the wool trade; grew grapes, made and traded in wine; built churches, castles and cathedrals; operated stone quarries; were millers, merchants and miners and founded an international banking system that lent money to priests, prelates and popes, nobles, kings and emperors. Yet, despite this almost unbelievable record of achievement, they are still sometimes described by their critics within the Catholic Church as 'illiterates'.

Accused, with some justification, of arrogance, they were, in their later years, regarded with suspicion due to the respect they gave to the religious beliefs of their Muslim opponents. Finally, arrested en masse under charges of heresy, their leaders were tortured by the Inquisition before being ritually burnt over a slow fire and, despite the fact that they were never convicted of any crime, the order was disbanded by the pope because it had fallen into disrepute.

Since their demise and the subsequent suppression or destruction of their records, the story of the Knights Templar has given rise to a wealth of rumour, legend and fantasy that has clouded the facts that explain their rapid rise to power and the truth about the heretical belief system that inspired them to such great achievements. In recent years, Templar legends have proliferated due to a flood of publications, especially those following in the footsteps of Baigent, Leigh and Lincoln's controversial best-seller *The Holy Blood and the Holy Grail*, such as *Foucault's Pendulum* and, more recently, *The Da Vinci Code* which has fired the public imagination to a phenomenal degree.

The Templars have been described as 'Knights of the Holy Grail', yet the true meaning of that phrase was a closely gurarded secret that has only recently gained widespread public recognition. The Grail sagas are an allegorical description of a search for spiritual enlightenment. A form of transformative spirituality, used by the elite in ancient Egypt, that pervaded the religious life of the high priesthood of biblical Israel and went underground, to be followed in secret when Christianity became the dominant religious power in Europe.

Those who sought the Grail in medieval times risked persecution as heretics, yet, nonetheless left clues as to their beliefs that could only be discerned by the initiated. Thus, to understand the full implications of the true origins and beliefs of the Knights Templar we need to briefly examine the history of the people who transmitted this form of spiritual teaching down through the ages from ancient Egypt to medieval Europe.

GNOSTICISM, JUDAISM, CHRISTIANITY & ISLAM

The Order of the Knights Templar arose and flourished in the context of a series of wars between Christian Europe and the Muslim Empire known as the Crusades. To come to any degree of meaningful understanding of these events and how they shaped not merely the destiny of the Templars but that of the modern world we live in, we need to examine the roots of Judaism, Christianity and Islam.

While Christianity claims to be founded on the example of Jesus of Nazareth, the truth is that, despite the fact that it carries within it some of the teachings of this divinely gifted Jewish teacher more correctly called Jesus the Nazarene, the man regarded by many Church historians as 'the father of Christianity' was another Jew entirely, namely Saul of Tarsus, better known as St Paul.

CHAPTER 1

The Parting of the Ways –
Conflict Between Truth & Church Dogma

Considerable evidence of the importance of the initiatory tradition can be found in ancient Egypt, where we find the earliest demonstrable source of a sustained system of initiation preserved by a hereditary priesthood. The earliest surviving references to this spiritual pathway occurs in the Pyramid Texts,[1] which refer to a succession of priestly initiates who transmitted an extraordinary body of sacred knowledge from master to pupil down through the generations. The English author John Anthony West paraphrased the views of one leading scholar, Schwaller de Lubicz, when he stated that Egyptian science, medicine, mathematics and astronomy were all of an exponentially higher order of refinement and sophistication than most modern scholars will acknowledge, and that the whole of Egyptian civilization was based upon a complete and precise understanding of universal laws.[2]

SACRED GNOSIS

The incredibly sophisticated levels of gnosis attained through initiation were not used for personal gain by the priestly and royal initiates of the Egyptian temple mysteries. While rank and royal birth undoubtedly had their privileges, the sacred knowledge of subjects such as astronomy, agriculture, architecture, building, medicine, mathematics, navigation and metallurgy were used for the benefit of the entire community. Protected by the desert that surrounded it and sustained by this divinely inspired gnosis, Egyptian civilization developed a stability and complexity that has never been exceeded. This vast body of esoteric knowledge was recorded in part in the Pyramid Texts, the Edfu Texts and the Books of the Dead as well as being encoded on temple walls and elsewhere. After the Exodus, this initiatory tradition was continued in emerging Judaism.

Scholars such as Sigmund Freud[3] and Ernst Sellin,[4] have described the overwhelming significance of Egyptian thought on early Judaism. In the Old Testament, for example, both Abraham and Melchizedek, the priest-king of Jerusalem, use the same phrase to describe the deity – the Most High God – one of the common terms used in Egypt for the supreme god of the pantheon. Abraham also adopted for himself and all his children the Egyptian custom of circumcision, ostensibly at God's command. Circumcision, while an unusual practice elsewhere, had been mandatory among Egyptian royalty, the hereditary priesthood and the nobility since 4000 BCE.[5]

When we read the scriptural accounts of the religion followed by the Jews during the Exodus, we find direct links to previous Egyptian practice. The creation of an hereditary priesthood based upon the tribe of Levi followed the example of Egyptian priests who were also a hereditary caste and who acted as the guardians of sacred knowledge. The Levitic hereditary priestly clan was created by extending the rank, rights and privileges of the Egyptian priesthood to their Levitic successors who continued the transmission of sacred wisdom among their number in the traditional manner.

It is clear that the Jews treasured their own mystical and initiatory religious traditions and stressed their importance in the inspired writing of the Old Testament composed during the Babylonian Exile. The mystical vision of the prophets was extolled time and time again, the role of the priest-kings David and Solomon was revered and the initiatory concept of ascending degrees of holiness pervaded Jewish life and the very precincts of the Temple itself.

There was also a distinctive trend of charismatic Judaism that had Galilean roots,[6] as well as a multifaceted mystical trend of truly Egyptian/Hebraic origin. From the 2nd century BCE the devir, or Holy of Holies, that had once held the Ark of the Covenant, God's throne on earth, became the focus for visionaries who imagined ascending directly to God's heavenly palace and approaching his celestial throne. We read of Jewish mystics preparing for this mystical ascent by special disciplines.[7] Other mystical speculations in the Talmud focus on the *maaseh bereshith* (the work of creation) described in the first chapter of Genesis, and the *maaseh merkabah*, (the divine chariot) in the account of Ezekiel's vision. These mystical doctrines were carefully guarded and it was forbidden to expound them except to a few chosen disciples in the traditional Egyptian manner.

There are also 'the Psalms of ascents' in the Bible and the Ascents tradition in the Kabbala: that is the ascent through the various degrees of neo-Platonic enlightenment or gnosis – ascents to the higher heavens – another variation of the Merkabah tradition, also known as *Hekaloth*.[8] The Kabbala itself, or the tradition that was received from Aaron, is the major Jewish mystical tradition. One of its better-known tenets is the idea of the Zaddik or the Righteous One.[9] The Righteous Man, as Ezekiel puts it, will not suffer for someone else's sin. He will not die.

'The man who has sinned ... is the one who must die. A son is not to suffer for the sins of his father, nor a father for the sins of his son.'[10] In the Sefer HaZohar it is written that Noah was a righteous one of whom it was said: 'The Righteous One is the Foundation of the World', and the Earth is established thereon, for this is the Pillar that upholds the world. So Noah was called 'Righteous... and the embodiment of the world's Covenant of Peace'.[11]

The Old Testament began to take its present form during the Babylonian Exile and the process continued for several centuries after that. Within it we find repeated references to the 24 *ma'madot*, the hereditary priestly teams who took turns in serving in the Temple in Jerusalem.[12] These hereditary high-priestly families all claimed descent from Aaron and Zadok the Priest, and governed all religious life in Israel from the return from the Babylonian Exile until the reign of the pagan Selucid king, Antiochus IV who deposed the last true Zadokite high priest in 175 BCE and appointed his own nominee in his place. The deposed high priest's son built a rival temple at Leontopolis in Egypt. The other zealous Zadokite priests of the *ma'madot* withdrew from the Temple in a body and formed their own sect in the wilderness near Qumran, basing their form of worship on strict rules of purity and observation of the Torah under the leadership of the man they called the Teacher of Righteousness.

The Jewish historian Flavius Josephus describes four main sects within Judaism in the 1st century of the Common Era: the Essens, the Sadducees, the Pharisees and the 'fourth philosophy'.[13] The Essens, now more commonly called the Essenes, were thus the direct descendants of the Zadokite priests of the *ma'madot* who had withdrawn into the wilderness after the defilement of the Temple by Antiochus and the later appointment of non-Zadokite high priests by the Maccabeans.[14] This group of hereditary high priests held their goods in common, lived austere lives, maintained ritual purity, believed that the soul was immortal, and held as the major aspect of their belief an almost fanatical insistence on 'doing Torah', that is, living life in strict accordance with the law of God. Josephus wrote of them: 'They exceed all other men that addict themselves to virtue, and this in righteousness.'[15]

The family of Jesus were most certainly one of the 24 families of the *ma'madot*, for Jesus' brother, James the Just, is recorded as being a high priest in the scriptures, the works of Josephus and those of some of the early fathers of the Christian Church. Therefore it is not suprising to discover that the teachings of Jesus the Nazarene were not regarded as the foundation for a new and distinctly different religion by Jesus, his family, or the Apostles who walked and talked with him throughout his ministry. These men and women were all, without exception, strict, devout, fundamentalist and nationalistic Jews. No one among them took the teachings of Jesus as an indictment of Judaism, nor was the Crucifixion regarded as a means of salvation. The only difference between the beliefs of the followers of Jesus and those of other Jews, was their fanatical adherence to Jesus' interpretation of the Law. They were completely devoted to 'doing Torah' in the way Jesus had taught them. There was absolutely nothing in the teachings of Jesus, as they understood them, to cause any breach with traditional Judaism. On the contrary, as the priestly and kingly Messiahs, John the Baptist and Jesus, both of whom were members of the Nazorean (or Nazarene) sect of the Essenes, were regarded as the fulfilment of Jewish religious thought and belief, not its contradiction. Such conflicts that did arise between many of the priestly and Saducean factions and the followers of Jesus did so because those in a position of power and privilege felt that his teachings undermined their priestly authority and power.

The allegedly 'divine' origin and nature of Jesus, which later became such a divisive and controversial issue, was not a problem to the disciples who knew him. They knew from firsthand experience that he was a man supernaturally endowed by God, a *Teacher of Righteousness* and his followers were not Christians as we now understand the term, but zealous members of an offshoot of the Essene community, the Nazarenes. Nothing in the words or actions of their master, in his teachings or in the scriptures – which they, as Essenes, knew intimately – gave them any cause to think otherwise. Indeed, according to one of the earliest apologists for the Christian faith, Aristides, the worship of the first Jerusalem 'Christians' was fundamentally more monotheistic than that of other Jews, for Jesus' brother James the Just, who is described in the Acts of the Apostles as 'the first bishop of Jerusalem', was, as mentioned above, one of the hereditary high priests who was granted entrance to the holy of holies in the Temple.

After the Crucifixion, James took on the role of the priestly Messiah which had previously been held by John the Baptist prior to his execution by Herod. James exerted great power and authority among the Jews for many years after the Crucifixion of Jesus and was clearly acknowledged by all the Apostles, including Paul, as a much more significant figure than the later Christian Churches have ever admitted.

> He was of the lineage of David…and moreover we have found that he officiated after the manner of the ancient priesthood. Whereof also he was permitted once a year to enter the Holy of Holies (i.e. on the Day of Atonement), as the Law commanded the high priests, according to that which is written; for so many before us have told of him, both Eusabius and Clement and others. Furthermore he was empowered to wear on his head the high priestly diadem as the aforementioned trustworthy men have attested…[16]

The pre-eminence and importance of James is referred to repeatedly in a variety of ancient documents yet, nonetheless, Church teaching about him is sparse, vague and inconclusive. The question that arises inevitably from this is: Why has his role been minimized by the Church so that the laity and most of the clergy know little about it? Indeed, two characters called James are described in Church teaching, James the Great and James the Less. Were there in fact, two James' operating among the followers of Jesus at that time? Why have the actions and importance of James the Just been either suppressed or glossed over and why was his importance diminished by being called James the Less? Some biblical scholars have even suggested that the character known as 'James the Great' is a complete fabrication conceived by the Church to distract attention from James the Just, the brother of Jesus.

MARY, THE MOTHER OF JESUS, AND HER FAMILY

Developing Church doctrine gave rise to other problems. Once the concept of Jesus' divinity had been established and the alleged 'virginity' of his mother Mary had been proposed and accepted, the Church found that it had painted itself into a corner from which there was no escape. How could one who was dogmatically declared to be 'ever virgin' be described as having a large family? The Church could not deny the uncomfortable fact that in the Gospel according to St Mark it is recorded: 'is not this the carpenter, the son of Mary, the brother of James, of Joses (or Joseph), and of Juda (or Judas) and Simon? and are not his sisters here with us?'[17] A similar passage occurs in St Matthew's Gospel, which states: 'Is not this the carpenter's son? Is not his mother's name Mary and his brethren, James, and Joses, and Simon and Judas?'[18]

The tactic used by the Church to resolve the problem of explaining how someone 'ever virgin' could have such a large family, was simple evasion. Patriarchal religions, such as Judaism and Christianity, have always devalued the role of women, and Mary's role was marginalized by, paradoxically, exalting her in her role as 'the Mother of God' to the exclusion of all else. Omission was used to overcome the Gospel statements that Jesus had siblings, through the denial of their existence to a flock who were not allowed to read the scriptures and only to hear selected passages read to them. However, as doctrine developed and they were challenged on this point by the privileged few who were permitted to read the New Testament, theologians evaded the issue by claiming that in this context, 'brothers and sisters' meant fellow believers or 'cousins'. Yet the early Church father, Clement of Alexandria, referred to James as the brother of Our Lord, and bishop of bishops.[19] Much later in the Vulgate translation of the Bible, St Jerome used the Latin word *frater*, which translates unequivocally as brother, and never uses the Latin for cousin. The Vulgate still remains a translation of the Holy Scriptures that carries the *imprimatur*, or official seal of approval, of the Roman Catholic Church to this day.

Another brother of Jesus whose relationship and importance the Church has marginalized is Didymus Judas Thomas, the Judas referred to in the passages quoted above and the author of 'The Gospel of Thomas'. Thomas's role has been cleverly devalued in the canonical Gospels by referring to him as *Doubting Thomas*, thus casting doubt not only upon his commitment and spiritual insight, but also upon his personal knowledge of Jesus himself. Why should such a slander be cast upon one of the Apostles? Yet, the Gospel of Thomas circulated widely for the first three centuries of Christian history for it was written by the twin brother of Jesus, was regarded as authoritative and seriously rivalled the canonical Gospels as a source of both authority and teaching. This situation was one of grave concern to an emerging

Church hierarchy so this Gospel was eventually suppressed and disappeared from sight for over 1,500 years until it was rediscovered at Nag Hammadi in 1945. In it we find the following:

> The disciples said to Jesus: "We know that you will depart from us. Who is to be our leader?"
>
> Jesus said to them: "Wherever you are, you are to go to James the righteous, for whose sake heaven and earth came into being."[20]

Do these words of Jesus indicate, as many scholars and initiates have known for centuries, that James' role as the priestly Messiah was superior in some way to that of Jesus as the kingly Messiah?

Another problem arises when we discover that no explanation is offered in the Acts of the Apostles or the Epistles as to why, or how, the new 'Christian' community was formed in Jerusalem immediately after the Crucifixion of Jesus. How could a handful of 'peasants and fishermen' create such an elaborate and effective form of organization with such speed? The Acts of the Apostles claims that this seemingly *ad hoc* structure sustained a massive influx of new Jewish adherents to the teaching of Jesus from throughout the Diaspora.

How indeed did such a complex and efficient system of governance develop? It was ruled by a triumvirate, which consisted of James the brother of Jesus and two of the Apostles, Simon Peter and John, assisted by area supervisors and administrators, later renamed by the Church as bishops and deacons. The three leaders were called 'the pillars' by Paul: 'And when James, Cephas and John who seemed to be pillars, perceived that grace was given me, they gave to me and to Barnabas the right hand of friendship.'[21] These three 'pillars', James, Cephas and John, replicated the ruling trio of the Essene community from which they and Jesus sprang. Furthermore, it is highly likely that they were all brothers of Jesus. James the Just is described in the scriptures as the Lord's brother. According to the French author Robert Ambelain, Simon Peter and the Simon listed among Mary's children are one and the same. It is interesting to note that the Nazorenes, the sect from which Jesus himself sprang, later called the Ebionites, continued to conform with the hereditary traditions of the *ma'madot* and elected their leaders from among the family of Jesus until well into the 2nd century CE.[22]

THE MARRIAGE OF JESUS

The Church has always taught that Jesus, as God, while having a human nature, remained celibate and did not have children. If they had admitted this possibility it would have implied that the children and descendants of Jesus, who they claimed was divine, would have had far more authority than the Church itself. Yet the Professor of New Testament theology at the École Biblique in Jerusalem, Father Jerome Murphy O'Connor, stated in a BBC radio broadcast, that:

> (St) Paul was certainly married… Marriage is not a matter of choice for Jews, that's why you have so few in the early centuries who weren't married and that's why… Paul… must have been married because this was a social obligation whose social fulfilment was obvious.[23]

Despite the obvious truth of this statement, neither Fr. Murphy-O'Connor, nor any other clergyman has ever applied the same compelling logic to the case of Jesus, notwithstanding the fact that there is no mention in the New Testament that Jesus was unmarried, a situation that would have provoked considerable comment at the time.

11

However, indications of Jesus' marital status and clues as to the identity of his wife still remain in the Gospels.

The English scholar, A N Wilson, claims that, 'The story of the wedding feast at Cana contains a hazy memory of Jesus' own wedding',[24] and the Muslim scholar, Professor Fida Hassnain states of the same passage:

> The question arises who is the guest and who is the bride? I would suggest Mary is the host for she orders the procuring of the wine for the guests, which Jesus deals with. One wonders whether it is *his* own marriage with Mary Magdalene, and whether the whole episode has been kept under camouflage… I believe that Mary Magdalene behaved as the chief consort of Jesus, and he also took her as his spouse.[25]

The story of the wedding is found in the Gospel of John:

> And on the third day there was a marriage in Cana of Galilee; and the mother of Jesus was there:
>
> And both Jesus was called, and his disciples, to the marriage.
>
> And when they wanted wine, the mother of Jesus sayeth unto him, they have no wine,
>
> Jesus sayeth unto her, Woman, what have I to do with thee? Mine hour is not yet come.
>
> His mother sayeth unto the servants, whatsoever he sayeth unto you, do it.[26]

The Gospel story continues with the 'miraculous' changing of the water into wine and Jesus then ordering the servants to distribute it. Jewish custom of the time reveals that only the bridegroom or the groom's mother would have the necessary authority to give orders to the servants at a wedding feast,[27] therefore it must be Jesus' own wedding that is being described.

Later in the same Gospel we read of circumstances that, interpreted in the light of the strict religious and cultural customs of that time, reveal the full nature of the relationship between Jesus and his obedient wife, Mary Magdalene.

> Then Martha, as soon as she heard that Jesus was coming, went and met him: but Mary sat still in the house…
>
> …And when she had so said, she went her way, and called her sister secretly, saying, the Master is come and calleth for thee.
>
> As soon as she heard that, she arose quickly, and came unto him.[28]

In the Gospel of Luke we find the following: 'And she had a sister called Mary, which also sat at Jesus' feet and heard his word'[29] The Mary in question is Mary of Bethany, better known as Mary Magdalene, the wife who would be the only woman permitted to sit at a man's feet indicating, according to Jewish custom, that Jesus and Mary Magdalene were husband and wife.

The Catholic theologian, Margaret Starbird, was so incensed at the apparent heresy of Jesus' marriage as described in the controversial best-seller *The Holy Blood and the Holy Grail*, that she set out to refute it. It is a credit to her spiritual and intellectual integrity that the book she published after several years of detailed research, *The Woman with the Alabaster Jar*,[30] is a superbly argued and detailed exposition of the conclusive evidence proving the marriage of Jesus to Mary Magdalene and their founding of a dynasty. The alabaster jar in question contained expensive perfume that Mary poured on Jesus' head:

While Jesus was in Bethany in the home of a man known as Simon the Leper, a woman came to him with an alabaster jar of very expensive perfume, which she poured on his head as he was reclining at table.[31]

According to Jewish custom, and to other Near-Eastern traditions from Sumer, Babylon and Canaan, the king's head was ritually anointed with oil, usually by the royal priestess or royal bride in her ancient role of goddess. The Greeks called this ritual *hieros gamos,* or the sacred marriage. This ritual union with the priestess was crucial if the king were to be recognized in his divinely blessed and royal status, as the true 'anointed one' or the 'messiah'.[32] As a result, Western art and Church iconography nearly always portray Mary Magdalene as the lady with the alabaster jar.

Although he never used the title himself, Jesus was later referred to as *a Son of God*, a phrase which, to the Jews of biblical times, meant something very different indeed from the one ascribed to it by Christians today. To the Jews this ranked Jesus with the many other 'Sons of God' mentioned in the Old Testament, such as Adam, Abraham, Moses and David. The status of 'Son of God' was held to be attainable to all of those who followed Jesus' teaching and who attained enlightenment. Jesus himself said as much, as reported in The Gospel of Thomas: 'He who will drink from my mouth will become like me. I myself shall become he, and the things that are hidden will be revealed to him.'[33]

THE DEIFICATION OF JESUS
BY ST PAUL

The canonical scriptures leave us in no doubt whatsoever that it was St Paul who first preached the blasphemous doctrine that Jesus was divine and which was later adopted by the Church. Yet, according to his own account, Paul never met the living Jesus. Today, in a world completely indoctrinated by the idea that Jesus is God, it is perhaps difficult at first to accept that Jesus himself never claimed divine status. The fact is that Jesus was born, raised and taught as a Jew. His followers regarded themselves as a Jewish movement. The doctrine of a divine human being is diametrically opposed to the Jewish concept of God at the time of Jesus and no practising Jew who subscribed to the faith of his fathers and who sought acceptance by other Jews, could present himself in such a manner without being stoned to death for blasphemy. However, the deification of humans was agreeable to current heathen notions, as the history of the Roman Empire confirms. Therefore, the deification of Jesus was an intrusion from gentile or heretical sources and is most certainly not fundamental to the integrity of Jesus' message. Proof of this is found in the fact that Jesus' deification was staunchly resisted by the original Apostles and those Jews who believed that he was the Messiah, thus confirming that this blasphemous concept was entirely alien in origin and that Jesus himself could not have entertained it.[34] Indeed Jesus, like all his disciples, was an ultra-orthodox and devout Jew who was well steeped in esoteric Hebraic Gnosticism. The origin of the word Essene is held by many to mean *those with the light within*, and Jesus was an Essene initiate. In the Holy Qur'an, Jesus is called by the name of Issa. One explanation of this name is *an initiate of Isis* and it must be remembered that the Egyptian mysteries pervaded the entire esoteric belief system of biblical Israel from the time of Moses onwards. Another translation of the name Issa that is often put forward is *an initiate of Light.* Was Jesus not called the Light of the World?

Another major, fundamental and theologically important divergence from the beliefs of James and the Apostles is demonstrated by Paul's use of the phrase *Christ died for us.* Since the time of Abraham, no Jew could perform a human sacrifice or become one, and those that transgressed this teaching were castigated for it. Furthermore, the sacrifice of an innocent man for the guilt of others also went against the basic religious principle that the innocent should not suffer for the guilty, enunciated centuries earlier by the prophet Ezekiel.[35] Thus the mere idea of a vicarious human sacrifice of this nature would again be viewed as outright blasphemy by devout Jews, as was the alleged 'divinity of Jesus'. Yet both ideas were totally in keeping with the traditions of the Greeks and Romans to whom Paul was preaching, where a noble, sacrificial death would be extolled.

While Paul referred to Jesus as God, Peter, who according to Catholic teaching at least, was made the founder of the Church by Jesus himself, described Jesus as a man: 'Ye men of Israel, hear these words; Jesus of Nazareth, *a man* approved of God among you by miracles and wonders and signs, which God did by him in the midst of you, as ye yourselves also know.'[35] (my emphasis)

The complete change in the way Paul viewed the nature of Jesus is echoed clearly in many of his later letters:

> Here is a trustworthy saying that deserves full acceptance: Christ Jesus came into the world to save sinners – of whom I am the worst.
>
> But for that very reason I was shown mercy so that in me, the worst of sinners, Christ Jesus might display his unlimited patience as an example for those who would believe on him and receive eternal life.

Now to the King eternal, immortal, invisible, the only God, be honour and glory for ever and ever. Amen.[36]

...while we wait for the blessed hope – the glorious appearing of our great God and Saviour, Jesus Christ.[37]

It was because of this type of teaching and his repudiation of the validity of the Law, that it has been claimed that Paul was indeed *the Wicked Priest* referred to in the Dead Sea Scrolls, and the man described as *the Liar*, *the Scoffer*, and *the Spouter of Lies*. Paul was certainly despised and disliked by James and most of the other disciples. As this view is in conflict with that of many Christians, is there any evidence to back it up?

There is at least one other document of similar age to the Synoptic Gospels, written in the early years after the Crucifixion, known as the *Kerygmata Petrou*. This important, yet little known, document describes the 'Apostle' Paul, venerated by the Church as the 'Father of Christianity', as *the hostile man who falsified the true teachings of Jesus*. It was written by the Ebionites, the people closest to Jesus throughout his ministry and who possessed the deepest understanding of his teaching. They were brutally dismissive about the Church's elevation of Paul to the rank of Apostle which, to them, was a title reserved solely for those who had accompanied Jesus during his ministry.

The implications of Jesus' involvement with the Ebionites created havoc among later Church theologians and Iraneus, Bishop of Lyon, writing during the late 2nd century, showed the mental convolutions that only a Catholic theologian was capable of in his explanation of this relationship. He claimed that Jesus whom he, of course, believed was God, had been in error, practising 'the wrong religion'.[38] Now Jesus, in his view at least, was divine and therefore incapable of error, yet, according to this esteemed theologian, God had boobed when incarnate on earth and had led his flock into the wrong religion. The mind boggles! Furthermore Iraneus condemned the Ebionites, who had walked and talked with Jesus himself, as heretics for claiming that Jesus was a man and not God, as defined by the Church. He freely admitted that the Ebionites spurned the Pauline Epistles and that they also rejected Paul outright as *an apostate of the Law*. The early Church historian, Eusebius, writing in the 4th century, records that the Ebionites '...had poor and mean opinions concerning Christ. They held him to be a plain and ordinary man who had achieved righteousness merely by the progress of his character and had been born naturally from Mary and her husband.'[39] He also stated that the Ebionites '... affirm that Christ was born of Joseph and Mary, and suppose Him to be a mere man'.[40]

CHAPTER 2

St Paul, the Gospels & Emerging Christianity

The bizarre and complex character who became known as 'the Father of Christianity' was Saul of Tarsus, better known as St Paul who claimed never to have known Jesus when he was alive. He also claimed to be a Roman citizen and a Pharisee who had spent some considerable time vigorously persecuting the follow-ers of Jesus in the years immediately after the Crucifixion.[1] Then, after his miraculous conversion on the road to Damascus, this fanatical opponent of Jesus' followers did a complete religious *volte-face* and changed both his religion and his name. Following an unexplained period of three years in Arabia[2] he then joined James the Just and his followers in Jerusalem to learn the 'true way' as taught by Jesus.[3] After this, he began a series of evangelical journeys that took him to some of the most important cities of the eastern Mediterranean. Yet, despite his undoubted evangelical zeal, he became the subject of scathing crit-icism by James and Jesus' disciples in Jerusalem.

New Testament accounts and other sources make it absolutely clear that there was a fundamental difference between 'the Way', as interpreted by James and the original disciples and the new version taught by Paul. The conflict is mentioned, in a distinctly 'sanitized' manner, in the account of the Council of Jerusalem recorded in the Acts of the Apostles. This revised version of events claims that, after heated discussion, Paul's teaching was deemed to be acceptable.[4] However, when we consider Paul's actions in the light of the absolute dedication to the Torah that was characteristic of James and the disciples, namely their strict prohibition against mixing with gentiles and their rigid adherence to the dietary laws of Judaism, this is an incredible scenario.

PAUL'S EXPULSION BY JAMES THE JUST

Paul mixed almost exclusively with gentiles and, in his view, God's covenant with Abraham and its laws no longer applied and circumcision was no longer necessary for converts. Furthermore, he taught that faith, and faith alone was all that was required for eternal salvation. The renowned biblical scholar Robert Eisenman has found among the Dead Sea Scrolls and other early Christian documents, accounts that enabled him to reconstruct a far more accurate and credible rendition of the dispute that arose from Paul's preaching to the gentiles and his repeated denial of the validity of the Torah. This led to a dramatic confrontation between a man called 'the Liar', namely Paul, and 'the Teacher of Righteousness', who at that time was, most probably, James the Just. The word treachery occurs in the texts, referring to the factional strife within the community.[5] The Essenes' absolute commitment to ritual purity and their refusal to eat food sacrificed to idols, was divinely ordained and, therefore, irrevocable and their fanatical insistence on 'doing Torah', that is, living life in strict accordance with the law of God, meant that the strictures against social contact with gentiles were rigidly enforced. In the Qumran Community Rule we find the following unequivocal statement:

> Any man who enters the Council of Holiness walking in the Way of Perfection as commanded by God and, whether overtly or covertly, transgresses one word of the *Torah* of Moses on any point whatsoever… shall be expelled from the Council of the Community and return no more. No Man of Holiness shall associate with him in monetary matters or in approach *on any matter whatsoever*.[6] (my emphasis)

This is precisely what happened to Paul and, as a result, Barnabas, who had been his constant companion, now deserted him. Paul himself tells us this in his Epistle to the Galatians[7] which also lists his total repudiation of the Law, his teaching that salvation is by faith alone and his denial of the Torah, which he claimed was worthless.[8]

Any analysis of the differences between the teachings of Paul and those of James and the other disciples in Jerusalem, demonstrates that Paul had committed blasphemy in respect of his controversial views on the Torah and was also responsible for the 'deification' of Jesus. If one scours the New Testament in its entirety, the earliest reference we have to the claimed divinity of Jesus can be found in one of Paul's Epistles when he writes '…while we wait for the blessed hope – the glorious appearing of our … great God and Saviour, Jesus Christ.'[9] It was also Paul who conceived the notion that contradicted all of Jewish tradition from the time of Abraham onwards, that at Golgotha, Jesus had become some form of vicarious 'sacrificial lamb' and had 'died for us'.[10] Thus Paul repudiated the Law, condemned circumcision and circumcisers, namely the entire Jewish people, validated the pagan concept of human sacrifice and deified Jesus.

The reaction to Paul's blasphemous views from the strict Jewish community that centred on James the brother of Jesus in Jerusalem was predictable. Even the staunchly Catholic historian Paul Johnson admits that from this time onwards the evangelical mission of St Paul steadily lost ground to missions mounted by evangelists carrying written accreditation from James the Just in Jerusalem. Paul was scathing about this practice of accreditation and wrote, 'Or do we need, like some people, letters of recommendation to you ...'[11] Johnson makes it quite clear that if it were not for the destruction of Jerusalem by the Romans, Paul's efforts might well have been forgotten altogether.[12] The hatred and distrust felt by the followers of James in Jerusalem towards Paul was mutual. Paul describes his position vis-à-vis the first 'Christian' community in Jerusalem, in the following terms:

> Therefore stand fast in the freedom with which Christ has made us free and do not (submit) again to the yoke of slavery... Everyone who accepts circumcision is obliged to do the whole Law. Whosoever is justified by the Law *are set aside from Christ*.[13]
> (my emphasis)

Paul was also derided for adopting a two-faced approach, or, to use his own words, of being simultaneously a 'Law-Keeper to those who keep the Law' and a 'Law breaker to those' who did not.[14] It is not surprising, therefore, that this quarrel did not end with Paul's expulsion from the first Christian community in Jerusalem. Indeed it soon turned from bitter, verbal argument and mutual abuse to murderous violence.

PAUL'S ARREST AFTER HIS ASSAULT ON JAMES

Recorded in the 'Pseudo-Clementine Recognitions' and in a lost work about James from which Epiphanius quotes several passages, the *Anabathmoi Jacobou – the Ascent of Jacob* is the serious accusation that Paul tried to kill James the brother of Jesus by throwing him headlong down the steps of the Jerusalem Temple thus breaking his legs. The most scholarly and superbly researched study of this appalling event can be found in Robert Eisenman's masterwork, *James the Brother of Jesus*.[15] After this, Paul was arrested.[16] The Acts of the Apostles claims that this was because he had inflamed the Jewish mob at the Temple by preaching the Gospel. The truth would appear to be that this was a protective arrest to save the Roman citizen, Paul, from a mob that wished to kill him for his attempt on the life of James who was supremely popular with the people. When warned of another plot to kill him, the Roman arresting officer[17] took Paul to Caesarea under an escort of 200 soldiers, 70 cavalrymen and 200 spearmen.[18] A suspiciously large escort for a mere Jewish blasphemer whom the Romans could easily have handed over to the Sanhedrin, who would have sentenced Paul to death by stoning. Yet few historians and certainly no Christian scholars have ever questioned why such a large expenditure of scarce military resources should be employed to protect Paul at a time of potential rebellion. The answer can actually be found within the New Testament: Paul is not only a Roman citizen, but also a member of the Herodian ruling family and a long-term friend of Rome. These uncomfortable facts can be found in Paul's own letters where he wrote: 'Greet those who belong to the household of Aristobulus. Greet Herodian my relative.'[19]

These politically charged links to the ruling family explain how Paul became a member of the Temple guard authorized by the high priest to persecute the followers of Jesus. The nationalistic zealous members of the Jesus group were a prime target for the Sadducees of the Temple bent on suppressing rebellion against their Roman masters. A N Wilson claims that, 'It does not seem unreasonable to suppose that he was in the same position in the Temple guard when Jesus was arrested.'[20] The political 'clout' that flows naturally from royal connections also explains Paul's comfortable status during his two-year 'imprisonment' at Caesarea under the orders of the Roman governor Felix.[21] The Jewish contemporary historian Josephus records that Antipater, the father of Herod the Great, had been awarded hereditary Roman citizenship for services to Caesar.[22] Therefore Paul, as a Herodian related to King Agrippa II,[23] had inherited a highly privileged position which he exploited to the full. The Epistle to the Philippians, mentions one of Paul's converts, Epaphroditus, a senior advisor of the Roman Emperor Nero[24] and Paul writes, 'Greetings, especially those in Caesar's household'.[25] Paul, or Saulus as the Romans and Herodians knew him, had friends and relatives in very high places which tends to explain how Paul, allegedly a humble tent-maker, managed to travel the world with comparative ease, had so many 'miraculous' escapes from prison and was so frequently welcomed as the guest of people of power and political influence.

The community at Antioch, who, according to the biblical scholar Robert Eisenman, were the first group of believers to be called Christians, were mainly drawn from members of the Herodian family. These Herodian and pro-Roman links explain why Paul neutered Jesus' message so thoroughly, stripped it of all Jewish and nationalistic intent and then diluted it further by issuing firm instructions to obey all lawful authorities. Paul, like Herod the Great, wore his Judaism very lightly, otherwise it is difficult to conceive how any Jew, especially one of a self-confessed studious and devout Pharisaic background, could preach the anti-Semitic and anti-Torah message he repeated so vehemently in his Epistles.

Thus Paul's message of subservience to 'lawful' Roman authority and his preaching of a New Covenant that denied the Torah was the complete negation of the teaching of Jesus and his brother and successor James. James' fanatically Jewish stance, on the other hand, also had distinct and overt political dimensions, for his pro-Torah, nationalistic, anti-Herodian and anti-Roman policy resulted inevitably in a head-on collision with the authorities in Jerusalem, namely the Sadducee high priests and their principal ally, Paul's kinsman King Agrippa II.

Indeed, Paul's attitude created what the staunchly Catholic and conservative Church historian Paul Johnson describes as 'monstrous difficulties' by his divergence from the teachings of Jesus.[26] From other comments that he makes later in the same letter, it would seem that he is also being accused of taking some sort of financial advantage from his evangelical efforts.[27]

THE 'TRUTH' OF THE GOSPELS

In the accepted chronology of New Testament composition, the Epistles of St Paul are now recognized as being the earliest, having been written in the late 40s CE. The Gospels and the Acts of the Apostles came very much later; Mark during the 70s, Matthew in the 80s, Luke, the Acts and the Gospel according to John early in the 2nd century. Thus, all the Gospels were written after the fall of Jerusalem, and originate in the era when James and the disciples in the Jerusalem Church had been killed or scattered and Paul's followers had the field to themselves.

In the academic sense at least, the Gospels and the Acts of the Apostles are an extremely unreliable source. The Acts of the Apostles and at least three of the canonical Gospels were written long after the events they describe, by people who were not present at the time of Jesus and who based their accounts on hearsay evidence arising from the teaching of Paul, rather than on historical truth. The Gospel of St John, on the other hand, despite its many later additions, may have been written by, or at the behest of, an eyewitness, which may explain some of the significant differences between it and the Synoptic Gospels known to us as Matthew, Mark and Luke. The three Synoptic Gospels were based, to one degree or another, on a mysterious source document known in scholarly circles as 'Q' which has never been traced. There is a startling consensus among scholars regarding Q's content and style that has resulted in the virtual recreation of the document. Burton L Mack, Professor of New Testament Studies at the Claremont School of Theology in California writes:

> The remarkable thing is that the authors of Q did not think about Jesus as the Messiah or the Christ, nor did they understand his teachings to be an indictment of Judaism. They certainly did not regard his crucifixion as a divinely inspired, or saving event. Nor did they believe that he had been raised from the dead to rule over the world. They thought of him as a Jewish prophet whose teaching made it possible to live an attainable and righteous life in very troubled times. As a result they neither gathered to worship in his name, honoured him as a god – which to them, as devout Jews would have been the ultimate blasphemy – nor celebrate his memory through hymns, prayers or rituals.[28]

Yet the Gospels, largely based on information from the Q document, speak of Jesus as a divine figure. Close and unbiased examination of this concept, however, soon displays the *a priori* improbability of the doctrine of the deity of Jesus.

Q is not the only important scriptural document to have vanished without trace, or been suppressed by the Church. Professor Morton Smith discovered in 1973 a letter from Clement of Alexandria which refers to a 'secret apocryphal Gospel of Mark'. Clement's writings disclose a wide-ranging knowledge of early Christian documents, many of which have since been lost or suppressed. Clement was of the opinion that all knowledge of the existence of the secret Gospel of Mark should be denied, in spite of its authenticity, because this document claimed that Jesus had been a pupil of John the Baptist and had continued his baptismal cult, in direct contradiction to Church teaching.[29] Another Gospel that survived for many centuries and has also been lost is the controversial 'Gospel of Love' used by the Cathars who are described in a later chpater. This is now accepted to have been a Gnostic variation upon the Gospel of St John, possibly the original version itself. Thus, the canonical Gospels were written long after the events they purport to describe, to evangelize according to a belief structure that had arisen under Paul's guidance in the gentile world, and therefore they record an authoritative and seemingly historical basis for beliefs founded on the teaching of Paul, not Jesus.

The Gospels were also subjected to waves of amendment, alteration and distortion in order to bring them to an even closer approximation with the teaching of Paul and the developing doctrine of the Church. Insertions, some glaringly obvious, some not, are many and varied. Which books were accepted as part of the official canon was also a matter of argument and vehement debate, which was finally settled by a show of hands. Hardly what we would reasonably expect to learn when we hear clergy of various denominations talking about scriptural authority, divine inspiration and *the inerrant word of God* as they so often do.

THE TRIUMPH OF PAUL'S TEACHING

The killing of James the Just, the priestly Messiah who had inherited the mantle of John the Baptist, triggered a series of events that eventually led to the explosive revolt of the Israelites against the hated Roman oppressors. One early Church father, Origen, wrote that Josephus recorded: 'James was of such great Holiness and enjoyed so great a reputation among the people that the downfall of Jerusalem was believed to be on account of his death.'[30] With the death of James and the scattering of the remaining Essenes and Ebionites, Pauline teaching was virtually unopposed and rapidly became the foundation for emerging Christian teaching and belief. After the Church had grown and eventually become 'established' by the Edict of Milan in 312 CE, its Pauline theological base became the foundation for a sustained campaign of suppression directed against all of its rivals – pagan temples, local deities and the wide range of mystery cults and Gnostic groups, Christian or otherwise.

Constantine the Great

When his decisive victory at the battle of the Milvian Bridge in 312 CE ended a brutal civil war, Constantine the Great became the ruler of the Roman Empire. Later the same year he passed the Edict of Milan which granted religious freedom to the previously persecuted Christians.[31] The almost inevitable and immediate result of the Edict was to increase the accumulation of wealth by the Church, which led, in its turn, to corruption. New bishops were soon being appointed for their high birth, personal wealth or administrative skills rather than for their piety. Constantine's motives for favouring Christianity were far from altruistic however, he wished to use the Christian religion with its teachings of 'render unto Caesar what is Caesar's' and 'obey all lawful authorities', as a form of social cement to unite the peoples of the empire who had been torn apart by the recent civil war.[32]

Constantine, however, was soon to be disappointed in his choice of a healing mechanism, for among the most divisive factors within the empire were the continuing bitter doctrinal disputes within Christianity. In fact the state was in grave danger of being torn apart by the vituperative theological arguments within the Church.[33] Not surprisingly, the most vigorously disputed question arose from the ever-present debate about the true nature of Jesus, or Christ as he was now more commonly called. To the Pauline Christians, Jesus was not merely divine he was 'the only begotten Son of God.' To the Arians, on the other hand, God the Father was the 'One True God' and although Jesus was divinely guided, he was not God, but man. According to Arius (d. 336 CE), it was even possible for Jesus to have sinned. This idea caused uproar within the Church and provoked theologians to attain the heights of absurdity and vitriolic abuse in their attempts to defend and clarify Paul's blasphemous idea that Jesus, the ultra-orthodox Jewish rabbi, was God. The only way to stop to this increasingly bitter internecine strife was to come up with a binding definition that clarified precisely in what sense Jesus was God. As the emperor placed political stability far higher in his list of priorities than either religious or historical truth, it was deemed imperative to impose his will on the squabbling clerics who threatened to tear his empire apart, and so he convened the first ecumenical council of the Church at Nicea in 325 CE.[34]

The Council of Nicea

The Council of Nicea in 325 CE was convened by Constantine to end all controversy over the nature of Jesus, buttress the power of the clergy and condemn heresy in all its forms; furthermore it created an effective power base for the Church that it has continued to use, strengthen and exploit ever since. However as a means of ending all religious disputes, it was a dismal failure, but it did accomplish one vital political objective in a novel manner. Decisions of the carefully chosen delegates were promulgated as official Church doctrine, binding on all believers, and this was to have devastating long-term effects. Church and state were now officially in line with one another under the authority of the emperor. Needless to say, the teachings of Arius were condemned as heretical.[35]

Constantine also incorporated Mithraic mythology into Christianity, such as the myth of a holy birth in a grotto attended by shepherds, an apocalyptic judgement day, the concept of a 'Holy Trinity', first suggested by another sun-worshipper, the Pharaoh Akenhaten in Egypt, the resurrection of the body and the second coming of a god, only this time it was Jesus who was to come again, not Mithras. Sunday, the day previously dedicated to Sol Invictus, the Sun god of the Mithraic cult followed by Constantine, was now to be the official Sabbath instead of the ancient and revered Jewish one of Friday dusk until Saturday sundown. The Creed of Nicea, not to be confused with the later Nicene Creed, stated unequivocally that Jesus was divine and the equal of God the Father in every way. To ram this point home, the council decreed that anyone who did not accept the divinity of Jesus was to be excommunicated, thus laying the foundations for centuries of repression to come and sowing the seeds of future antagonism towards Jews and Muslims. One of the emperor's final actions was to impose sentences of exile on all the bishops who refused to sign the council's decrees, thus illustrating the freedom of conscience he had accorded to them. A year later, he sent a letter to the newly defined heretical sects informing them that their places of worship were to be confiscated[36] and in 333 CE, the emperor promulgated a further decree that stated:

> ... if any teatise composed by Arius is discovered, let it be consigned to the flames... in order that no memorial of him whatever be left. .. if anyone shall be caught concealing a book by Arius, and does not immediately bring it out and burn it, the penalty shall be death; the criminal shall suffer punishment immediately after conviction.[37]

Thus was created the first official Church/state establishment in Europe, founded firmly on fear and repression that was to set the scene for much of what was to come. Yet, despite all this, the vexed question about the true nature of Jesus was to bedevil the Church for the next five centuries. This repressive Church/state alliance, however, was to last, in one form or another, for centuries to come and was described by the modern Catholic theologian Matthew Fox as, 'An abortion in the womb of the Church.'[38]

Soon after the Council of Nicea, Constantine made it clear that the benefits he had granted to the Christian Church, 'must benefit only adherents of the Catholic Faith,'[39] who were defined as those who accepted without reservation the doctrine enunciated in the new creed and the supreme ecclesiastical authority of the bishop of Rome. Later emperors continued the same policy and membership of a heretical sect incurred a degree of infamy and a loss of civil rights. By the time of Emperor Theodosius in the 5th century, these restrictions had multiplied until there were over 100 statutes aimed at heretics.

Heresy

Theodosius I was responsible for the exile and expulsion of Nestorius, the Patriarch of Constantinople, who made the assertion that to argue about whether Jesus was 'God' or the 'Son of God' was irrelevant as everyone knew that he had been born to a human father and mother like anyone else. Exiled with Nestorius was a large group of Greek classical scholars; in this manner, all the benefits of centuries of Greek intellectual speculation and learning, philosophy, mathematics, and science were wiped from the memory of European man as if they had never existed.[40] Thus the Church, which claimed to be based upon the redemptive sacrifice of the risen Christ, was brutally unmerciful to those who disagreed with it on matters of faith.

The Church historian David Christie-Murray defines heresy as, '... an opinion held by a minority of men which the majority declares unacceptable and is powerful enough to punish'.[41] The necessity for punishment, however, created the need for a more precise definition, which was provided by St Augustine (354–430), who became Bishop of Hippo in 396 CE. He redefined heresy as, 'the distortion of a revealed truth by a believer or an unbeliever'. The ambiguous term 'revealed truth' was simply defined, by the Church of course, as, 'what the Church itself had declared to be revealed truth'. The hierarchy used this circular argument, along with St Augustine's other pronouncements on heresy, to establish a total monopoly on all access to the sacred.[42]

The Church has always seemed to believe that heresy exists wherever and whenever any man exercises his God-given gift of free will in matters of faith. In 1990 Cardinal Ratzinger, who was in charge of the Congregation of the Doctrine of the Faith, the modern equivalent of the Inquisition, and who is now Pope Benedict, claimed: 'The freedom of the act of faith cannot justify the right to dissent'.[43] To show how little has changed over two millennia, the New Catholic Catechism, published the same year, states that, 'The task of giving an authentic interpretation of the Word of God... has been entrusted to the living teaching office of the Church alone.'

THE POPE CONSOLIDATES HIS POWER

After the Council of Nicea, the Church claimed that the Bishop of Rome and the hierarchy were God's representatives on earth and that, therefore, all their pronouncements had divinely approved authority. In this manner, the position held by James the Just, the first 'bishop' of Jerusalem was completely reversed. James, as the hereditary high-priest at the Temple in Jerusalem, had humbled himself in the Holy of Holies as the representative of his people, praying to God for forgiveness. Now, the position had irrevocably and completely changed, and the pope was declared to be the representative of God before the people and therefore ruled over them all in God's name. James had humbly and devoutly served his people, the pope now proudly and arrogantly ruled his.

In order to legitimize its claim to spiritual supremacy, the Roman Church used the completely unjustifiable assertion that both St Peter and St Paul had been martyred in Rome, despite contemporary evidence that Peter had been crucified in Jerusalem, and the uncomfortable fact that there simply is no evidence to suggest that Paul was executed by the Romans or by anyone else. This fabricated Petrine foundation myth, classed as 'tradition' by the Church, was then used to substantiate the even more spurious claim to 'apostolic succession' used to assert the primacy of the Bishop of Rome over all Christians.

Laurence Gardner, the English writer, records that Pope Sylvester informed a group representing the *Desposyni*, the descendants of the family of Jesus, that they and their teachings now had no place in the new Christian order.[44] The pope told them that the teachings of Jesus had been superseded by Church doctrine which had been amended in conformity to the emperor's wishes. Despite the fact that at the Council of Nicea Jesus had been elevated to equal status with God the Father, the pope now declared that salvation rested not with Jesus, but with the Roman emperor Constantine the Great.[45] The *Desposyni* were regarded as so important throughout the Jewish Diaspora and among the followers of the true teachings of Jesus that, for many centuries to come, both the Roman emperors and the bishops of Rome continued to persecute them[46] as had the emperors Vespasian, Titus, Domitian and Trajan before them.[47]

Not surprisingly in the circumstances, particularly after their rebuke from the pope, the *Desposyni* and other members of the Essenes and the

Ebionites went underground to ensure their survival.[48] Scattered throughout Europe, Arabia, Egypt and the Near East, these descendants of the *ma'madot*, the 24 high-priestly families of biblical Judaism, learned to dissemble in order to survive. Outwardly they followed the prevailing religion of their time and place; in secret they preserved the true initiatory teachings of Jesus. Like all the high-priestly families before them, they kept strictly to the marriage laws that bound the Cohen clan. Levites, the hereditary holders of minor priestly duties at the Temple, were allowed to marry outside their clan: the Cohens, as hereditary high priests, could only marry other Cohens. As heirs to a hereditary office that traced its origins back to the first dynasties of Egypt, this restriction was sacrosanct and inviolable. Henceforth they called themselves Rex Deus or, more simply, 'the Families'.

The Church Tightens its Grip

The Rex Deus families, the last truly authoritative group that could give the lie to the Church's dogmatic and blasphemous assertion that Jesus was God, were now scattered and silent. A silence that was vitally necessary for survival, for the Church could brook no rivals, persecuted all those it classified as heretics and swept away all other sources of knowledge of the spiritual world. It campaigned vigorously for the destruction or closure of all the temples and centres of worship of rival faiths throughout the empire, often hijacking these sacred sites for its own use. Thus the Greek mystery temples were rendered defunct and the oracles silenced for all time.[49] The Church slammed the doors that gave access to the spiritual and cultural heritage of the people and it resented and feared any access to the realms of either sacred or secular knowledge that it did not control.[50] Who knows what might happen if people were encouraged into education, intellectual adventure and inquiry? Education was therefore restricted to the clergy and holy orders became the essential prerequisite for basic literacy.

By restricting access to books, education, understanding and the world of the spirit, the Church revealed its real aims and objectives: total power and control over kings, emperors and princes; over territories, peoples and individuals; over this life and entrance to the next. With the Church's stranglehold on all forms of education, intellectual adventure was stifled and the superstitious populace remained quiescent in a state of ignorance and fear. Thus with the effective end of the Arian faith in the 5th century, a period of calm and unity of religious belief appeared to pervade the intellectual and spiritual desert that was Europe in the Dark Ages.

CHAPTER 3

The Rise of Islam
& its Empire

After the fall of Jerusalem in 70 CE, a large number of Jewish families fled to Arabia and these were joined later by others fleeing from Judea after the failure of the Bar Kochba revolt in 135 CE. They preserved their own culture, remained unwavering in their monotheism and were at all times sustained by the certain knowledge that they were the chosen people. By the 7th century the native Bedouin tribes of Arabia, on the other hand, had to live in fierce competition with one another in order to gain even the bare necessities of life and this gave rise to an ideology called *muruwah* which stressed the supreme importance of courage in battle, patience and endurance in suffering and, above all, absolute and unequivocal dedication to the welfare and needs of the tribe.[1] They worshipped the fixed stars and planets, angels and a wide variety of inferior deities whom they believed could intercede on their behalf before 'the most high God' al-Lah.[2] The term 'most high god' was identical to the phrase used by both Abraham and Melchizedek in the Bible.

In the city of Mecca in the Hijaz, stood the *Kabah*,[3] a huge block of stone said to be the seat of the Nabatean god Hubal which was the focus for an annual pilgrimage for Arab tribesmen. For the duration of this pilgrimage, or *haj*, all hostilities between the various tribes were banned and Mecca became a thriving centre of trade as well as the hub of a series of caravan routes to nearby Yathrib and more distant destinations such as Egypt, the Yemen and Syria.[4] The advanced civilizations of Byzantium, Persia, Iraq, Syria and Palestine, however, regarded Arabia as a barbaric place but, nonetheless, a degree of intellectual and spiritual life arising from both Jews and Christians alike slowly began to affect the Arab people.[5] Furthermore, many of the northern tribes on the borderland between the Persian and Byzantine empires had converted to Nestorian Christianity[6] which, as I have indicated earlier, firmly believed that Jesus was both a man and a prophet but not divine. Around Mecca and Yathrib, the influence of Monophysite Christianity which taught that in the person of Jesus there was only one single, human, nature, was even stronger.[7]

MUHAMMED IBN ABDALLA

By the time of the birth of Muhammed in or around 570 CE, Jewish tribes were settled at Fadak, to the north of Mecca,[8] in Wadi al-Quara and Tayma[9] and a further Jewish community, the Khaybar, lived about 100 kilometres to the north of Yathrib. Almost half the population of Yathrib, now the city of Medina, were Jewish and were known as the Kahinan;[10] they included the tribes of the Banu Nadir, the Qurayza, Qaynuqa and others who were descendants of the *ma'madot*, the hereditary high-priestly families of Jerusalem. These direct family links to the true teachings of Jesus, stimulated the circulation of a variety of writings associated with James the Just and the Ebionites among both Jews and Christians in Arabia.

In about the year 610 an Arab merchant, Muhammed ibn Abdalla of the Quraysh tribe, who lived near Mecca in the Hijaz, underwent a deep spiritual experience while on retreat during the month of Ramadan. Muhammed spent this time of spiritual retreat praying to the High God of the Arabs, al-Lah, and distributing food and alms to the poor who came to visit him during this sacred period.[11] He believed that al-Lah, the High God of the Arab pantheon, whose name simply means 'the God', was the identical deity to that worshipped by the Jews and the Christians, yet Muhammed, like all Arabs, was acutely aware that al-Lah had never sent them either a prophet or a scripture of their own, despite the fact that he had his shrine in their midst since time imme-morial, for while the Kabah in the heart of Mecca was dedicated to the Nabatean deity Hubal, most Arabs believed that originally it been ded-icated to al-Lah.[12]

Muhammed recounts that he was forcibly awoken from his sleep on the 17th night of Ramadan in 610 CE, and immediately felt himself enveloped by a divine presence. He later recounted that an angel had appeared to him and given him a curt command: Recite! (*iqra*). Like the Hebrew prophets of antiquity, who were often reluctant to utter the Word of God, Muhammed refused because for him a reciter was a *kahin*, an ecstatic fortune-teller who claimed to recite inspired oracles. Then, he recounted, the angel enveloped him in an overpowering embrace again with such force that he felt as if all the breath was being squeezed from his body. The angel released him and commanded him again to 'Recite!' Once again Muhammed refused and the angel embraced him a third time, and at the end of this third terrifying embrace, Muhammed heard the first words of a new sacred scripture pouring from his mouth:[13]

Recite in the name of thy Sustainer, who has created — created man out of a germ-cell! Recite — for thy Sustainer is the most Bountiful, One who has taught (man) the use of the pen — taught him what he did not know!'[14]

When he recovered his senses, terrified in the extreme, Muhammed rushed from the cave with the intention of throwing himself off the mountain to his death. Yet, as he left the cave he heard a voice from heaven which declaimed 'Oh Muhammed! Thou art the Apostle of God and I am Gabriel.'[15] Then, according to the English author Karen Armstrong, Muhammed, experienced 'that overpowering apprehension of numinous reality which the Hebrew prophets called *kaddosh*, holiness, the terrifying otherness of God.'[16] When he consulted his wife on these matters, she suggested he talk to her cousin Waraqa ibn Nawfal who was a Christian and well versed in the scriptures. Waraqa was in no doubt whatsoever as to the truth of what had just happened: Muhammed had indeed received a revelation from God. The God of Abraham and of Moses and the prophets had indeed appointed Muhammed as an apostle of God and the divine envoy to the Arab people.

The Prophet, who had suffered periods of self-doubt after his first visionary experiences, soon became convinced of the innate truth of the revelations that had been granted to him and 'knew' that he was indeed a 'messenger of God' in the time-hallowed tradition of Abraham, Moses, Elijah, John the Baptist and Jesus.[17] However, Muhammed no more thought of himself as the founder of a new religion than had Jesus before him, indeed he was absolutely convinced that he was restoring the one true monotheism that had existed since ancient times, and was the last in a long line of prophets who testified to the same religion of 'the one true God'. Indeed, he regarded himself as 'The Seal of the Prophets'. According to the Prophet, the 'One Truth' had been revealed to both Jews and Christians but they had either distorted the message or ignored it. [18]

The Holy Qur'an

Later, Muhammed dictated these visions to scribes who recorded them as the Holy Qur'an which, in its 114 chapters, or *suras*, preaches pure and unalloyed monotheism and beautiful, yet simple, instructions of how to submit to God's will. When one considers that Muhammed himself believed he was re-establishing true monotheism it is not surprising that there are strong similarities and parallels between the Judaism of the Ebionites and the teachings of the Qur'an. Indeed, during his visionary sessions, Muhammed had a deep mystical experience in which he was magically transported to Jerusalem and then ascended through the seven heavens, an almost identical replication of the ascents to the throne described in the Jewish Hekkaloth mysticism. It has also been suggested that the Prophet was a direct descendant of Simon, one of the younger brothers of Jesus and the implications of this are simply that he too was of the Rex Deus line and tradition.[19] Prince Michael of Albany, who also claims to be of the Rex Deus line, writes that one of Muhammed's ancestors, Ilyas, was the son of Simon's grand-daughter, and indeed the Jewish name of Ilyas, or Elisha, does occur in the Prophet's genealogy.[20] Whatever the truth of this may be, the fact remains that however many times God chooses to reveal his will for mankind, when these revelations are authentic, the divinely revealed truth within them will always be the same after making allowance for differences in language and culture.

Islam

The Prophet decreed that new converts should bow down in ritual prayer (*salat*) five times a day, an external gesture signifying an internal humility towards God. In time, this religion became known as *Islam*, a form of existential submission to al'Lah. A Muslim was anyone, male or female, who surrendered their whole being, body, soul and spirit, to the Creator of all. The instructions within the Holy Qur'an led to the foundation of a pious, just and equitable society in which the poor, the sick and the vulnerable are treated with respect and dignity. The principle of alms-giving (*zakat*) and prayer (*salat*) became two of the five essential pillars (*rukn*) of Islam. Ritual fasting, or *saum*, during the month of Ramadan was, at first, a matter of voluntary self-denial but later this too became one of the obligatory 'pillars of Islam'.[21]

Theological speculation of any kind was dismissed as *zanna*, or self-indulgent guesswork about matters that would be forever beyond the understanding of any mere mortal. This contrasted starkly with Christian practice where the Church's views on abstruse theological matters as 'The Holy Trinity' or 'The Incarnation' became matters of dogma, binding on all believers, and led to the persecution of all who dissented. Furthermore the suras teach Muslims to glimpse the Divine in the 'signs' of nature; the Qur'an urges all true believers to view the world as an ongoing epiphany in which they need to be constantly aware in order to perceive the transcendental divine reality that unites everything in the diverse and complex world of God's creation. Muslims were therefore encouraged to use their God-given powers of reason to decipher these 'signs' or divine messages, which led to a healthy attitude to both intellectual endeavour and curiosity which, in its turn, stimulated a remarkable development of the study of natural science that was, in their opinion, fully in keeping with God's will. The Christian Church, on the other hand, had an innate distrust of intellectual adventure that ultimately led to the perception that science was a danger to the Christian faith.

Muhammed's Mission

Muhammed preached to the citizens of Mecca, warning them against social indifference and the perils of their newfound materialism, and vehemently opposing the prevalent polytheism on which they believed

41

that their recent prosperity depended.[22] This was perceived as a threat to Mecca's wealth and trade, and the Prophet and his followers were forced to move to Yathrib in fear of their lives. The date of this move, or *Hegira*, in 622 CE marks the beginning of the Muslim calendar. Yathrib itself was soon renamed as *Medinat-al-Nabi*, the city of the Prophet, now known as Medina.[23] From that time onward, the first 'pillar of Islam' was to be the *shahadah*, the profession of faith: 'I bear witness that there is no god but al-Lah and that Muhammed is his messenger.'[24]

The Holy Qur'an insists that all the People of the Book[25] were not necessarily in error and that, fundamentally, all religions based upon revelations from God were, essentially, one. Thus, the Prophet never expected Christians or Jews to convert to Islam, for they too had received authentic revelations from God. The revelations of the Qur'an had neither cancelled out nor devalued previous scriptural sources but, indeed, had confirmed and completed them, for each prophet had confirmed the revelations of his predecessors and developed those insights according to the will of God.[26] The Holy Qur'an instructs all Muslims to create a just society and the new followers of Islam took this duty very seriously indeed.

Faced by enemies in Mecca and elsewhere, Muhammed spent the last ten years of his life in a struggle against opposing forces and converted people at phenomenal speed, thus vastly expanding the territory he controlled. By the end of his life, most of the Arabian tribes had joined him. He conquered the city of Mecca two years before he died and instituted the *haj*, or pilgrimage to that city as the fifth pillar of Islam, a sacred duty every Muslim is bound to make at least once in his life, if circumstances allow.

The Death of the Great Prophet

Muhammed died unexpectedly in June in 632 CE, without having nominated a successor. Despite the shock, Islam stood firm; Muhammed had not only been the divinely chosen vehicle for a new revelation, but his military success had laid down a solid political and temporal foundation on which his successors could build. The Prophet was succeeded by Abu Bakr who reigned from 632 to 634. It was he who arranged for the compilation of the first written version of the Holy Qur'an. His authority was such that he was able to forge what had been a loosely connected group of disparate tribes into a cohesive and devout community and he assumed the title of caliph, from the Arabic *khalifa*, or representative, as did the others that followed him.[27] He was succeeded as caliph by another of the Prophet's early converts, Umar ibn al-Khattab (634–44 CE), a man renowned for his piety, humility, courage and strength of will, who is regarded as the true founder of the Islamic Empire.

ISLAMIC CULTURE AND THE CONSOLIDATION OF EMPIRE

After the accession of Caliph Uthman (644–56 CE) the first in the Umayyad dynasty, the empire spread with formidable speed due to the warlike prowess of the Arab tribesmen. Yet, while these vast territorial gains were undoubtedly made by the sword, it must be clearly and unequivocally stated that the spread of Islam as a religion was not. The forcible conversion of other faiths was absolutely contrary to all the fundamental principles of choice and religious toleration that Islam espoused. Indeed, the People of the Book – Jews, Christians and Zoroastrians – were treated with such respect within the Islamic world that they became willing subjects of the caliphate, for their legal status under Islam was infinitely better than that accorded to them by the Byzantine Christians in Syria, Palestine and Egypt, the Sassanids in Persia or the Visigoths in Spain. The newly subjected peoples who did become followers of Islam in vast numbers were attracted to that religion by its spiritual purity and the relevance of its message to their daily lives. In the predominantly Christian countries of Iraq, Syria and Egypt, the advent of Islam bestowed religious freedom to many 'heretical' Christian sects that had previously been persecuted by their earlier Byzantine rulers. This gave rise to a renaissance of minority Churches, the rebuilding of many monasteries, and ultimately to the recruitment of many Monophysite Christians as officials within the administration of the new state.[28]

Perhaps the greatest gift the Jews received from their new conquerors was the final lifting of the centuries-old prohibition against Jews residing in Jerusalem, first imposed by the Romans and maintained by the Byzantine Christians, and so several families took up residence in the Holy City.[29] Furthermore, in Palestine and throughout most of the East prior to the 7th century, the Jewish economy had been primarily an agricultural one but, as a direct result of the *dhimmi*, the new poll and land tax imposed by the Arab conquerors, many Jews left the land and sought their livelihood in the far more lucrative world of commerce.[30] By the end of the 8th century this resulted in Jewish traders exerting a predominant influence on the caravans connecting the East to the West.

Jews had certain advantages as traders for they operated under a unified legal code, benefited from having supportive Jewish communities strategically placed along the trade routes and, above all, had a fluent mastery of the two major international languages, Arabic and Hebrew. These Jewish merchants became important cultural agents, bringing the teachings of their religious school, or *yeshiva*, in Baghdad to all the Jewish communities of the Diaspora and thus contributing to its increasing authority.[31] In fact, the Islamic Empire brought a high degree of unification to Jewish communities throughout the Diaspora[32] and within a short space of time over 90 per cent of the Jewish settlements in the world was subject to Islamic rule. With the establishment of the capital of the Abbasid dynasty at Baghdad the largest and wealthiest Jewish communities always remained close to the seat of real political power.[33]

Baghdad had long been an important Christian city and was home to the Nestorian patriarch and contained monasteries belonging to the Nestorian, Jacobite and Melekite obediences. It was also, as mentioned above, the intellectual capital of Judaism with its Talmudic schools and the presence at court of the exilarch.[34]

The Founding of Baghdad

In 756 CE, the Abbasid caliph al-Mansur (754–75 CE) began the construction of a capital in Baghdad which soon assumed a preeminence in the sciences, literature and the arts that it would maintain long after the city had lost its political power.[35] Under the rule of the caliphs al-Mansur, his son al-Mahdi (775–85) and then his nephew Harun al-Rashid (786–808), the study of philosophy, law, history, geography, poetry and architecture flourished as never before. When Harun's son, al-Mamun (813–33) became caliph he founded the 'House of Science', otherwise known as the 'House of Wisdom' (*bait al-hik-ma*) to preserve and disseminate the accumulated learning of Greek Antiquity.[36] Baghdad became the epicentre of an empire and a vibrant culture that was undoubtedly the most sophisticated in the world outside of China.

Thus, it was the Muslims, and not the Christians, who rekindled the flames of classical Greek science. The scholars of Baghdad knew that the world was round, and could measure a degree of longitude many centuries before their European Christian counterparts. They revived the astronomy of the Chaldeans, encouraged Jewish alchemists and men of medicine and translated the works of Galen, the 2nd-century Greek physician, into Arabic. The quality of Islamic art and architecture was of such renown that architects and mathematicians from as far away as Constantinople and Sammara came to the empire's centres of learning.[37]

Al Andalus – Moorish Spain

At the beginning of the 8th century, the Visigothic Empire, Spain, was in a state of political turmoil, and it is feasible to suppose that both Byzantine and Jewish merchants in Spain may have asked the nearby forces of Islam in North Africa for help to combat Visigothic persecution.[38] Musa ibn Nusair, the governor of the Islamic province of Ifriqiya, dispatched his most able general, Tariq ibn Zihad, in April 711 with an army of 7,000 Berbers.[39] Tariq landed at Gibraltar (the name derives from the Arabic *Jebel al-Tariq*, or the Rock of Tariq) and pushed inland. In a lightning campaign which met with little resistance, he captured Malaga, Grenada and Cordova and then, on 19 July 711 at the Battle of the Rio Barbate, destroyed the Christian army after which the demoralized Christians fled in disarray to the north, and Tariq occupied the royal city of Toledo. Musa himself landed in June with 18,000 Arab troops and conquered Seville and Mérida before joining Tariq outside Toledo.[40] Resistance to the Muslim invasion was sparse and ineffective. The flight of the Christian armies was panic-stricken, and this incredibly rapid conquest of most of Spain was typical of the way in which the Muslim armies combined prudence with audacity.[41]

Forays into Christian Europe

The new conquerors crossed the Pyrenees in 719 CE and invaded and plundered parts of the Frankish Empire. Some years later the Muslim armies conquered Carcassonne and ravaged territory on the far side of the Rhône as far as Autun in Burgundy. One Governor of al-Andalus, Abd-al-Rahman al-Gafiqui, ranged as far as the Loire and sacked

Tours. In October 732, however, at the famous Battle of Poitiers, he was defeated and killed by a Frankish army under the command of Charles Martel (688–741) known thereafter as Charles the Hammer, who was the grandfather of Charlemagne.[42] Frontier disputes continued for many years and after 791 Muslim troops once again captured Carcassonne and Narbonne.[43]

CONSOLIDATION AND CULTURAL EXCELLENCE

The rule of the Umayyads in the 9th century saw the peak of cultural achievement, not merely in Spain but in the entire European continent. The rise of Cordova was ensured by Abd al-Rahman II (822–52), who devoted much time to cultural matters and began the construction of public buildings in the city that are a source of pride today. During his reign, the Jewish population of Granada was estimated to be over 5,000, thus it is no wonder that the Muslims called the city *Gharnatat al-Yahud*, the City of the Jews.[44]

It was Abd al-Rahaman III (912–61) who finally unified the Islamic territories in Spain, reconquering Seville and Mérida. Exploiting the political weakness in the Christian lands, he concluded a treaty of protection with the kingdoms of León and Navarre who, in consequence, recognized Abd al-Rahaman III as the de facto ruler and arbiter in all Spain. Even the strong Christian kingdoms of Castille and Barcelona in the Spanish March paid him tribute. When, in January 929 he named himself caliph, Cordova became the third caliphate in Islam along with the caliphates of Baghdad and Cairo.[45] The new caliph created a new and a strictly centralized internal administration and ensured the country's rapid growth in prosperity based upon extensive irrigation and efficient agriculture.

The arts flourished along with agriculture, and Muslim sophistication paved the way for the new rulers to found trade guilds for skilled
craftsmen who were prized and well rewarded.[46] The formulation of
an effective and just tax system resulted in overflowing state coffers and
allowed further trade concessions for the Jews. All these factors, allied
to sound municipal administration, enabled al-Andalus to become the
most populous country in Europe at that time. Cordova, its capital,
thrived as an economic and cultural centre to such an extent that it was
compared favourably with Constantinople, the capital of the Byzantine
Empire and may even have even exceeded that city as a centre of
learning.[47] Indeed it boasted 80,000 market stalls, 1,000 mosques and
900 bath houses, a completely unknown luxury in the Christian lands
beyond the Pyrenees.[48]

The caliph's son, Crown Prince al-Hakkam (961–76) shared in government from the age of 40, and later, as caliph, continued to build upon
his father's achievements. He surrounded himself with scientists and
scholars, and amassed many books, following the example of previous
emirs who had also owned great libraries and attracted poets, philosophers and mathematicians to their courts.[49] He created a library of
400,000 books in Cordova, which were indexed in 44 catalogues, and
he added his own commentaries to many of these volumes.[50] This
became the greatest library in Europe and was second only to the greatest
in the world which was located in Baghdad at the heart of the Islamic
Empire. This almost insatiable passion for learning stimulated the production of between 70,000 and 80,000 bound volumes each year, which
not only reflected local demand but also demonstrated the country's
capacity for a phenomenal high-volume, top-quality production, many
centuries before the invention of printing. Muslims had learned the
secret of papermaking while in Samarkand and had spread the art
throughout the empire; Spain, Cordova, Valencia and Toledo became

vibrant centres of this new industry, stimulated by the seemingly insatiable demand for books and documents.[51] Sciences, such as geography,
agriculture and irrigation, astronomy, medicine and mathematics were
actively encouraged; as was the serious study of philosophy based prin-
cipally on classical Greek thought. With the expulsion of the persecuted
Nestorian scholars from Europe as a result of Christian intolerance, the
Arab world had become home to this vast collection of Greek learning,
and to mathematics.[52] It was not just the fruits of Greek civilization that
impinged upon European consciousness from Islamic roots, but also
more recent advances in medicine, art and architecture. Much of the
classical knowledge of ancient Greece that we now treasure and take
for granted would have withered away had it not been preserved and
enhanced by Islamic scholars.[53] As caliph, al-Hakkam now commissioned
many scholarly works on ethics, statecraft and history, taking a personal
interest in popular literacy and education, establishing schools and centres
of learning open to people of every social class. Thus, his reign is rightly
renowned as the apotheosis of science, scholarship and poetry in the
history of Moorish Spain.[54]

The Jews, who were being treated as second-class citizens in
Christian Europe, enjoyed a rich cultural renaissance of their own[55] and
the large Christian population was also allowed full religious liberty in
Spain as throughout the Islamic Empire. Most Spanish Christians were
extremely proud to belong to a highly advanced and sophisticated culture
that was light-years ahead of the rest of Europe.[56] The full extent of the
contribution of Moorish Spain to the development of European culture
is incalculable and Spanish Christian scholars later supplied much of the
raw material for the emerging literature of the West.[57] Thus, the
variety of literary creation in Spain was both broader and richer than
that which arose in the caliphate of Baghdad or North Africa.[58]

Under the rule of the Umayyad caliphs, Moorish Spain gained

international renown for the poetry, literature and learning of both Cordova and Granada. The well-attended and richly endowed colleges in Andalusia were later to provide a model and a template for those founded in Oxford and Cambridge in England.[59] In an era when the vast majority of European Christian nobles, kings and emperors were illiterate, the Islamic Umayyad court at Cordova was the most splendid in Europe; one that provided a haven and an oasis of peace wherein philosophers, poets, artists, mathematicians and astronomers could pursue their studies.[60] It was in Muslim Spain that Jewish science found its most fertile soil and made substantial and important contributions to medicine, geography, cosmology, the development of instruments for measurement, cartography and navigation, and, as importantly, the translation of works from Greek into Arabic and from Arabic into Latin and other European languages. The Jews became the most important cultural link in the transmission of scientific knowledge from one culture to another and in this manner Jewish scholarship became crucial to the emergence of modern science.

In Andalusia, as in the Muslim world at large, the Jews wrote their scientific, medical and philosophical treatises in Arabic, a language that they found best suited to this branch of human learning. It was through this combination of Islamic respect for learning and Jewish scholarship that the West first came into contact with classical Greek science and its Arabic commentators. It was in Toledo and in centres in Septimania – a broad stretch of land, once settled by soldiers discharged from the Roman Seventh Legion, that ran from Arles in the Rhône delta to the Pyrenees and had supported a large Jewish population since Roman times – that Jewish scholars translated works in philosophy, mathematics, geometry, physics, astronomy, astrology, medicine, and magic and laid down the foundations for the Latin science that evolved during the central and late Middle Ages.[61]

Spiritual Schools in Muslim Spain

Religious and spiritual schools abounded in all three of the main religious communities; Muslim madrasas, Jewish yeshiva and Christian seminaries worked side by side in this tolerant country, each operating according to the religious requirements of their own community. Jewish yeshivas refined and enhanced the various oral traditions of mysticism within the Hebraic tradition, such as the *maaseh bereshith*, based on the work of creation described in the first chapter of Genesis, and the *maaseh merkabah*, founded on accounts of Ezekiel's vision of the divine chariot; 'the Psalms of ascents' that is, the mystical ascents to the higher heavens, or the ascent through the various degrees of neo-Platonic enlightenment or gnosis in a variation of the Merkabah tradition known as Hekaloth.[62] These now developed into a written form known as the kabbala, allegedly the oldest Jewish initiatory, mystical tradition first received from Aaron and passed down from master to pupil in an oral form of teaching that only attained its written form in the 13th century CE. The Sefer HaZohar or Book of Splendour expressed its principal aspects, mainly Jewish Gnosticism tinged with Sufi mysticism, recently synthesized neo-Platonism and magic.[63] It was written about 1280 and spread into Christian Europe from the rabbinical schools in Moorish Spain and Septimania. Later, during the 14th and 15th centuries, the kabbala spread into Christian Europe and a Christianized form of it became popular among scholars of a mystical inclination.

Sufi Schools in Spain

The Sufi mystery schools in Spain were the principal open and accessible sources of Muslim mystical teaching in a continent wherein the Christian Church actively discouraged spiritual exploration.[64] Sufism is a mystical tradition that derives its inspiration from the Qur'an and the teaching of the Prophet; the Sufi orders were all founded by men who claimed spiritual and/or genealogical descent from Muhammad and, therefore, from the family of Jesus. Thus, the Sufi masters are, most probably, a valid branch of the Rex Deus tradition. However, unlike their counterparts within the Christian world who had to operate in secret for fear of persecution, the Sufis were able to operate openly within Islam and contributed significantly to its development. The poet and mythologist Robert Graves claims that Sufism, in fact, dates back to 2500 BCE and alleges that he found a 'Sufic signature' in accounts of the building of Solomon's Temple in Jerusalem.[65] The grandson of Judaism's greatest thinker, Moses Maimonides (1135–1204 CE), also claimed that the Sufi tradition is Hebraic in origin when he wrote that Sufism is 'the pride of Israel bestowed upon the nations'.[66] Undoubtedly, the greatest medieval mystical writer was the Sufi teacher from Seville, Mohieddin ibn Arabi (1165–1240) who described the Great Prophet Muhammed as the manifestation of the 'Perfect Man'. Renowned as a mystic, philosopher and poet, ibn Arabi is known among the Sufis as *Shaykh al-Akbar*, or the greatest teacher. In the West he became known as Doctor Maximus, an accurate translation of his Arabic title. His sublime poetry, which is even more popular today than it was in the medieval era, profoundly influenced such leading scholars as Friar Roger Bacon, Dante Alighieri, Cervantes, Averroes, St Francis of Assisi and Chaucer. From these brief examples, it is clear that Moorish Spain had a more profound influence on the development of European thought, scholarship and culture than any other single country in European history.

Classical Learning spreads to Christian Europe

Jewish scholars who could move with ease between Latin, Hebrew and Arabic, provided a vital link in the international dissemination of knowledge.[67] Knowledge of the Greek classics crept back into European consciousness via the theological college founded at Chartres by Bishop Fulbert (960–1028). His pupils were probably the first in Christian Western Europe to read the works of Plato, Aristotle, Pythagoras and Cicero as well as being familiar with mathematics, science and recent Arabic inventions such as the astrolabe.[68] This repository of knowledge at Chartres came from Moorish Spain, translated, not from Greek, but from Arabic by Jewish scholars. How did this knowledge get from Spain to Chartres? The answer lies in the Rex Deus connection whereby nobles of the hidden family group passed translations of the classics sent by members in Spain to another of their group, Bishop Fulbert.[69]

CHAPTER 4

The Dark Ages
in Christian Europe –
From the Fall of the Roman Empire
to the First Crusade

The western Roman Empire breathed its last in August 476 CE, when the last emperor, Romulus Augustus, was deposed as a result of the Visigoth invasion of Italy and their sacking of Rome. The eastern empire, with its capital at Constantinople, continued to flourish and thus was born the Byzantine Empire. The name Byzantine derived from the old Greek name for the city in pre-Roman times, namely Byzantium.

With the collapse of the Roman Empire, the Church was the only surviving institution with any determined sense of purpose that possessed the organizational skills necessary for survival. As it extended its influence over the barbarian tribes, it also became the major lawmaker in the declining empire. The clergy, who were not only the scribes but also the final arbiters against whose decisions there was no appeal, codified the traditional laws of the tribes of Europe. The clergy recorded the oral legends, myths and stories of the various tribes, adding their own distorted religious gloss, omitting all that was offensive to accepted doctrine, retaining this, adding that, subtly changing the histories and forming the mould for a new and essentially Christian, culture.

Thus the Church distorted the histories of entire cultures, increased its grip on the current reality of the tribes, on their past and their ancient cultural heritage.[1] Pagan festivals were incorporated wholesale into the new Christian calendar. The festival of Astarte, the Phoenician goddess of love and fertility, became Easter; the summer solstice became the feast of St John the Baptist; the pagan feast of the winter solstice, amalgamated with the birthday of Mithras, the Persian god of light, on 25 December, came to be celebrated as the birthday of Christ or 'Christmas'.

The fathers of the expanding Church believed they could legislate away all knowledge of the spiritual world, and that they could control all access to spiritual powers and this delusion influenced the thinking of Church leaders for centuries to come. The evidence that has come down to us is found in the truly horrendous stories of the persistent and vicious persecutions that were the inevitable result of such an illusion.[2] However, even in the well-named Dark Ages, there were glimmers of hope – little points of light battling against the seemingly all-pervading darkness imposed by the Church's monopoly on education and salvation. This hope sprang from the Ebionite/Rex Deus tradition that preserved the true teachings of Jesus.

CELTIC CHRISTIANITY

The first of these portents of truth was to be found in Ireland within the Celtic Church. The British Isles had been evangelized within four years of the Crucifixion, long before St Paul had confected the blasphemous dogma of the deification of Jesus. Evangelists who had been accredited by James the Just in Jerusalem arrived in Britain and Ireland

and founded the first 'Christian' church in the British Isles. According to St Gildas, writing in 542 CE[3] and the early Christian historian Freculpus,[4] this evangelical effort spawned a distinctive religion known as Celtic Christianity. In the tolerant atmosphere created by this new religion, the older Celtic religion of Druidism lasted for several centuries in Britain after the advent of the new faith. Most Druids had no difficulty with this form of initiatory Christianity and even became priests of the new religion, while continuing in their privileged position as members of an intellectual class created by their ancestors 1,000 years before.[5] Columba, the great Celtic saint, is on record as saying that 'Jesus is my Druid',[6] perhaps the most accurate delineation of the initiatory form of Jesus' teaching ever made in the West.

The Celtic Church developed a form of monasticism, characterized by spiritual purity and simplicity, in which priests were encouraged to marry and the priesthood was, like that in the early Jerusalem Church, a hereditary office.[7] No images of the Crucifixion were used in their churches and infant baptism was forbidden.[8] Unlike its power-hungry rivals in Rome, the Celtic Church rejected all the trappings of power, and the simplicity and humility of the Celtic monks stood in stark contrast to the pomp and circumstance of the priesthood in the rest of Europe.

These long-haired Celtic mystics and monks, inspired by their initiatory belief system, exhibited a vibrant cultural dynamism and their artwork, scholarship and scriptural learning were exemplary. Education was treasured and the monasteries accumulated large and well-used libraries. Nomadic by nature, the Celts evangelized much of Western Europe,[9] crossing from Scandinavia in the north to Switzerland in the east. The 17th-century historian, Thomas Fuller, described these peripatetic missionaries as the 'wandering scholars' who were as learned in the classics as they were in Holy Writ, another point that distinguishes them from their Roman Catholic counterparts. Such was the quality and range of their classical learning, that Professor H Zimmer claims: 'It is almost a truism to state that whoever knew Greek on the continent of Europe in the days of Charles the Bald was an Irishman or had been taught by an Irishman.'[10] In fact, they were known as the 'snail men' who left a silver trail of knowledge behind them wherever they went. Their efforts were soon swamped by the pervasive and repressive attitudes of the corrupt Church in Rome, but all was not yet lost in Dark Age Europe.

The whole of Christendom had been shocked and appalled when Jerusalem fell to the armies of Islam in 638, but in line with the basic principles of their faith, the Muslim conquerors were surprisingly tolerant of their Christian subjects. Indeed, many of the Christians, now under the rule of the Islamic Empire, preferred the life they led under their new political masters to that which they had endured for centuries under a succession of Byzantine emperors who taxed them excessively and often persecuted them for their 'heretical' beliefs. Heretical at least in the eyes of the rulers of Constantinople but, nonetheless, firmly held beliefs in Palestine, Syria and Egypt. Their new Muslim overlords now allowed them to believe whatever they wished and worship as they thought fit.

REX DEUS DESCENT

Throughout the early years of the Dark Ages the scattered members of Rex Deus kept a very low profile indeed in order to avoid persecution. The families descended from the *ma'madot*, who included the descendants of Jesus known as the *Desposyni*, secretly spread throughout Europe, Asia Minor and the East. Keeping their own 'heretical' beliefs secret and outwardly conforming to the religious and social practices of their district and time, Rex Deus members in Europe successfully avoided the unwelcome attention of the increasingly powerful Catholic Church. Many used their natural talents, literacy and Jewish contacts to gain and consolidate positions of power both among the landowning classes and the few trading families, usually also of Jewish origin. Several members of Rex Deus gained positions of power close to kings, both minor and sometimes major, and used their influence to ensure that other members of the family group were appointed to positions of aristocratic power and privilege.[11]

While great stress has often been placed on the Frankish Merovingian connections to the Rex Deus families, no evidence can be produced to validate the overwhelming importance placed upon this theory by the authors of *The Holy Blood and the Holy Grail*.[12] Indeed Michael Baigent, Richard Leigh and Henry Lincoln have signally ignored the family that truly wielded all power in the later years of the Merovingian era, the family identified over 50 years ago by Dr Walter Johannes Stein as the true 'family of the Grail',[13] the stewards of the palace who eventually usurped the crown, namely the Carolingians.

The Carolingians were illustrious in their own right and achieved fame both as statesmen and as generals. When Charles the Hammer conquered the Moorish army of Abd el-Rhaman at the Battle of Poitiers in 732 CE and halted the Islamic expansion into France and the whole of Europe, he was the mayor of the palace serving the Merovingian dynasty. It was Pepin the Short who actually deposed the Merovingians, won papal recognition for the Carolingian house, and went on to conquer Aquitaine, limiting Lombard power in northern Italy before finally driving the Moors from the Languedoc.[14] He died in 768 and his kingdom was divided between his son Charles, later known as 'the Great' or Charlemagne, and Pepin's younger son, Carloman. Carloman died in December 771 and subsequently Charlemagne reunited the kingdom and then initiated a series of wars to expand it. Eventually he ruled a vast empire that reached from the Danube to the Mediterranean. Charlemagne made several forays into Moorish Spain and while these were signally unsuccessful in the north, in the south his efforts were crowned with considerable success where he captured the important areas known as the Spanish Marches and consolidated the gains his father had made in Septimania, now the Languedoc/Rousillon.

Jewish Septimania

Shortly before the Moorish invasion, Jews fleeing from persecution in Visigothic Spain had settled in Septimania. This Jewish community became influential under the rule of Pepin the Short. One Latin romance, as well as several Hebrew and papal documents, attests to the fact that that the Jews of Narbonne delivered the city to the Frankish armies under Pepin in return for a promise of self-government under their own king.[15] Following the capture of Narbonne in 759 CE, the Jews of Septimania were a highly privileged group, richly endowed with freehold estates granted to them by the Carolingian kings.[16] Their protection continued under the reign of Charlemagne who could see where the commercial interests of his empire lay, for he knew that the Jews were the keys to success in international trade. Therefore, both he and his nobles actively encouraged Jewish immigration into the empire as a matter of consistent policy and many charters granting protection and privileges to Jewish merchants are still extant.[17]

The emperor Charlemagne used a Jew, Isaac by name, as an interpreter for the ambassador he sent to Harun-al-Rashid, caliph of Baghdad, in 797 which resulted in the first *nasi*, or Jewish prince of Narbonne, Rabbi Makhi being sent from Baghdad to Septimania, where Charlemagne endowed him with great possessions.[18] There is a long-standing tradition among European Jews that Charlemagne also encouraged the transfer of the main centre of Torah studies from Baghdad to Narbonne.[19] There may well have been another reason for Charlemagne's protection of the Jews, for the renowned historian of the Carolingian era, P Munz, writing long before any disclosure of the Rex Deus traditions, asserted that Charlemagne claimed succession from the biblical kings of Israel and concluded that Charlemagne engineered the situation in Septimania to arrange a marriage between his family and that of the nasi. This liason between two families both descended from the Davidic line, would demonstrate that the Carolingian dynasty had divine sanction as rulers.[20]

The major responsibility of the new Nasi Makhir was to lead the Jews of Septimania and the Toulousain in their defence of the Spanish frontier and the Mediterranean coast, against raids by the Umayyad Moors of Spain and North Africa.[21] Thus Charlemagne's motivation was many-faceted: it was commercial and directed towards trade; furthermore it encouraged Jewish scholarship, it also had a strong defensive element; and finally, it created the opportunity for the union in marriage of two royal houses descended from the House of David. This complex range of aims and objectives succeeded beyond all expectations.

The Jews of Septemania, under the leadership of their nasi, were steadfast supporters of the Carolingian dynasty throughout their long reign. The Jewish community in Narbonne prospered, grew, and lasted until the expulsion of the Jews from France under King Philippe le Bel in 1306. Archival records demonstrate that Jews maintained considerable estates in the Narbonnais from the time of Pepin the Short until the middle of the 11th century. Indeed one Christian commentator, Peter the Venerable, wrote in 1143, denigrating the 'Jewish king' of Narbonne and claiming that he could not accept any king of the Jews unless he reigned in the Holy Land.[22] The noted Jewish chronicler, Benjamin of Tudela, also writing in the 12th century, stated:

Narbonne is an ancient city of the Torah. From it the Torah goes out to all lands. Therein there are sages, magnates and princes (nas'im) at the head of whom is R. Kalonymo… a descendant of the House of David as stated in his family tree. He holds hereditaments and (other) landed properties from the rulers of the country and no one may dispossess him by force.[23]

The extensive properties held by the Jews and their nasi at the time of their expulsion indicates that they occupied a sizeable portion of the countryside and city until the early years of the 14th century.[24]

Charlemagne's statesmanship, military prowess and commercial acumen led not only to a growing reputation but also to an ever-expanding kingdom. He became the perfect ally for any ruler under pressure. On his election as pope, Leo III who was under threat from the Lombards to the north of Rome, wrote to Charlemagne in very strange terms indeed, assuring the king of the Franks of his humble obedience and promising fidelity to his person.[25] To relieve the pressure on Rome, Charlemagne made a series of successful forays into the Lombard kingdoms of northern Italy, and, as an act of gratitude and insurance, Pope Leo crowned Charlemagne as the new Holy Roman Emperor in 800. The great historian Edward Gibbon recounts that:

… at his Imperial Coronation, Rome, which had been delivered by the sword, was subject, as his own, to the sceptre of Charlemagne. The people swore allegiance to his person and family: in his name money was coined and justice was administered; and the election of Popes was examined and confirmed by his authority.[26]

Charlemagne continued to expand his empire by a series of campaigns against the Saxons and a variety of internal wars suppressing rebellion within its boundaries. To keep order within his sprawling dominions, he founded a warrior aristocracy,[27] rewarding relatives, supporters and loyal aids with the gift of lands. Charlemagne created over 600 counties[28] to be ruled, under his aegis of course, by his newly created and loyal counts. The most trustworthy people he could appoint to these positions of power were members of Rex Deus, especially in the regions of greatest potential danger, the marches or borderlands, which were ruled by a marquess and, under him, a number of counts. Thus, by the time of Charlemagne's death in 814, much of Europe, particularly France, Chartres, Champagne, Toulouse, Septimania, Provence, northern Italy and Saxony, were administered by nobility of the Rex Deus line. Nonetheless, life for the majority of people in Europe from the fall of the Roman Empire to the Crusades, was short, brutal and barbaric when compared with that in Islamic Spain.

The events of history rarely conform to the needs of any thematic chronicler, so, in order to gain some understanding of the roots of the seemingly perpetual hostility that exists between the worlds of Christianity and Islam, we need to go back in time. At first, the response of the Christians in the west of Europe to the rise of Islam was minimal until the warriors of North Africa invaded Spain. Charles Martel effectively put a halt to Muslim expansion into mainland France and Charlemagne's policy of containment resulted in the creation of a series of buffer states that limited any further major advance of the forces of Islam into his territory. Thus Septimania and the Spanish Marches came into being.

Throughout the Dark Ages there was a general trend within European society towards destruction and decay except, perhaps, in

Charlemagne's time.[29] Long-distance trade had all but died, with the exception of that in luxury goods, such as jewellery, carved ivory, and incense for the Church which was mainly carried on by Jews and Levantines. Thus, each small community was forced to become as self-supporting and self-reliant as possible.[30] Even the extensive and powerful state that developed under Charlemagne was, compared to the Islamic Empire ruled by Harun al-Rashid, rather like a minnow placed beside a whale. Charlemagne's power depended upon the loyalty of a fundamentally unruly military aristocracy who secured their domains by force rather than morality or justice. Literacy was limited to members of the clergy and, even among them it was often only vestigial, at least at the lower levels. Reading and writing were skills that were not prized in Europe, as they were in the Islamic world. The learning of classical antiquity had been replaced with a narrow and limited 'Christianized' intellectual culture based on the Bible and the works of the early Latin Fathers of the Church, such as St Augustine of Hippo. A deeply conservative and narrow culture thus developed, that looked inwards and backwards to the early years of the Church and no further.[31]

When Charlemagne died, Islamic power dominated the western end of the Mediterranean from Catalonia in Spain to Tunis in North Africa. Moorish pirates preyed upon Christian shipping, the forces of Islam built castles in Italy and in Provence; Rome itself had been sacked by the Muslims in 846.[32] The Islamic conquest of Sicily had begun in 827 and for more than a generation between 843 and 871, the Muslims maintained an important toehold on the mainland at Bari in Apulia. When they were eventually expelled from Bari, they acquired another base near Naples which they held until 915. Once the hold on Sicily was secure, the maritime regions of Calabria were repeatedly attacked.[33] A troublesome nest of Moorish pirates controlled the area in Provence surrounding La Garde-Freinet some 30 miles inland from St Tropez until

972 CE.[34] Eventually, in the 11th century, various bands of Norman mercenaries established themselves in southern Italy and then, gradually, between 1060 and 1091, they successfully wrested both Sicily and Malta from Muslim hands.[35] However, the new Norman overlords were so impressed with the sophisticated lifestyle and administration developed by their Muslim enemies that they retained many aspects of Muslim life and granted a high degree of religious freedom to their new subjects.

In the century immediately prior to the crusades, famine was common in Europe in 48 years out of 100. By the 11th century Christian society had itself become barbarous, for war and brutality were endemic; each petty lord fought with his rivals, lords fought against kings, kings fought one another and there was no central authority with sufficient power to control them. The kings and lords were illiterate thugs who lacked any semblance of honour, who betrayed each other without a qualm, who lied, cheated, raided, tortured and killed in a nightmarish world fuelled by fear, greed and ambition.[36]

The Church did at least try, albeit ineffectively, to mitigate or limit the extent of this barbarity and the bishops of Aquitaine, meeting at the Council of Charroux in 989 CE, suggested that the Church had a duty to guarantee that the poor might live in peace.[37] Yet they could not effectively do so, and at a synod in Toulouse in Rousillon held in 1027, Oliba, the Bishop of Vichy, forbade all warfare during the hours of Sabbath.[38] This ban was later extended to include the feast days of the Church and, some time later, the Archbishop of Rouen proclaimed the 'Truce of God', which attempted to limit private wars to only three days a week.[39] The idea, if not the practice, of the 'Truce of God' was well established by the middle of the century and the Council of Narbonnne, held in 1054 CE, sought to coordinate it with the idea of the 'Peace of God', which aimed to protect the property of both the Church and of the poor from the effects of war. The basic principle, often stated, was that no

Christian should slay another, 'for he that slays a Christian sheds the blood of Christ'.[40] However, the innate bellicosity of the European nobility could not be easily quenched, and so it was deemed more practical to attempt to make use of this barbaric energy by diverting it into warfare against the infidel.[41]

THE KNIGHTS TEMPLAR

The mystery surrounding the foundation of the medieval monastic and military Order of the Knights Templar has been compounded by the actions of modern historians. They have arrived at a suprising consensus for the date of foundation of 1118/1119 based upon documentation from one man, Guillaume of Tyre, a monk who composed his work some 70 years later. Contemporary writers, however, give a far wider range of dates, some of which indicate that the order may have been started many years earlier and may even have begun before the First Crusade.

The rapid rise to power and influence of the new order along with its speedy expansion certainly give us cause to suspect that this had all been long planned and resulted from a wide-ranging conspiracy that linked some of the most influential families in Europe. The almost complete autonomy achieved by the Templars shortly after their foundation, their inexplicable rise to wealth, power and fame, and the wide range of their economic and political influence has never been equalled by any other monastic order before or since. Their military and diplomatic achievements are an almost incredible mixture of ubelieveable bravery, subtle negotiation, moderated only by the strategic incompetence that ultimately led to the loss of the Holy Land.

These factors and the order's dramatic fall from grace when charged with heresy have provoked intense speculation for over seven centuries. The loss, or suppression, of the orders' own records has left a vacuum that has given free rein to the myth-makers and the fantasists. Yet the facts that can be discerned are far stranger and more intriguing than any fiction.

CHAPTER 5

A Family Affair –
The Conspiracy that Led to the
Foundation of the Knights Templar

The Rex Deus families who outwardly conformed to the religion of their time and place, which in Europe was Christianity, secretly handed down an initiatory pathway based firmly on the true teachings of Jesus. They did not merely restrict themselves to this silent but essential task but sometimes, when appropriate, tried to influence the corrupt Church and attempt to change it from within. One glorious example of the success of this tactic came to fruition in 1007, when the great Bishop Fulbert was installed as Bishop of Chartres. Under the protection of the Rex Deus nobility of the area, he transformed this ancient cathedral city into an important centre of learning and further developed its traditional role as a focus of pilgrimage.[1] This theological school attained international renown and, during the 200 years of its major influence, attracted brilliant scholars from every part of Europe, including Bernard and Thierry of Chartres, William of Conches and John of Salisbury. The knowledge of the Greek Classics taught at Chartres came from that beacon of light in the Dark Ages, Moorish Spain, and were translated not from Greek, but from Arabic.

These important translations were made by Jewish scholars working in yeshiva under the protection of the tolerant rule of Islam. It was due to the network of the Rex Deus nobility that this knowledge was transmitted from Spain to Chartres. We find a strong indication of Rex Deus influence when we learn that under the outward guise of teaching the seven liberal arts of *gramatica, dialectica, logica, musica, mathematica, geometrica* and *astronomia*, Fulbert taught the seven steps of initiation, the same tried and tested initiatory pathway preserved by the 24 families of the *ma'madot* throughout the history of ancient Israel and preserved by the Rex Deus families of Europe.[2] Thus the mystery school at Chartres was able to practise a heretical initiatory pathway right under the noses of the repressive Church authorities. This was not the only time that Rex Deus tried to exert influence from within the Church. Others, following the steps of Fulbert, also took holy orders in an attempt to influence their corrupt enemy from within. The strange events that took place within one Rex Deus family in the county of Champagne eloquently illustrate the tensions that this strategy could provoke.

BERNARD OF CLAIRVAUX

A certain Burgundian nobleman, Bernard de Fontaine, expressed his desire to join the Church by becoming a monk in the relatively new and struggling Cistercian Order. His family were horrified when he first announced his intention but, for reasons that no one has ever satisfactorily explained, their attitude was completely transformed. All opposition to his plans vanished like snow off a hot shovel and, stranger still, a large number of his male relatives and friends chose to follow him into the order. No less than 32 of them became novices with Bernard when he joined in 1112.[3] This sudden and massive explosion of vocational fervour affected Bernard's elder brother who was heir to the family estate, his two younger brothers and his uncle, the knight Gaudri of Touillon and, as a result, nearly doubled the manpower of the struggling Cistercian Order.[4]

The modern Benedictine historian, Dom David Knowles described Bernard in the following terms:

> ... one of the small class of supremely great men whose gifts and opportunities have been exactly matched. As a leader, as a writer, as a preacher and as a saint his personal magnetism and his spiritual power were far-reaching and irresistible. Men came from all over Europe to Clairvaux and were sent out again all over the continent. ... For forty years, Citeaux-Clairvaux was the spiritual centre of Europe, and at one time Saint Bernard had among his ex monks the pope, the Archbishop of York, and cardinals and bishops aplenty.[5]

Bernard certainly rose to an informal but widely recognized position of power and influence within the Church with incredible speed, yet he never led the Cistercian Order and remained simply the Abbot of Clairvaux. Nonetheless, he attained an almost unbelievable position of influence not merely throughout the religious world, where he became the principal personal adviser to the pope, but in temporal affairs where he advised kings, emperors and the nobility. His *Rex Deus* membership was one obvious asset he exploited to the full to achive this high status.

Bernard rose to such a position of great power and influence both in the Church and in politics, not just because of his family connections but also as a result of his immense energy. Bernard suffered from ill health throughout his life yet he instigated the foundation of at least 68 Cistercian houses from his base at Clairvaux and his deep spirituality had such profound influence on the Cistercian Order that he is sometimes called its 'second founder'. Furthermore, his influence on other branches of the initiatory tradition was wide-ranging, for Bernard of Chartres and later leaders of the mystery school there, such as John of Salisbury and Alanus ab Insulis, were also Cistercians, as were many of the other Chartres masters.[6]

Bernard's deep commitment to initiatory teaching came into the open with the 120 sermons he preached based on the Song of Songs by King Solomon.[7] He also played a significant role in enhancing the spiritual tradition of that branch of the Compagnonnage, or Craftmasons, known as the Children of Solomon. While no archival evidence exists that adequately explains the bizarre burst of collective enthusiasm that led so many of his family and friends to join the Cistercians with him, later events do provide some indications. It would appear that Bernard conspired with other Rex Deus family members to achieve a common aim that was to leave an indelible mark on European history. This conspiracy was wide-ranging and included a variety of people including his cousin, who later became Patriarch of Jerusalem; his uncle André de Montbard; Hugues de Payen; the St Clairs and the Setons of Scotland; the Royal House of Flanders and one of the most important noblemen in Europe at that time, Count Hughes of Champagne.

COUNT HUGHES OF CHAMPAGNE

Hughes I, Count of Champagne, who ruled over an area larger than Wales that lay to the east of Paris, was the godson of King Philippe I of France who was nominally his sovereign. The count also owed allegiance to the Holy Roman Emperor and the Duke of Burgundy. The counts of Champagne were linked both by blood and marriage to the St Clairs of Normandy and Scotland,[8] the Capetian kings of France, the Duke of Burgundy, the Duke of Normandy, and the Norman and Plantagenet kings of England who were, of course, all members of the Rex Deus group. Hughes' power base was the city of Troyes in the county of Champagne which, under his benevolent rule, became a centre of learning that attracted scholars and intellectuals of considerable stature. At this time, large Jewish families often led by rabbinical scholars began to migrate from southern Europe and settle in the Paris basin, the lands of Champagne and on the banks of the River Rhine.[9] One such family, which settled in Troyes, produced a son who became one of the greatest Jewish biblical scholars of all time, Rabbi Solomon ben Isaac, known as *Rachi*.

Born in Troyes, Rachi studied at yeshivot in both Worms and Mainz before returning home to establish his own yeshiva in the city of his birth.[10] This great Jewish teacher became a frequent and welcome guest at the court of Hughes de Champagne and attained such intellectual repute that, as a biblical scholar, he is still unequalled, indeed, as a philosopher, even now he is still considered as second only to the incomparable Maimonides. Rachi was able to maintain a kabbalistic school of considerable stature in the city with the tolerant approval of Count Hughes of Champagne.[11] The kabbala was the principal spiritual pathway encompassing the traditional Hebraic/Egyptian pathway of initiation. Prince Michael of Albany claims that this school was influenced by Sufi teaching which crept in through the Rex Deus connections with Moorish Spain.[12] Hughes de Champagne, like the vast majority of the Rex Deus nobility, gave shelter and protection to the Jews and when, in the later part of the 12th century, they were expelled from the Isle de France, they retained both their security and residence in Champagne.

Hughes I de Champagne met with leading members of the Rex Deus families of Brienne, De Joinville, Chaumont and Anjou at a secret conclave in 1104.[13] Count Hughes then left for the Holy Land and did not return to Champagne until 1108 and, it is alleged, that a certain Hugues de Payen, one of his vassals who had taken part in the First Crusade, accompanied him on this visit. In 1114 he made yet another brief and mysterious visit to Jerusalem and on his return he made a donation of land to the Cistercian Order upon which the monks built a new monastery, the Abbey of Clairvaux. Bernard de Fontaine was immediately appointed as its first abbot.

These mysterious visits to the Holy Land and his donation of land to the Cistercians were merely the prologue to concerted and decisive action by the Families that would make its mark on the public conscious-ness in a manner that would last for over 800 years. This public resurrection of Rex Deus was to take place not in the county of Champagne where it had been planned, or even in Europe from where it drew its conspirators, but in the Holy City of Jerusalem. Here was founded an order of warrior monks whose name was to resound through the annals of European history down to the present day, *The Poor Knights of Christ and the Temple of Solomon*, otherwise known as the Knights Templar. However, we need to go back a little in time and examine how the crusades arose. This brutal series of wars not only set the scene for the order's foundation, but were the context in which we can discern its true *raison d'être* and some of the reasons behind its downfall.

HOLY WAR AGAINST ISLAM

In 1014 CE, King Sancho III of Navarre organized a league of Christian princes to fight the Moorish invaders and this effort soon acquired the status of a holy war when Pope Alexander II (1061–73 CE) promised an indulgence, the remission of all sins, to all those who fought for the

Christian cause in Spain.[14] Events within Muslim Spain conspired to facilitate this move to holy war and reconquest by the Christian armies which later became known as the *Reconquistà*. The 11th century saw the powerful state centred on Cordova fall apart as a result of civil war. It splintered into a number of petty principalities that became known as *taifa* kingdoms.[15] With the renewed onslaught by the Christians they fell one by one, until the Castillians captured Toledo in 1085 CE.

Events in Jerusalem

By the middle of the 11th century, the situation for Christians living in the Holy Land itself had seldom been so pleasant. The Muslim authorities were lenient, trade with Christian countries overseas was prosperous and increasing, and wealth also accrued from the ever-increasing flood of pilgrims from the West.[16] This continued until the last two decades of the century, as an unending stream of pilgrims poured into the Holy Land, sometimes travelling in parties numbering thousands, composed of men and women of every age and class.[17] However, successful pilgrimage to Jerusalem depended on two conditions: that life in the Holy Land and the countries around allowed the defenceless pilgrim to traverse in safety; and secondly, that the way should be kept open and cheap enough for the pilgrims to afford.[18]

The state of affairs that enabled such mass pilgrimage to take place, Muslim religious tolerance, apparently came to an end on 19 August 1071 CE when the Seljuk Turk, Atiz ibn Abaq, captured Jerusalem without a struggle and then occupied the rest of Palestine. In 1075 he took Damascus, and the Damascene and the rising tide of Seljuk domination not only included the lands of the Islamic Empire, but also overran a vast swath of land in Asia Minor that had been ruled for centuries by the Christian Emperor of Byzantium.

The Byzantine Empire

The Byzantines, who saw themselves as the heirs of the old Roman Empire, and viewed their capital, Constantinople, as the New Rome were perceived by the pope in Rome as heretics. A situation complicated by serious theological differences and the vexed question as to the real nature and extent of papal authority.[19] It was against this background that the Byzantine emperor had to act when faced with the conquest of much of his lands by the Seljuk Turks. Alexius I Comnenus (1081–1118 CE), the Emperor of Byzantium, appealed to Pope Urban II (1088–99 CE)[20] to help him rescue the Christians of the East and their churches from the tyranny of their new Turkish conquerors. The brutal reality of western Europe at that time imbued the whole idea of a holy war against the Turks to rescue the holy places of Christendom with a dreadful sense of inevitability; it seemed bound to occur to someone, sometime, and now it certainly appealed to Pope Urban. His words evoked such a response in the hearts and minds of ordinary men and women throughout western Europe that the history of both Europe and the world was to be dramatically changed by them, but in a way very different from that hoped for by the emperor.[21]

The Call for the First Crusade

Eventually Pope Urban summoned the bishops of France to join him at Church Council at Clermont, where Urban let it be known that he would make an important announcement at a public session on Tuesday 27 November. The pope, a great orator, claimed that the Christians in the East had recently appealed to him for help against the Turks who were advancing into Christian lands, maltreating innocent Christian men and women and desecrating their churches. The time had come for the Christians of Europe to stop making war on each other and wage a holy war against God's enemies instead. The pope claimed that God himself would lead them in battle and grant them a holy victory. Urban promised that absolution and remission of all sins would be granted to all who 'took the Cross'[22] and died in the battle to free the Holy Land from the Turks. This intoxicating message produced an immediate response – loud cries of *'Dieu le volt'* – 'God wills it'. A massive tidal-wave of enthusiasm spread from Clermont across France and spilled over its borders into every country in western Europe, one that set all the Christian peoples alight with fanatical fervour.[23] The brutal wars that followed were to leave a scar on the relationship between the Christian West and the World of Islam that would never fully heal – the Crusades.[24]

All over Europe, various groups prepared to set out when the summer had come, all firmly of the belief that God would be their guide.[25] That year, Europe was blessed by a plentiful harvest of both grain and wine, so that none should falter for lack of provisions on this holy enterprise. Hugh of Vermandois, the brother of King Philippe of France set out first; he was followed by Bohemund of Taranto, the Count of Apulia. Godfroi de Bouillon, the Duke of Lower Lorraine, travelled through Hungary while Count Raymond of Toulouse and his Provençal army along with Adhemar, Bishop of le Puy, crossed through Dalmatia. In October 1096, Robert, Duke of Normandy, set out for the Holy Land in company with Stephen of Blois and Robert, Count of Flanders.[26] Far from being a unified and coherent expedition, the First Crusade was, therefore, composed of a series of small, independent groups of warriors interspersed with what can only be described as ill-disciplined mobs of enthusiastic peasants who, unlike the warrior class, were singularly ill-prepared for the trials ahead. All seemed united by one simple aim, to kill the enemies of Christ.

The Massacres of the Jews

Numerous mobs of undisciplined, ravening peasants and townsfolk, usually led by fanatical clergy set out across Europe. However, before any of these people departed for the Holy Land they posed the question: 'Were there not enemies of Christ nearer home, who should be dealt with first?' Indeed, 'Why should they march over 2,000 miles through strange terrain to fight the Turks while some of the race who had crucified Christ were living in every great European city?' While the Jews had long enjoyed some degree of protection from the more tolerant among the Christian rulers, they were rarely popular among the ordinary people of Europe.[27] Thus, the early summer of 1096 saw numerous outbreaks of murderous anti-Semitic violence in many Christian cities.

During the summer of 1096, while the Jews of Germany and central Europe were being brutally killed in the name of Christ, the various princes and nobles who had taken the Cross were assembling their armies and supplies in preparation for their departure. They knew that no military expedition had any chance of success without careful planning.[28] While the Rex Deus noble Godfroi de Bouillon, the Duke of Lower Lorraine, was preparing to leave, he was given 1,000 pieces of silver by the Jews of Mainz and Cologne in order to speed him on his way, and also, it has been suggested, to induce him to leave them in peace. He then reassured them that he had no harmful intentions towards them, but, nonetheless, Godfroi accepted their generous offer to offset the heavy expenses of the campaign to come.[29]

As the restless, half-organized, savage bands of peasantry crossed eastern Europe, they robbed and pillaged as they went and this did little to endear them to the local populations, so petty wars and skirmishes broke out en route. When they and the brutal, yet visionary chivalry of western Christendom crossed the Bospherous, two very different cultures came into collision. Byzantine culture was very old, highly literate, sophisticated and immensely civilized. That of western Europe, which was barely emerging from total barbarism, was warlike, ruthless and fanatically intolerant.[30] As the various armies arrived, one by one, the Byzantine emperor kept them outside the city walls, entertained and presented gifts to their leaders and extracted oaths of allegiance from them.[31]

The oaths of allegiance taken by the various leaders of the First Crusade proved meaningless, for what oath could bind a western Christian to the emperor of a heretical sect that did not bow the knee to the pope. Many of the nobles on the crusade were landless younger sons of the nobility of Europe who sought to carve out an empire for themselves in the Holy Land of Palestine.

Despite all claims to standards of knightly chivalry, the warrior nobles of Western Europe were, in the main, greedy, dishonourable and brutal thugs. Chivalry and honour were values they had yet to learn from their Muslim adversaries. Their behaviour at the fall of Antioch clearly revealed the appalling reality of their Christian standards of chivalry for all the people of the East to see. The siege lasted nine months and the Emir of Antioch, Yaghi Siyan, defended the city with unprecedented bravery. When the city fell in June 1098, a truly barbarous massacre took place in which no one was spared; Turkish women and children were butchered along with their men and a good many Greek and Armenian Christians along with them.[32] This was to set a pattern that was, sadly, to be oft-repeated. Bohemund of Taranto became Count of Antioch despite further complaints from the emperor Alexius that yet another crusader had broken his solemn oath of allegiance. After the successful defence of Antioch against a Turkish siege, Bohemund and Count Raymond of Toulouse set the date of 1 November for the crusaders' departure for Jerusalem.

The 'liberation' of the Holy City

The crusaders' actions at the fall of Jerusalem have left a permanent and dark stain on any European pretensions to honour and chivalry. However, the actions of one man do stand out as a glowing example of what could have been achieved, for Raymond of Toulouse alone had behaved with honour and decency. In the battle for the Tower of David, the Muslim warrior Iftikhar who was fighting Raymond and his Provençal troops realized early in the afternoon that all was lost. Withdrawing into the Tower of David, he offered to hand it over to Raymond with a great treasure in return for his life and the lives of his men. Raymond accepted these terms and occupied the Tower, while Iftikhar and his men were safely escorted out of the city and permitted to join the Muslim garrison of Ascalon.[33] This was the sole instance of civilized behaviour shown by the crusaders when they took the Holy City, for once they were let loose inside the walls, they were overcome by an insatiable and terrible blood-lust. An account written by Daimbert, Archbishop of Pisa describes the fall of the Holy City: 'If you want to know what was done to the enemies we found in the city, know this: that in the portico of Solomon and in his Temple, our men rode in the blood of the Saracens up to the knees of our horses.'[34] The slaughter went on throughout the day and far into the following night until, when there was no one else left to kill, the victors processed through the corpse-littered streets to the Church of the Holy Sepulchre and there gave thanks to God for His manifold and great mercies.[35] The Jewish inhabitants of the Holy City fared no better than their European counterparts when they fled in a body to their chief synagogue, for no mercy was shown to them even there. The synagogue was torched and they were all burnt alive within its walls.[36] When Raymond of Aguillers went to visit the Temple area, he was forced to pick his way through corpses and blood that reached up to his knees.[37] No one can say with any degree of accuracy how many people were slaughtered, but Jerusalem was completely emptied of all of its Muslim and Jewish inhabitants. The massacre had an enormous impact on the world; many Christians were horrified and the Muslims, who might otherwise have accepted the crusaders as just another factor in the tangled politics of the time, developed a fanatical determination to drive the Franks out at all costs. According to Stephen Runciman, England's leading historian of the Crusades, it was this bloodthirsty proof of Christian brutal intolerance that rekindled the fanatical fires of Islam.[38]

Despite the concerted effort by the crusaders to capture the Holy City, no decision as to who would assume power over Jerusalem had been taken prior to the siege. Eight days after the massacre, a council of bishops and noble lords was charged with selecting a suitable king. They first decided to offer the throne to Raymond of Toulouse but, to the surprise of the assembled company, he refused the position on the grounds that there could only be one King of Jerusalem and that one was Christ. After that the council asked Godfroi de Bouillon, who agreed to assume the leadership but not the title of king.[39] After some deliberation, Godfroi de Bouillon took the title of *Advocatus Sancti Sepulchri,* the dedicated defender of the Holy Sepulchre.[40] He only reigned for one year but, on his deathbed, he named his brother Baldwin of Boulogne, Count of Edessa, as his successor.

The European conquerors proceeded to establish feudal fiefdoms with their own administrations. They now had a king in Jerusalem, new Catholic patriarchs in Jerusalem and Antioch and, under them, a network of Catholic archbishops and bishops throughout their new territories. Four major secular lordships emerged from the chaos of conquest: the principality of Antioch (now Antakya), the county of Edessa (now Urfa) the county of Tripoli (now Tarābulus) and, above them all, in name at least, the Kingdom of Jerusalem.[41] The Europeans had conquered their new lands due to a combination of two distinct and separate factors, firstly a high degree of disunity on the part of their Muslim adversaries and secondly their own secret weapon – heavy cavalry.

Cavalry Tactics

European success in battle depended on skilful use of specially equipped cavalry over carefully chosen ground,[42] backed up by infantry armed with spears, long Danish axes and crossbows who provided cover until the moment for a single decisive charge.[43] There was usually only need for one charge to scatter the enemy, which was perhaps as well, as most of the European knights would then scatter in search of loot or captives who could be ransomed. The knight's armour consisted of a conical steel helmet, a chain-mail tunic with sleeves and hood worn over a quilted undershirt, padded breeches and a kite-shaped shield – although as time progressed, the shield became smaller and the conical helmet was replaced with the helm covering the whole face. Mailed stockings were later adopted along with the habit of wearing a burnous and keffiyeh to ward off the sun. A lance was carried, couched under the arm, and a long double-edged sword and occasionally a mace.

While on the march the knight rode a hack, and only mounted his carefully trained warhorse when action was imminent. These warhorses, or destriers, were enormous animals – often 17 hands high and more akin to a drayhorse than a modern cavalry charger – and were taught to bite, butt and kick. To time the cavalry charge correctly, meanwhile restraining troops baking beneath the hot sun as they were being struck by the enemy's arrows demanded leadership of the highest quality.[44]

Not only were the Christian knights mounted on their destriers considerably bigger and heavier than the light cavalry of their Muslim opponents, but they were far better at infighting and dealt out terrible punishment. The perennial problem that haunted the Crusader State was how to muster enough of these panzer-like noblemen.

There was a chronic shortage of manpower throughout Outremer, as the Holy Land was now called, and its desert frontier was difficult to defend, however, the crusaders had sea power and built fortresses. Fleets from Genoa, Pisa and Venice soon controlled the sea lanes, captured seaports and established commercial colonies within them. By as early as 1100, Fulcher of Chartres recorded that only 300 knights and 300 foot soldiers remained in the vicinity of Jerusalem which would never be enough to protect the country.[45] So it was blatantly obvious from the very start that these newly conquered lands needed far more personnel, not just to settle the land but also to defend it against the Saracens.[46]

The entire economy of the Holy Land was founded firmly upon the vast pilgrimage trade that soon sprang up, but pilgrims were never safe once they left the confines of Jerusalem. One Russian abbot, Daniel by name, wrote of his visit to the tomb of St George at Lydda (in 1106 CE):

> … and there are many springs here; travellers rest by the water but with great fear, for it is a deserted place and nearby is the town of Ascalon from which the Saracens sally forth and kill travellers on these roads. There is great fear too, going up from that place into the hills.'[47]

He described Galilee as worse:

> This place is dreadful and dangerous… many tall palm trees stand about the town like a dense forest. This place is terrible and

difficult of access for here live fierce pagan Saracens who attack travellers at the fords.[48]

Within les than 13 years, this situation had degenerated still further. At Easter in 1119 CE, one group of over 700 pilgrims on the road to the Jordan river were attacked by Saracens with more than 300 pilgrims killed and some 60 being carried off into slavery.[49] At this point a French nobleman by the name of Hugues de Payen enters the story.

THE CO-FOUNDER AND THE FIRST GRANDMASTER OF THE TEMPLAR ORDER

The co-founder of the Knights Templar and its first Grandmaster, Hugues de Payen, was born at the de Payen château on the banks of the Seine, one of the principal castles defending Champagne, in 1070.[50] Some time between 1085 and 1090, he received the fiefdom of Montigny near Lagesse in the county of Champagne.[51] Hugues was the cousin of two of Europe's most powerful men, Bernard of Clairvaux[52] and the Count of Champagne who was also his overlord.[53] He was also related, as was the Count of Champagne, to Raymond, Count of Toulouse, who was the effective leader of the First Crusade and who had refused the throne of Jerusalem. Other relations included Godfroi de Boullion and King Baldwin of Jerusalem. Known also as 'Hugues the Moor' because of his lineal descent from the emir of Cordova[54] and the Prophet Muhammed, he was not merely Rex Deus, but one of the *Desposyni*, a descendant of one of the brothers of Jesus.

In 1094, before the First Crusade, Hugues de Payen had helped yet another relative, his cousin Henri of Burgundy after his marriage to Teresa of Portugal, to consolidate his position as Count of Portugal.

In this manner Hugues acted as the midwife to the birth of the infant Kingdom of Portugal which only reached maturity when it was confirmed in 1139. The price demanded by Hugues for this intervention was a strange one for a man who was apparently to devote his life to unending warfare against the forces of Islam; it was, quite simply, the condition that the Muslim population of the emergent state would be left to worship according to their own conscience. A remarkable act of tolerance in Christian Europe at that time.[55]

According to the historian Desmond Seward, Hugues arrived in Syria in 1115, and by 1118 had become the self-appointed protector of pilgrims, who were ceaselessly harried on the dangerous road from Jaffa to Jerusalem by Saracen raiders based at Ascalon. This ragged eccentric persuaded several other French knights to help him, and they took a solemn oath before the Patriarch of Jerusalem to protect pilgrims and observe poverty, chastity and obedience.[56] King Baldwin was so impressed with their piety and courage that he gave the poor knights a wing of the royal palace, the Mosque of al-Asqua, thought to be the Temple of Solomon. He also joined the patriarch in subsidizing them.[57] It was in this strange manner, according to the general consensus of modern historians at least, that the Order of the Knights Templar came into being. Most historians content themselves with the bald statement that The Order of the Poor Knights of the Temple of Solomon, more commonly known as the Order of the Temple or the Knights Templar, was founded by the French Nobleman Hugues de Payen in or around the year 1119 in Jerusalem.[58]

The Templars were the first military order ever to be founded in the history of the Catholic Church, but, strange to relate, contemporary 12th-century writers are actually far from reaching any real sense of agreement as to how or when the order actually began. The modern consensus is almost entirely based on the work of Archbishop William of Tyre, who wrote a history of the Crusader States between 1165 and 1184. Thus his account was not written until some 70 years after the order's alleged date of foundation. Furthermore, he frequently displays a distinct anti-Templar bias in his work. Nonetheless, he wrote that the first Templars were a group of noble knights, 'devoted to God, religious and God-fearing', who entrusted themselves into the hands of the patriarch (Warmund of Picquigny) to serve Christ. However another religious scribe, the monk Simon of the monastery of St Bertin near St Omer, wrote, somewhat earlier in around 1135–7, that the first Templars were simply crusaders who stayed in the Holy Land after the First Crusade instead of returning home: then, allegedly on the advice of the princes of God's army, they dedicated themselves to God's Temple under this rule:

> … they would renounce the world, give up personal goods, free
> themselves to pursue chastity, and lead a communal life wearing
> a poor habit, only using weapons to defend the land against the
> attacks of the insurgent pagans when the necessity demanded.[59]

The modern historian Professor Helen Nicholson admits that this account was written within a generation of the founding of the Templars and so, must be given some credence.[60] Furthermore, Anselm, the Bishop of Havelburg in 1145, dated the foundation of the order to the time of the First Crusade. In 1153, yet another monk, Richard of Poitou, who was at Cluny, dated the foundation of the Templars to 1109.[61]

Thus, as we have seen, the contemporaries or near-contemporaries of the order's foundation were not sure when the Order of the Temple began. In the opinion of Professor Nicholson, they also did not know why it began or who was responsible for its beginning.[62] While many accept the work of William of Tyre, modern historians tend to disagree.

Baigent, Leigh and Lincoln claim an earlier date for its foundation, citing a letter from a leading Catholic Church dignitary in support of their claim. Indeed, in 1114, Ivo, Bishop of Chartres did write to Count Hughes of Champagne, rebuking the count for abandoning his wife and vowing himself to the 'knighthood of Christ', *militiae Christi*, a name later used to describe the Templars. As the Templars were the first military order in Christendom, to whom else is the bishop referring? The bishop continued his tirade against Count Hughes by accusing him of taking up 'that gospel knighthood', *evangelicum militiam*, by which 2,000 may fight securely against him who rushes to attack us with 200,000,[63] a distinctive phrase later used by Bernard of Clairvaux in describing the Templar Order. Prince Michael of Albany dates the foundation of the order to circa 1094, but sadly does not cite any verifiable data to support this theory.[64] In some respects, however, he may well be right as the conspiracy which led to the order's foundation certainly had its roots at that time.

Michael Baigent, Ricahrd Leigh and Henry Lincoln claimed, in *The Holy Blood and the Holy Grail*, that Hugues de Payen was married to a certain Catherine de St Clair,[65] a marriage to which, at first at least, I gave some credence. However, having searched through countless archives, I have to admit that not only have I not found any valid document inferring any matrimonial alliance between Hugues and the wider St Clair family, but, I have discovered the work of a French author, Thierry Leroy, who has found documents confirming that Hugues de Payen was indeed married, but to a French lady called Elisabeth and that the marriage took place sometime between 1108 and 1114.[66] Despite many allegations that Hugues died without issue, he did father at least one son, Thibaud de Payen, who became the abbot of the monastery of Sainte-Colombe in 1139. One contemporary chronicle describes the new abbot in the following terms: '*Theo Aldus de Pahens, filius Hugonis primi magistri templi Jerosolymitani*',[67] which translates as 'Thibaud de Payen, son of Hugues, first master of the Temple in Jerusalem'.

Hugues was not the only well-connected co-founder of the Templar Order, André de Montbard, Hugues' closest associate in the new knightly enterprise and the order's second grandmaster, was the uncle of Bernard of Clairvaux,[68] a kinsman of the Duke of Burgundy and yet another vassal of the house of Champagne. Geoffroi de St Omer, who is also listed among the original founders, was the son of a leading Flemish nobleman, Hughes de St Omer.[69] Payen de Montdidier and Achambaud de St-Amand were related to the royal House of Flanders, whose sons Godfroi de Boullion and his younger brother Baudouin of Brittany, were rulers of the Kingdom of Jerusalem – Godfroi as protector of the Holy Sepulchre and after his death, Baudouin as King Baldwin I.

I have mentioned previously that there are some historians who place the foundation of the Templar Order at a far earlier date than that of 1119 claimed by William of Tyre. Indeed, some claim that land donations to the order, made by the rulers of Portugal, Henri and Teresa, date from as early as 1108, 11 years before William of Tyre's date,[70] thus, there is no substantive agreement among historians ancient or modern as to the true date of this powerful order's real beginning. However certain facts are now coming to light which are tending to clarify this confusing situation. While the conspiracy to found the order certainly dates from about the beginning of the First Crusade, the first actions that are discernible in bringing this plot to fruition can be gleaned from the life of Bernard of Clairvaux.

An old and respected Provençal tradition recounts that Hughes of Champagne, Hugues de Payen, André de Montbard and several of the other founding knights of the Templar Order visited the small church at Roquebillière in February 1117, stayed a few days and then crossed the Alpes Maritimes by the Col de Turini to Seborga where they met with Bernard of Clairvaux. One of the many Cistercian houses he founded stands in Seborga in northern Italy and, according to local tradition, it was established in 1113 to protect 'a great secret'.[71] Under the direction of its abbot, Edouard, were two monks, Gondemar and Rossal, who had been knights before they became Cistercians and, it is alleged, that along with Edouard, they had all joined the order at the same time as Bernard. One document in the archives at Seborga claims that in February 1117, Bernard came to the abbey where he was joined by several companions. Releasing Gondemar and Rossal from their vows, Bernard then solemnly blessed the whole group which departed for Jerusalem in 1118. The document further states that prior to their departure, Bernard nominated Hugues de Payen as the Grandmaster of 'the Poor Militia of Christ' who was then consecrated in that rank by Abbot Edouard.[72]

The account by William of Tyre, written over 70 years after the events it describes, may, therefore, contain some degree of truth. While other accounts of an earlier foundation may also be plausible, William of Tyre's description relates to the first overt and public manifestation of the fruits of the Rex Deus conspiracy. Granted quarters on the Temple Mount by King Baldwin II within a few weeks of the new king's accession to the throne,[73] the order took the name of the 'Poor Fellow-Soldiers of Jesus Christ' and were recognized as 'the Knighthood of the Temple of Solomon'.[74] The founding members of the order were its first Grandmaster, Hugues de Payen, André de Montbard, Geoffroi de St Omer, Payen de Montdidier, Achambaud de St-Amand, Geoffroi Bisol, Godfroi, Gondemar and Rossal. [75]

Thus, this supposedly randomly assembled group of knights, apparently united only by their religious dedication was, in fact, a tightly knit group of relatives, members of Rex Deus who were all closely associated with Count Hughes I of Champagne. Hughes, as mentioned above, had already made at least two visits to the Holy Land prior to the foundation of the order. There is one further anomaly regarding Hughes de Champagne. He repudiated his unfaithful wife and disinherited his son, whom he believed was not his, and made his estate over to his nephew, Theobald and then returned to the Holy Land in 1125.[76] He then took the unprecedented step of joining the Order of the Knights Templar and swore unquestioning obedience to its first Grandmaster, his own vassal, Hugues de Payen.

Recognition of the Order

The Knights Templar received recognition from the Patriarch of Jerusalem at the Council of Nablus in 1120.[77] The patriarch, yet another distant cousin of Bernard of Clairvaux, then granted the order permission to wear its first insignia, a red two-barred cross that later developed into the Cross of Lorraine. Orderic Vitalis (1075–c.1141), writing in the Norman monastery of St Évroul, recorded that in the 1120s Count Fulk V of Anjou joined the 'knights of the Temple' for a period of time during his pilgrimage to Jerusalem. On his return to Europe he continued to pay them 30 pounds of Anjou for their support. Orderic described the new order as *venerandi mitlites*, knights who should be held in great respect or admiration, and wrote that they devoted their lives to the physical and spiritual service of God, despised all worldly things and faced martyrdom daily.[78]

The publicly proclaimed and primary purpose of the new order of warrior monks was to be the protection of pilgrims en route from the Mediterranean coastal port of Jaffa to Jerusalem. Now, Hugues de Payen was 48 years old at that time and as most of his companions were of similar age, it is hard to imagine how nine knights who were hardly in the 'first bloom of youth', were going to accomplish this mammoth task. A problem that is rendered particularly intractable when one studies their bizarre actions during the first nine years of their existence.

CHAPTER 6

The Early Years &
the Council of Troyes

Most accounts of the history of the Knights Templar are vague or uninformative about the activities of the knights during the first eight or nine years of the order's existence, from the time of its foundation *circa* 1118/1119 CE until the Council of Troyes in 1128 CE. It is usually assumed that the knights of the new order spent that time fulfilling their stated purpose of protecting the pilgrim routes, especially the road from the seaport of Jaffa to Jerusalem. While those duties may well have been discharged, the knights' primary purpose at this time was very different, and was not discovered until the later years of the 19th century when a certain Lieutenant Warren of the Royal Engineers and his companions began the mammoth task of excavating a strange series of tunnels that he discovered under the Temple Mount in Jerusalem.

Lieutenant Warren's excavations lasted for some considerable time and extended into the early years of the 20th century. The tunnels they found were truly extraordinary, firstly there was a vertical 80-foot shaft reaching downwards through the solid rock that led to a system of tunnels radiating horizontally for a considerable distance. Warren discovered a variety of Templar artefacts in the tunnels that he explored which included a spur, the remains of a lance, a small Templar cross and the major part of a Templar sword. These fascinating relics are now kept in Edinburgh by the Templar archivist Robert Brydon, who has shown some of them to me along with a letter from Captain Parker who accompanied Warren on his explorations. Captain Parker had written to Robert's grandfather in 1912 and entrusted the finds to him for safekeeping.

Thus we may conclude that, far from simply patrolling the bandit-infested roads between the coast and Jerusalem, the first Knights Templar spent much of their time excavating beneath the Temple Mount, directly under their headquarters.[1] The discovery of these tunnels leads to some interesting questions: 'Were these excavations the primary purpose that lay behind the founding of the order?' If so, 'What exactly were they seeking?' Furthermore, 'Did they find it?' Perhaps more importantly, 'How did they know precisely where to excavate?' Finally, 'How did they obtain quarters immediately above their chosen site of excavation?' These questions are impossible to answer from any archival sources but they do lead, inevitably, to some interesting speculation that is, seemingly, backed up by some strange symbolism and theories that do have a basis in fact.

One tangible indication of what the knights may have been seeking is carved on one of the outer pillars of the north porch of Chartres Cathedral, the porch known as the Portal of the Initiates. The carving depicts the Ark of the Covenant being transported upon a wheeled cart.[2] The Bible recounts that the Ark of the Covenant was carried on men's shoulders by poles inserted into rings on each side of the Ark, and well-established tradition from the time of biblical Israel recounts that, later, the Ark was buried deep beneath the Temple in Jerusalem long before the Babylonian invasion. A long-standing esoteric legend within Europe claims that Hugues de Payen was chosen to retrieve it and bring it back to Europe.[3] The same legend goes on to tell us that, on its arrival in Europe, it was at first hidden beneath the crypt of Chartres Cathedral which was, at that time, under the control of the Chartres masters. It is a little strange that in the carving in the Portal of the Initiates, the Ark is not depicted being carried on poles, but being transported on a wheeled cart, an idea that has absolutely no biblical justification whatsoever.

Some historians have further claimed that, found along with the Ark was a vast quantity of ancient documents. Naturally, considerable speculation has arisen as to the precise nature of these documents and a reasonable consensus has emerged that they probably contained, among other things, copies of the Dead Sea Scrolls material found at Qumran, treatises on sacred geometry, ancient science and other aspects of the Hebraic/Egyptian Gnostic tradition. The translation of the Copper Scroll found at Qumran tends to confirm this otherwise bizarre speculation, as it lists a variety of sites where Temple treasure and items of sacred import were hidden immediately prior to the destruction of the Temple in 70 CE. It is curious, to say the least, that in several of the sites listed in the Copper Scroll that were excavated by John Allegro, the Dead Sea Scrolls scholar, he found many artefacts relating to the Knights Templar of the 12th century, but nothing whatsoever from the era of the destruction of the Jerusalem Temple by the Romans in 70 CE.

The only rational explanation that can be offered to clarify this strange set of circumstances, and the question I have already posed as arising from them, is that 'the knowledge of these secret hiding places was passed down through the generations for over 1,000 years, via the oral traditions of the Rex Deus families.' The man responsible for granting them quarter placed immediately above the hiding place of the treasure they sought, was King Baldwin II who was obviously part of the conspiracy, and it is further indicative of this, that the order first 'went public' within a few weeks of his accession. Furthermore, despite having made several visits to the Holy Land during the reigns of Godfroi de Boullion and his brother Baldwin I by both Hughes de Champagne and Hugues de Payen they made no attempt whatever to found the order until Baldwin II acceded to the throne.

THE RETURN TO EUROPE

After their excavations under the Temple Mount were complete, Hugues de Payen asked King Baldwin II to write to Bernard of Clairvaux requesting him to intercede with the pope for formal papal recognition of the order. Bernard was the ideal man to make an intercession such as this as he was not only party to the conspiracy, but was the principal advisor to Pope Honorius II and his former teacher.[4] Shortly after this, Hugues de Payen and his fellow co-founders set out for Provence, then Normandy where he met King Stephen of England, who made gifts of both money and land to the new order and gave permission to Hugues to visit nobles both in England and Scotland. Stephen's wife, Queen Matilda, also gave the order the valuable manor of Temple Cressing in Essex.[5] The Templars then travelled through England to Scotland where they stayed with the St Clair's of Roslin.

King David of Scotland gave the Templars the lands of Ballantrodoch that became the headquarters of the order in Scotland and has since been renamed Temple. This land bordered on the St Clair estates so that communication between the ancient Rex Deus family of the St Clairs of Roslin and the new Knights Templar could be easily maintained. As an immediate result of this visit to Europe the order was given estates in England, Scotland, Champagne and Provence.

There is still considerable dispute as to which of these estates was the first to be given to the order but it is most likely that the lands around

Les Arcs-sur-Argens in Provence were first; Temple Cressing in England shortly after, Balantradoch third and Troyes fourth. This matter is complicated by the fact that the gifts were first given orally and only confirmed by legal deeds of donation long after the knights had taken possession. The fact is that these donations of land had been long-planned and were soon to be followed by a veritable cascade of gifts of estates, castles, towns, farms and villages throughout Christian Europe.

The development of the new Templar property at Troyes became the template for estate management in the future. This became the model for a new concept, that of 'preceptories' throughout Europe. These estates, which were eventually to be found in every country within Europe, acted as provincial supply bases used in support of Templar operations in the Holy Land. They operated as recruiting and training depots, instructed new members in the 'Templar Rule' and, a real innovation in medieval times, were used to give basic training in fighting as a highly disciplined unit.[6]

However, most of these other gifts of property and money only came in after the pope's official recognition of the order and the award of its first 'rule' by Bernard of Clairvaux. Bernard had already expressed his approval of the principles that lay behind the foundation of the Templar Order when, in 1124, he disputed with the Cistercian abbot of Morimund who had proposed setting up a Cistercian monastery in the Holy Land. Bernard gave short shrift to this project and remarked that: 'the necessities there are for fighting knights, not singing and wailing monks.'[7]

The Rule of the Templars

In response to the missive from King Baldwin, Bernard of Clairvaux did bring the order to the attention of the pope who not only gave his blessing to the warrior monks but also, and more importantly, commanded Cardinal Matthew d'Albano, the papal legate in France, to call a council of Church and temporal dignitaries in order to legitimize the new order and give the knights their first religious rule. The council opened at Troyes on 14 January 1128 under Cardinal d'Albano's presidency. It was attended by the archbishops of Rheims and Sens, the bishops of Orleans, Paris, Soissons, Auxerre, Meaux, Chalons, Laon and Samur, the abbots of Vezelay, Citeaux, Pontigny, Trois-Fontaines, Saint-Remy de Rheims, Dijon, Molesmes and, of course, by Bernard the abbot of Clairvaux, the archconspirator himself.[8] Temporal power was also well represented by the new Count of Champagne, Thibaud IV, by William II, Count of Nevers, and another leading nobleman André de Baudemant.

On 31 January 1128, the Grandmaster, Hugues de Payen, and his fellow knights appeared before the council to receive the new 'rule' that had been written by Bernard of Clairvaux.[9] Later, between 1139 and 1145, the pope issued a series of three bulls that bestowed almost total power on the order. It was one of the most remarkable turnarounds of the Middle Ages, if not of all European history.[10] Ten years after the Council of Troyes, Pope Innocent II issued the papal bull *Omne datum optimum* which made the Templars responsible, through their Grandmaster, to the pope and the pope alone, thus freeing them from the authority of bishops, archbishops, kings and emperors. It also exempted the order from paying tithes. A further bull issued by Pope Celestine II in 1144, *Milites Templi*, instructed the clergy that they should make a collection for the Knights Templar. The following year, his successor, Pope Eugenius III issued yet another bull, *Militia Dei*, once more directed at the clergy that granted the military order further privileges. These papal actions, made little more than 20 years after the Templars' foundation, made the knightly order wholly independent of all prelates and princes and, thereby, the most independent religious order in the Christian world. It was soon to become the most powerful, both in wealth and military might.

Growth of the Order

Less than two years after the Council of Troyes the order had acquired more land in Portugal through its close relations to the rulers. Donations in eastern Spain came more slowly but followed a similar pattern with the order acquiring property in Aragon soon after 1130. By the early 1140s they had gained enough land and had recruited sufficient members to mount and sustain simultaneous military operations on two fronts, both in the Holy Land and the Iberian Peninsula. They took part in most of the king of Aragon's campaigns against the Moors, and also acted in an advisory capacity to him. Their numbers in these campaigns were never great, but they could mobilize quickly and remained in the field as long as required;[11] in fact, both in Europe and the Holy Land they were the first full-time, professional standing army since the fall of the Roman Empire.

The grants of land, castles and property came in so fast and furious in the years following the Council of Troyes that, in some cases, the order had to defer garrisoning their new properties and castles for some time owing to an acute shortage of manpower, for their main priority was always the protection of the Kingdom of Jerusalem. Thus, all the early recruits, knights and those capable of military service, were sent to the East as soon as possible. They were following their Grandmaster's example, for Hugues himself, accompanied by 300 knights drawn from the noblest families in Europe who had rushed to become members of the order, returned to the Holy Land in 1129.[12] This contribution alone almost doubled the military strength of the forces of the Kingdom of Jerusalem in one fell swoop.

Bearing in mind the difficulties in communication within Europe in the early years of the 12th century, and allowing for the time it took to arm and equip these men and then transport them to a rendezvous point within Europe, this massive influx of recruits and their

rapid transportation to the Holy Land is a classic example of sustained, long-term and efficient planning of the highest order.

These recruits and the ever-growing list of donations of land and
property did not all originate directly from the families of Rex Deus,
for Bernard of Clairvaux was a master of the art of public relations and
publicity, and deployed all his skills and reputation to the full. Bernard
wrote a pamphlet, what we would now describe as a 'publicity blurb'
or advert, *de Laude Novae Militiae* – In Praise of the New Knighthood
– to attract recruits and inspire donations. The Knights Templar found
themselves heroes almost overnight, with donations pouring in from the
kings of Aragon and Castille, from the Count of Flanders and many other
princes. Hugues was especially well-received in England and Scotland,[13]
while in France the Archbishop of Rheims instituted an annual collection.[14] The tract extolled the virtues of the new order and listed the
immense spiritual benefits that would accrue to those who supported
its aims with acts of personal service, donations of land or good old-
fashioned money. In it he wrote:

> Rejoice, brave warrior, if you live and conquer in the Lord, but
> rejoice still more and give thanks if you die and go to join the
> Lord. This life can be fruitful and victory is glorious yet a holy
> death for righteousness is worth more. Certainly 'blesssed are they
> who die *in* the Lord', but how much more so are they that die
> *for* Him.[15]

Bernard was not in the business of pulling any punches and was
explicit in describing the order's principal duties:

> ... such are they whom God chooses for himself and gathers from
> the farthest ends of the earth, servants from among the bravest in

Israel to guard watchfully and faithfully his Sepulchre and the Temple of Solomon, sword in hand and ready for battle.[16]

One enigmatic paragraph that occurs towards the end of this document gives an overt clue to the secret objective of the Templars when Bernard wrote:

Hail, land of promise, which, formerly flowing only with milk and honey for thy possessors, now stretchest forth the food of life and the means of salvation for the entire world.[17]

The central dogma of the Christian Church was the irrevocable and essential belief that more than 1,100 years before, Jesus had died on the Cross at Golgotha in the supreme sacrificial act of salvation and that this sacrifice had redeemed mankind and saved us all from sin. Bernard, Abbot of Clairvaux, a senior member of the Church, was the advisor to a series of popes, at least two of whom had been his pupils, and had supposedly dedicated his life to furthering mankind's understanding of this dogma which the Church regards as a fact. So what exactly did he mean when he wrote: 'Now *stretchest* forth the food of life and the means of salvation for the entire world'? Or as rendered in alternative trans-lations, 'From which *will come* salvation for the entire world'? (my emphasis). Was Bernard referring to the documents found under the Temple Mount and their translation? Or the re-emergence of the true teachings of Jesus that he hoped for in this era of Rex Deus resurgence?

Unless further documentary evidence comes to light we can never be sure. What can be proved, however, is that following the circulation of *In Praise of the New Knighthood*, recruits and gifts of land and money flowed into the arms of the Knights Templar in a tidal wave of devout generosity. The Templars were not the sole beneficiaries of this burst of generous donations; the struggling Cistercian Order, which had revived appreciably after Bernard and his companions had joined its ranks, also began an extraordinary period of expansion. During Bernard's lifetime they established over 300 new abbeys, and this was the most rapid expansion recorded of any monastic order before or since. Furthermore, during Bernard's lifetime the Cistercians and the Templars were regarded as two arms of the same body; one a contemplative monastic arm, the other the strong, swift, military arm. Bernard himself regarded Hugues' new brethren as military Cistercians.[18]

France, Provence, Champagne, Bar, England, Tuscany and Occitan (the area now known as the Languedoc/Roussillon) became the major centres of Templar power and influence within Europe, closely followed by Aragon, Gallicia, Portugal, Scotland, Normandy and the Holy Roman Empire. At the peak of their power the Templars owned estates, castles and churches that reached from the Baltic to the Mediterranean and from the Atlantic coastline to the Holy Land. The vast profits from all these estates were devoted to one aim, and one aim alone – to maintain the standing army and fortifications in the Holy Land. Everything was devoted to this one end, and the order left no stone unturned to maximize its profits and increase its efficiency and power.

CHAPTER 7

The Order's Commercial Activities

By the time that Hugues de Payen returned to the Holy Land with his army of over 300 knights, after the Council of Troyes, the order had received many prestigious donations of land and money, and Hugues had already established an administrative network in Europe. Brother Payen de Montdidier, one of the original knights, was deputed as the 'Master of France'[1] and Brothers Hugh Rigaud and Raymond Bernard were charged with overseeing developments in Occitania and Spain. Raymond Bernard was in Portugal, in March 1128, when Queen Teresa of Castile presented the Templars with the castle of Soure, near Coïmbra and, over the next two years she persuaded others to give gifts to the knightly order. Meanwhile Brother Rigaud was at work in the valley of the Aude promoting the interests of the new order. Within four years the Templars were given the castle of Douzens and received the main bulk of the commanderie in the early 1130s.[2]

The careful planning that spawned this new structure began to pay off at a meeting between senior European Templars and leading members of the Trencavel clan who virtually ruled southern Occitania. These included Roger I of Béziers (d.1150), his brothers Raymond Trencavel I (d.1167) Bernard Atton V (d.1159) and their recently widowed mother, Viscountesss Cecily (d.1150). They donated to the order one man, Pons the Gascon, all of his his family and a *mas*, or small farmhouse under the walls of Carcassonne.[3] Indeed, small as it was, this gift was typical of the vast majority of Templar holdings in Europe, for most were not great castles, except in Spain and Portugal where these were needed in their battles against the Moors, but mainly consisted of farmhouses, mills, barns, small apsidal chapels and commanderies. In major cities, some strongholds were erected to hold treasure in transit or troops en route to the Holy Land. It must also be remembered that the knights were warriors who needed servants, farriers for their horses and armourers; their farms required labourers, blacksmiths, carpenters and herdsmen; their ships needed crews, carpenters, sail-makers, oarsmen, senior officers and navigators; their churches had their own chaplains and, as we shall see later, they needed masons and craftsmen in stone. The so-called warrior monks owned land in every climatic zone in Europe; they owned farms, vineyards, pasturage for sheep and cattle, quarries, mines, mills, smithies and stud farms. They became, in effect, the first multinational conglomerate in history.

In many areas where the Templars owned only a few small tracts of land it was not efficient to cultivate it themselves and so the order let out such lands to tenant farmers. Like other religious orders they had the right to collect tithes, the tenth of all produce from the lands over which they held sway, and thereby would amass large amounts of grain from their tenants. The Templar's storage barns at their commandarie of Temple Cressing in Essex survive to this day, and have recently been restored.[4] In England they owned lands as far west as Penzance, in remote places such as the Isle of Lundy, in the Midlands, Home Counties, Lancashire and Yorkshire. In Scotland, according to the Victorian scholar Maidement, the Templars owned some 614 separate properties.[5] Wherever the order produced corn in its fields, or collected it as tithes, it needed mills to grind the grain and such mills were an important means of generating income either by operating these mills themselves or renting them out for payments in money or grain or other benefits in kind.[6]

King Henry II of England gave the Templars two forges in Fleet Street in 1246, for which the order received 18d. a year in rent.[7] They also had royal permission to hold annual fairs at Witham in Essex, Baldock in Hampshire, Walshford in Yorkshire which was later changed to Weatherby, and at Temple Bruer.[8] Where the order, like its Cistercian brethren, was involved in wool production, one profitable byproduct was cloth manufacture. Under the Templars, the process of fulling cloth was mechanized, for instead of the cloth being washed and pounded by hand, they used huge wooden hammers powered by a water mill. The Templars owned at least two fulling mills in England by 1185, one at Newsham in Yorkshire and the other at Barton on Windrush near Temple Guiting in Gloucestershire.[9]

Like other religious orders, the warrior knights were also involved in industries such as the mining of coal and metal ores, the smelting of metal and its manufacture into tools and armaments. On the Palestinian coast at Castle Pilgrim, the Templars distilled seawater to produce salt[10] and at the village of as-Sumairiya in the Kingdom of Jerusalem they owned a glass factory.[11] The range of their commercial activities was such that the modern American consultant in business management, S T Bruno, described their commercial acumen in the following words:

> The fact of the matter is that the Templars ran a 'world wide' system of farms, shipping concerns and financial services. They pressed olives in the Jordan Valley, made wine in France and traded wool in Ireland. Agriculture was, of course, only one activity. They also shipped lumber from Edessa, and carried pilgrims across the

Mediterranean from Lombardy to Acre. They even provided a medieval form of 'travellers cheque' to pilgrims and loaned money to kings. Although one might envisage their primary military 'product' as singularly focused on the conquest of the Holy Land, the resource branch of the order operated in a number of different markets.[12]

Truly the organizational and administrative skills needed to manage this vast, international, multifaceted enterprise, and keep a standing army in the field at the same time, were staggering. Yet the Templars did it superbly. Despite all this evidence, however, many of their critics within the Church and, sadly, some modern historians still describe the Knights Templar as 'illiterates'! Yet, Bruno claims that the Templars managed their organization for over 180 years with skills that were consistent with the most sophisticated and best management practices understood today in the 21st century.[13] One charge that is sometimes levelled against the Templars was that, although they had been granted massive privileges, only a small number actually fought against the infidel while the vast majority were employed on the 9,000 or so estates that had been given to the order.[14] While this charge is undoubtedly true, it patently ignores the fact that without the revenues from its European lands, the order could never have maintained a standing army in the Crusader States.

THE MEDIEVAL PACKAGE TOUR INDUSTRY

The order's principal stated objective of protecting pilgrims en route to the Holy Land, was rapidly and profitably extended to providing transport and shelter for all devout pilgrims, whether they journeyed to

Jerusalem, Rome, Chartres, Mont St Michel, Rocamadour or Compostela. The Knights Templar, in effect, became the first effective and commercial travel agents in the world. Thus the 'package tour industry' is far from being a modern phenomenon, it was born in the 12th century when the Knights Templar began what I called in an earlier work, *Halo Tours Inc.* They used the Benedictine tract, the *Codex Callextinus*, to describe the precise route from most parts of Europe to the shrine of St James at Compostela. One folio within this four-volume work describes how to avoid thieves, bandits and dishonest innkeepers while travelling. Another lists appropriate hymns and prayers to be made while on the pilgrimage. With their financial skills, and a nose for profit, the Knights acted as bankers to the pilgrims themselves, the rest houses, the monasteries, and all the cathedrals, churches and chapels visited while en route.[15]

The prospective pilgrim knew that he or she was about to embark on a long, arduous and potentially dangerous enterprise; one that was costly and full of risk. Before departing, the pilgrim would deposit a large sum of money at their local Templar commanderie and receive a coded chit in exchange. Whenever they had to pay bills or give alms or donations to the religious establishments on the way, a visit to the nearest Templar establishment would be made, instructions given and the chit recoded. On their return home, the pilgrim would hand in his chit to the original issuer and either a bill or any unused balance would be presented to him. The chit was the precursor of the credit card.

In the religious pecking order of the medieval era, the pilgrimage to Compostela was second only in importance to the pilgrimage to Jerusalem, and far more important than any to Rome. In straight commercial terms it was the most important single enterprise in Europe. The pilgrimage to the shrine of St James of Compostela was known to the public as the *Shell Pilgrimage*. To the mystics and hidden Gnostics within the Knights Templar and their spiritual heirs, however, it was known as either the *Alchemist's Pilgrimage* or *the Pilgrimage of Initiation* – that is, an outward journey through the sacred landscape which mirrored an inner, mystical journey along the path of learning.[16] It is interesting to note the reason why this special pilgrimage was accorded such spiritual importance. The pilgrimage to Rome was easily accessible and associated by the Church with both St Peter and St Paul, but greater significance was attached instead to a small, obscure and relatively inaccessible corner of northwest Spain; to the city associated with James the Great, son of Zebedee, and also to James the Less, who we know better as James the Just, the brother of Jesus and the first leader of the original disciples in Jerusalem after the Crucifixion.

LONG-DISTANCE TRADE

Before the foundation of the order, long-distance trade in Europe was mainly seaborne and was conducted mainly by the northern Italian cities of Venice, Genoa and Pisa. These city-states prospered greatly from trade with both the Byzantine and Islamic empires to the east. Then northern Europe, in its turn, underwent sustained commercial development and offered timber and woollen cloth in exchange for the spices and silks of the East. But, prior to the Templar era, long-distance overland trade was fraught with difficulty as local barons imposed heavy tolls on goods passing through their lands, and all goods and money in transit were prey to the many bandits who infested the countryside.

Under the watchful eyes of the Templars, this chaotic and bandit-infested countryside was dramatically changed. Templar estates scattered throughout Europe proved to be the ideal bases from which the knightly order could fulfil their primary function of protecting the pilgrimage routes. Long-distance travel and trade therefore became safer and more practicable and, as a result, large regional markets began to flourish, which, in turn, stimulated further mercantile activity. The counts of Champagne encouraged merchants to bring their business to the market at Troyes and thereby created a climate of security and freedom that facilitated the growth of an international market near the midpoint between the emerging trading centres of the Low Countries in the northwest and the prosperous city-states in northern Italy. Other powerful nobles soon followed this example and trade was further facilitated by Templar action.

Travel and the transport of goods could only take place in safety if the roads and trade routes were effectively protected. The Order of the Knights Templar ensured that this was indeed the case and, as a result, played a significant part in creating the conditions required to facilitate the accumulation of capital. These conditions, which already applied in the great trading centres of northern Italy, were now, thanks to the security provided by the Knights Templar, spreading rapidly throughout Europe to the main centres of population.

The political results that flowed from the commercial success of the trading cities of northern Europe included an increasing independence for many areas from their nominal rulers in the Papal States or the Holy Roman Empire, and this was reflected in a sustained and cumulative shift in the balance of power throughout Europe. Power shifted from the feudal barons to the emerging mercantile class in the cities. In some areas under the rule of Rex Deus nobility, such as Toulouse for example, this developed into an embryonic form of democracy, as city councils flexed their muscles and rivalled the powers of their overlords.

Their reputation as fighting men, renown as defenders of Christianity, their ownership of estates in every corner of Europe and their financial acumen and reliability led to Templars being appointed as ambassadors, advisors to kings, popes and emperors and other positions of considerable responsibility in nearly every kingdom in which they operated. Thus, the Templars rose to positions of almost incalculable power and influence throughout the European continent. They wielded power and influence in military matters, in diplomacy, in international politics and in finance.

TEMPLAR SHIPPING

The Knights Templar had, from time to time, a relatively large fleet which they needed primarily to transport men, horses, supplies and weapons to the Holy Land. They also carried many pilgrims on a commercial basis. Thus, the majority of their fleet would have consisted of transport vessels rather than warships or fighting galleys. Most of the evidence for Templar shipping activity can be found within port records or royal dispensations for exporting goods at times of war when ports were normally closed. At La Rochelle on the French Atlantic coast, the Templars were given several vineyards during the 12th century. There they produced wine for their own consumption and for export and the cartulary of that port discloses that the Templars were exporting wine in their own ships.[17]

By the final decades of the 12th century, Templar ships are recorded as being at Acre. By the early 13th century their presence is noted at Constantinople and in the Bay of Biscay.[18] King Henry III of England hired, in 1224, the Templar ship known as the 'Great Ship' with its captain, a Brother Thomas of the Temple of Spain, for use in his wars in France. Later, he bought the ship from the Master of the Temple of Spain for 200 marks.[19] Apart from terrorizing enemy shipping in an early form of privateering, Templar ships appear in the records as carrying pilgrims, grain, military personnel and equipment from the western Mediterrannean to the East. As I have mentioned above, during times of war, rulers would close all ports and forbid exports by sea, including those made by the Templars to the Crusader States in the East. The order would then be obliged to negotiate permission to export their essential supplies to the Holy Land.[20]

TEMPLAR BANKING

This growing and prosperous trade cannot flourish unless the financial infrastructure to sustain it is present.[21] The Order of the Knights Templar had developed systems for the collection, safe storage and transport of large sums of money and other valuables collected from all of Europe, to its ultimate destination, the Crusader Sates in the Holy Land.[22] Despite what many historians claim, coin and bullion was actually carried from the West to the East. Therefore the Templars needed ships to carry their money as well as agricultural produce, horses and troops for the East. Their ships also acted as a secure transport service for pilgrims who found this safer and cheaper than using the services of a commercial carrier.[23]

The Templars, who were well used to working in a variety of currencies and transporting gold and money safely to finance their military operations in the Holy Land, began to offer financial services to the emerging trading classes. They set themselves up as bankers using a device they had learned from the Sufis of Islam, namely the 'note of hand', to make financial transfers from one part of Europe to another. This encouraged trade still further and led to vastly more profits for the order. Thus, they soon developed a reputation for being reliable bankers and became, in effect, Europe's first great Christian bank. They developed a system of credit notes whereby money deposited in one Templar preceptory or commandarie could be withdrawn at another upon the production of the appropriate documentation.[24]

The Templars provided annuities and pensions, for frequently a donation of land or money would stipulate that the order must provide for a man and wife until they died, indeed there were very few ways of effectively providing for one's old age or the welfare of one's dependants except by making a gift to a religious order or institution.[25] They lent money to merchants, the nobility, princes and prelates and all their financial dealings were backed by their reputation for probity, accuracy and safety.

King Louis VII of France was among the first of a number of European monarchs who was saved from financial ruin by a Templar loan. In this instance, however, the size of the loan brought the order close to bankruptcy, for it is alleged that the order provided Louis with 2,000 marks of silver and 30,000 *livres parisis*. The true size of this provision can be gauged from the revenues from French royal lands which, even 20 or so years after the Second Crusade, were only about 60,000 *livres parisis* per year.[26] By the reign of Philip II (1180–1223) the Templars were, effectively, the French Royal Treasury. Here their financial acumen paid off to the benefit of France, for during his reign, they increased the revenues from royal estates by 120 per cent and became heavily involved in Philip's highly effective restructuring of the Capetian finances.[27] The papacy also came to be financially dependent on the warrior knights' banking services. The Templars began to act as Pope Alexander III's (1159–81) bankers in 1163 and were also used by Pope Innocent III when he undertook to reorganize crusading finances at the time of the Fourth Crusade.[28]

That the Templars proved themselves to be so successful as bankers is due to their meticulous record-keeping and their objectivity in dealing with their clients. No business was done on holy days such as Christmas Day, Easter and Ascension, and also on the feast days of saints who had a particular relevance to the order, such as John the Baptist. But, outside of these dates, the hours the Temple was open for business depended almost entirely on the needs of the clients.[29] This reputation for probity, reliability and availability explains why this warrior order soon rose to be the wealthiest financial institution in the Christian world.

CHAPTER 8

Military Activities
in Europe

The activities of the Templar Order extended right across Europe to the Holy Land and their stated objective of protecting pilgrims was extended to the holy shrines of Europe, such as Canterbury in England, the cathedral of St James of Compostela in Spain, to Chartres, Mont St Michel and Rocamadour in France as well as to the many sites where the Black Madonna was venerated. A complex network of routes linked all parts of Europe to Rome, Compostela, and the other pilgrimage sites. While their primary focus was the protection of the Kingdom of Jerusalem, the orders wealth that sustained those campaigns came from Europe, where over 30 per cent of their estates were in the Languedoc-Rousillon area of the south of France. The growth in their revenues was such that by the early 1140s they had acquired enough land, recruits and resources to maintain simultaneous military operations both in the Holy Land and in the Iberian Peninsula. Thus, their activities in Europe were not entirely peaceful and from as early as the 1140s the order played a major role in the *Reconquistà*, the fight to retake land from the Moors in the Iberian Peninsula, and later, albeit to a lesser degree, in conflicts in eastern Europe.

THE *RECONQUISTÀ*

The war against the Muslims in the Iberian Peninsula was given papal recognition as a crusade in an extant letter from Pope Alexander II (1061–73) which stated that those who intended to journey to Spain should confess their sins but not do penance as their visit to Spain would be penance enough,[1] and offered incentives to those who fought in Spain that are remarkably similar to those granted to the later crusaders to the Holy Land. After the First Crusade, the pope recognized the war in Spain as a full crusade. In both 1100 and 1101, Pope Paschal II (1099–1118) forbade Spanish knights from joining the crusade to the Holy Land while the Moors were still a force to be reckoned with in Spain. He also granted those who fought in the *Reconquistà* the same remissions from sin that the papacy had offered to those on the crusade to Jerusalem.[2]

Thus, Europe in the 12th and 13th centuries was not only fighting the Muslims in the Holy Land but also on her southern flank in Spain, where the Moors were retreating step by step as the Taifa Kingdoms fell one by one to the Christian forces. As a result, the threat posed by the Islamic state within Europe itself was gradually fading. In 1248, the Castilian conquerors of Seville initiated what we would now call 'ethnic cleansing' by expelling every Muslim from the city in an attempt to create an exclusively Christian territory. However, the new conquerors soon discovered that the city no longer functioned without the previous inhabitants and they grudgingly allowed the Muslims to return. These returnees became known by the Arabic term *al-mudajjar*, meaning those 'permitted to remain'.[3] The *Reconquistà* did not come to an effective halt until some considerable time after 1280. At that time the Christian forces had taken the Kingdom of Murcia, which left only the little kingdoms of Granada and Malaga under Muslim control.[4] Therefore, by 1300 the whole of the Iberian Peninsula, with the exception of Granada, was back in Christian hands for the first time in 750 years.

I have mentioned earlier that the Templars enjoyed a close relationship with the rulers of Portugal and soon after the order's foundation had received numerous donations of land there. However, donations on the eastern side of Spain came more slowly. The man who instigated the *Reconquistà*, King Alfonso of Aragon, gave considerable donations of land to the order and granted them many privileges in 1130.[5] However, as was usual elsewhere, the properties in the Peninsula were used purely as a source of income to support the knights in the Holy Land and it was not until 1143 that, under pressure from Alfonso's successor, the Templars committed the order to military action in Spain. This situation arose because under the terms of Alfonso's will, the order stood to gain very considerable power and wealth indeed.

King Alfonso's Will

In 1131, the childless King Alfonso of Aragon had bequeathed a third of his kingdom to the Templars, with the other two-thirds to be divided equally between the Knights Hospitaller and the Church of the Holy Sepulchre in Jerusalem.[6] However, when Alfonso died in 1134, his will was ignored. Ten years later, after prolonged and bitter negotiations, the new ruler of Aragon granted the Templars: a number of fortresses; exemption from various taxes; a fifth of all land captured from the Moors;[7] a fifth of all the booty they took in the expeditions they made; an income of 100 *sous* a year from Saragossa (Zaragoza); a tenth of all royal revenues; and also promised to give substantial assistance to the order in building castles and fortresses.[8] From this time on, the Templars played a major role in the fight against the Moors. They acted in an advisory capacity and took part in all the campaigns directed against the Muslims. Although small in numbers, their strength lay in their ability to mobilize quickly and remain in the field, unlike the secular nobles and their forces who, once they had served their 40 days, returned to their homes and farms.

Two factors combined to limit the Templars involvement in the *Reconquistà*. They suffered substantial losses in the Holy Land during the 13th century and the decline in pious donations forced the order to focus more intently on the campaigns in the Holy Land. Furthermore, Spanish kings were also demanding that the Templars not only defend the kingdom against the Moors but also fight against Christian enemies, which the knights refused to do.

Other Military Orders

The kings of Castile often preferred to use certain other military orders such as the Knights of Santiago, the Knights of Alcantara and the Knights of Calatrava, for they were proving to be far more reliable as they were less likely to withdraw their forces from Spain to fight in the Kingdom of Jerusalem. They too could mobilize just as quickly, spend long months on campaign and of course their entire resources were devoted solely to the Spanish cause. However the use of these orders had its drawbacks for they had far fewer resources and, being far smaller, were unable to act independently.

The Spanish orders of the Knights of Santiago, the Knights of Alcantara and the Knights of Calatrava were all products of the prolonged eight-century campaign against the Moors in Spain. The Knights of Calatrava were founded in 1164 as an order fully affiliated to the Cistercians, like the Templars before them and, later the same year, they also gained papal recognition as an order of warrior monks. Shortly after the founding of the Knights of Calatrava, an order of warriors was formed to protect pilgrims en route to the shrine of Santiago of Compostela. In 1171, the papal legate, Cardinal Jacinto, granted them a rule and Pope Alexander III gave them papal recognition as the Order of Saint James of the Sword in 1175. The Order of Santiago had been born.[9] What distinguished the Order of Santiago from the other military orders was that married men were accepted as full members right from the beginning. Prior to 1170, an armed brotherhood known as the Knights of San Julián de Pereiro began to transform itself into the Order of Alacantara. Thus, the concept of warrior monks had developed from its small beginnings, supposedly protecting the pilgrimage routes to Jerusalem, into a complex web of military orders fighting the Christian cause from the Baltic to the Bospherous, freeing Spain from its Moorish conquerors and, above all, defending the Kingdom of Jerusalem and the other Crusader States.

EASTERN EUROPE

The frontier region of eastern Europe at that time was comparatively underpopulated and undercultivated. One very efficient way of populating the empty land was through donations to the monastic and military orders. Colonization meant increased wealth and prosperity for the landowner and was the main reason for encouraging the orders into the area. The knights could be used as protectors for the proselytizing monks and the new converts, who were prime targets for attack by the local pagans. They raided pagan territory taking booty and prisoners, in whose conversion they could then play a part.

From the late 12th century the Templars began to receive generous donations in the German Empire; in Bohemia and Moravia the majority of the donations of land went to the Hospitallers and Teutonic Knights, with the Templars only receiving their first donation in 1230. They had a house in Prague, founded soon after 1230, which had a chapel with a round nave replicating that of the Church of the

Holy Sepulchre in Jerusalem.[10] Their role in Bohemia was not that of warrior but purely to encourage colonization of the area. In Hungary they were receiving donations from the 1160s though in general their holdings were limited.

In 1241 the Mongols attacked Hungary and the Templars played a leading role in the ensuing battle. The king of Croatia, his archbishop and the Templar master, James of Montreal, took action. They rushed into the fray, but were heavily outnumbered and, though their losses were fewer than the Mongols, they were forced to withdraw. When the Hungarians finally joined the battle, the Templars again launched an attack but were forced to retreat. The king of Croatia and the archbishop barely escaped with their lives; the Templar master and the army were slaughtered.[11] Poland was also attacked by the Mongols in 1241, and the Templars' possessions were devastated. These battles were not fought as part of a holy war but in defence of their lands.

Substantial donations of land continued to come to the Templars, mostly on frontiers within Christian territory and on underdeveloped land within the region, though their presence was more symbolic than military. In both the Iberian Peninsula and eastern Europe the Templars acted as the representatives of the landowner, looking after the land and protecting it from any would-be invaders, creating wealth for all and raising much-needed funds for the support of their fellow knights in the Holy Land.

THE ALBIGENSIAN CRUSADE

Protected from invasion by the Pyrenees and buffered by the growing strength of the Spanish kingdoms of the Spanish March, the southwest-ern corner of France, the present-day departments of the Languedoc and Roussillion, prospered quietly under the benevolent rule of their local Rex Deus aristocracy and, during the 12th and 13th centuries, gave birth to a truly dazzling civilization; one illuminated by the principles of emerging democracy, love and, above all, religious toleration.[12] The local nobility encouraged trade, economic stability and a level of creative freedom that was truly exceptional in Europe at that time.[13] The feudal rule of the local counts was subjected to a degree of democratic moderation by the wealthy bourgeoisie who were assisted by groups of lawyers in the more prosperous towns and cities.[14] The influence of the Catholic Church had almost totally vanished in some areas and was in marked decline in the rest of the southwest.[15]

The local nobility, tolerant of the large Jewish community in their midst, who had seen the economic and intellectual benefits that flowed from their presence, now extended this toleration to a religious group known as the Cathars, people who claimed to follow the 'True Teachings of Jesus'. Within the Cathar faith, the congregation were known as 'the hearers' and the priests as '*les bonshommes*' or the good men[16] who lived according to the ideals laid down by their Essene precursors, yet their hostile critics within the Christian Church called them '*perfecti*', a corruption of the Latin term *hereticus perfectus*; they were also known as the Cathari, the pure ones.[17]

At the end of the 11th century, Count Raymond of Toulouse had raised a considerable army to participate in the First Crusade and liberate his Rex Deus homeland from the infidel, however, attitudes had changed by the mid-12th century and the local nobility, who were growing in confidence in an atmosphere of declining Church power, were becoming openly anticlerical. Indeed, according to the Catholic historian Giraud, the nobility of the Laurageais, the prosperous and populous area between Carcassonne and Toulouse, were almost completely Cathar.[18] The Cathars encouraged the establishment of a class of skilled craftsmen within local society and supervised the operation of workshops specializing in the manufacture of textiles, leatherwork and one useful skill that had crossed over from Muslim Spain, paper-making.[19]

The Cathar Religion

Insofar as it can be established, the Cathar religion was a dualist form of Gnosticism whose roots can be traced back to early Zoroastrian religion,[20] the school of Pythagoras and the cult of Mithras; with this strange melange of beliefs transformed by contact with early Christianity. Some historians also claim that it was a derivative of Manichaeism, an initiatory Christian cult of Persian origin based on the teachings of the mystic, Mani.[21] Due to the rapid and considerable growth of the Cathar faith, four dioceses were established in the Languedoc by 1167: Agen, Albi, Carcassonne and Toulouse.[22] A fifth was later established at Razès.[23] One of the earliest references to the Cathars that can be found in Church documentation is a letter from Prior Ebwin of Steinfeld, dated 1145 and addressed to Bernard of Clairvaux, describing a group he called 'the Cologne Heretics' led by an apostate monk named Henry. After some harassment by the Church authorities, Henry wisely moved to the more tolerant territory[24] of Toulouse, where he was followed by Bernard of Clairvaux. Bernard later wrote to the Count of Toulouse and said:

> The churches are without congregations, congregations are without priests, priests are without proper reverence, and finally, Christians are without Christ.[25]

While Bernard described Henry as 'revelling in all his fury among the flock of Christ', this leading member of Rex Deus, important churchman and advisor of popes, described the Cathars as a people of simple

119

and devout spirituality led by a gifted priesthood: 'No one's sermons are more spiritual.'[26]

It has been claimed that this new religion arose when a priest known as Bogomil preached a dualistic form of belief in Bulgaria in about 930 CE.[27] Then, after the Crusades, when the empire of Byzantium strengthened the trade routes from Constantinople to both Venice and Genoa, it created a viable means of communication between eastern and western Europe for the first time since the fall of the Roman empire. Thus, paradoxically, the Crusades, the movement to Christianize the Holy Land, established the routes by which Eastern forms of heresy could infect Catholic Europe. The Cathar heresy was a pure form of initiatory Christianity whose only scripture, The Gospel of Love, otherwise known as The Secret Gospel of John,[28] taught the simple message that Jesus came to reveal and not to redeem. In this sense, the first identifiable parent of the Cathar faith can be found within the First Church in Jerusalem led by James the Just, the brother of Jesus.

The Response of the Church

The Cathar religion grew in power and influence throughout the Languedoc to the extent that it soon began to rival and sometimes completely displace the Church of Rome, which posed a threat that the Church could no longer tolerate. In response, the Church despatched a preaching ministry to the Languedoc headed by a fanatical Spanish priest, Dominic Guzman.[29] His preaching fell upon deaf ears and the terrifying finale to his fruitless evangelical mission was a brutal warning:

> For years now I have brought you words of peace, I have preached, I have implored, I have wept. But, as the common people say in Spain, if a blessing will not work, then it must be the stick. Now we shall stir up princes and bishops against you, and they, alas, will

call together nations and peoples, and many will perish by the sword. Towers will be destroyed, walls overturned and you will be reduced to slavery. Thus force will prevail where gentleness has failed.[30]

In 1209, Pope Innocent III declared a religious war against the Cathars giving this dubious enterprise the title of a Crusade, which meant that any participant who served for 40 days was granted a papal indulgence giving absolution for all their past sins and any they might commit during the crusade.[31] They were entitled to seize the property of any heretic, be he prince or peasant; thus they were granted a papal licence to murder, steal, rape and pillage, all in the name of Jesus. The clergy accompanied the crusading army and treated any suspected heretic with torture and the warm embrace of death at the stake.

In July of 1209, the crusaders advanced upon the prosperous city of Beziers. Viscount Raimond-Roger Trençavel, the lord of both Beziers and Carcassonne, knowing that the city was indefensible, left in some haste for the superbly fortified city of Carcassonne. The large Jewish community of Beziers who knew of the persecution that their fellow Jews suffered in the north of France, fled with him. The remaining people of Beziers took little notice of the appeals of their bishop, who advised an immediate surrender, and decided to defend the city.[32] The siege was short and on the eve of the final assault the leaders of the besieging army sought the papal legate's guidance on how to treat their fellow Christians in the battle to come. The papal representative ordered the crusaders to ' … show mercy neither to order, nor to age, nor to sex … Cathar or Catholic – kill them all … God will know his own when they get to him.'[33]

The following day, over 20,000 civilians were slaughtered without mercy, 7,000 being murdered in the cathedral precincts where they had fled for sanctuary. Pierre des Vaux-Cernay claimed that the massacre was a punishment for the Cathar blasphemy against Mary Magdalene, on whose official feast day, 22 July, the massacre of Beziers took place:

> ... Beziers was taken on St Mary Magdalene's day. Oh, supreme
> justice of providence! ... the heretics claimed that St Mary
> Magdalene was the concubine of Jesus Christ ... it was therefore
> with just cause that these disgusting dogs were taken and massa-
> cred during the feast of the one that they had insulted...[34]

One immediate consequence was the unconditional surrender of
Narbonne, whose leaders, both the viscount and the archbishop, not only
offered material support to the crusaders but also promised to surrender any perfecti in the city and any property that the Jews of Beziers
had owned within it.[35] The bestial brutality of the massacre at Beziers
was just the first in the long line of atrocities that punctuated the
Albigensian Crusade.

The first perfecti were burnt at Castres; after the siege and fall of
Minerve, 140 perfecti, both men and women, were burnt alive and all
who fought against the crusaders ran enormous risks. In 1210, the leader
of the crusade, Simon de Montfort, inflicted a terrible punishment on
the captured defenders of Bram by selecting a hundred of their number
at random and gouging out their eyes and also slicing off their lips, ears
and noses. One prisoner, who was only blinded in one eye, was ordered
to lead his maimed companions to the castle of Cabaret[36] as a warning
to the garrison there of the fate that awaited those who opposed the
crusading army. Cabaret did not fall!

De Montfort's army marched on to further conquests and after the
fall of Lavaur, the 80 knights who had valiantly defended the town were
sentenced to be hanged. The gallows collapsed under their combined
weight and so, as an act of mercy, Simon de Montfort ordered that their
throats be cut. Lady Guiraude, the chatelaine of the castle, was handed

over to the crusaders and repeatedly raped. Her bleeding body was then cast down a well and she was stoned to death as an adulteress.[37] After this victory, 400 Cathars were burnt on a huge fire; shortly afterwards 60 more were burnt at Lescasses.[38]

The king of Aragon who joined in the war in support of the Cathar cause, was mortally wounded at the battle of Muret on 12 September 1213, where the slaughter exceeded that of Beziers.[39] To add to the terror of the crusade and the routine execution of the heretics, a deliberate scorched-earth policy was instituted and the crops were routinely burnt to starve the people into submission.[40] The brutal war lasted 30 years. Guillaume Tudelle recorded that 5,000 men, women and children were simply hacked to pieces after the fall of Marmande in 1226.[41] All these routine acts of barbarity were justified by the Church, who claimed that the crusaders were defending the true religion against heretics who, by definition, had no rights.

The Albigensian Crusade ended in 1244 with the surrender of the last Cathar stronghold of Montsegur after a siege of nearly a year. For once, the crusaders behaved with some semblance of chivalry, for the fighting men of the garrison and all non-heretics within the castle were spared but, when they marched down the mountain, their path was lit by the flames arising from a vast funeral pyre where 225 perfecti were being burnt alive.[42]

The Warrior Order's Puzzling Inactivity

Despite the fact that the Albigensian Crusade was started at the behest of the pope, neither the Knights Templar nor the Knights Hospitaller played any significant role in it whatsoever.[43] I have no idea how the pope reacted to this abstention by the main body of warrior monks, but I do know of some of the arguments the orders used to justify their strange decision. The Languedoc was home to nearly 30 per cent of the

Templar's European holdings and also contained a large number of estates owned by the Hospitallers. Yet, despite the overt rivalry that almost inevitably strained the relationship between the two orders, there was a suspicious degree of unanimity in their response to the call for a crusade against the Cathars. Both claimed that their holdings in the province were purely commercial and agricultural, understaffed, unfortified and not capable of being garrisoned in a military manner and, thereby, unsuitable as bases or defensive strongholds in time of war. Furthermore, both orders claimed that the deeds of donation granting these estates to the orders specifically forbade their use for any warlike activity.[44] The Rex Deus foundation of the Templars, the fact that nobles from the same groups of families in the Languedoc had donated the lands in question, and that these same nobles supported the Cathars, certainly help to explain the strange reluctance of the Templars to join in the war.

Records demonstrate that there were clear links between the Knights Templar and the Cathars for as the crusade reached its height, Templars gave assistance to knights who had actively defended the Cathars against the crusading armies.[45] There is also a remarkable degree of correspondence between the names of leading Cathar families in the records of the Inquisition and those of leading Templars from that area.[46] Indeed, Cathars fleeing from the crusaders were often given shelter by the Templars who, in direct contravention of papal instructions, allowed them to be buried on consecrated ground, and this humane practice led to the obscene rite of disinterment by the Inquisition after which the rotting corpses were tried on charges of heresy. When convicted, the heretical cadavers were ritually burned at the stake.

It is also highly probable that both the Templars and the Hospitallers were simply displaying the same reluctance to fight against fellow Christians that had limited their usefulness to Spanish kings. After all, their primary role was to fight the infidel in the Holy Land.

CHAPTER 9

The Templars in the Holy Land

When Hugues de Payen returned to the Holy Land with a retinue of over 300 knights and their ancillary support, his new recruits more than doubled the forces available to defend the Crusader States. Thus, from that moment on, the Templars saw themselves, and were certainly perceived by many others, to be the most important defenders of Christendom. Although it was the first religious military order in Christendom, it was, substantively, no different from those that followed its example, such as the Knights Hospitaller or the later Teutonic Knights. The Templars undoubtedly played a major role in almost all of the military actions conducted within the Holy Land and the surrounding states.[1] The Knights Templar and the Knights Hospitaller took turns in acting as either the rearguard or the vanguard whenever the Christian army was on the march. For example, they protected the rear of the army on its march through Asia Minor during the Second Crusade. During the Third Crusade, on the march from Acre to Jaffa in 1191, the Templars played a prominent role in holding the army together at a time when the Christian forces displayed a marked lack of discipline. However, as far as the devout pilgrims to the Holy Land were concerned, the Templars' most important role was their protection, for Templar castles guarded the pilgrimage routes and the knights and sergeants provided military escorts for the pilgrims as they visited the holy places.

Many of the order's activities in the Holy Land drew criticism from clerical commentators who perceived it as being too independent and almost a 'church within the Church'. Nonetheless, the order was still regarded as the most significant single military force in the Crusader States. From the time of Hugues de Payen's return, the Templars maintained a standing army of over 300 knights in the Crusader States and in the Kingdom of Cyprus. Along with the knights were non-knights, known as sergeants, foot soldiers and ancillary personnel plus mercenaries, and light cavalry known as Turcopoles.[2]

After the death of Hugues de Payen in 1135, a general chapter of the Knights Templar assembled in Jerusalem to select a new Grandmaster and chose Robert de Craon. The bravery of this Grandmaster was soon established, for in one raid led by him against a far superior force near Hebron in 1139, many of the knights were slaughtered and de Craon was lucky to escape with his life. De Craon was a skilled administrator and was well aware that the order needed papal privileges to survive and consolidate its position. In 1138 he succeeded in securing the first of these from Pope Innocent II, whose bull *Omne datum optimum* made the Templars answerable to the pope alone, exempting it from all other ecclesiastical jurisdiction. Even the Patriarch of Jerusalem no longer had authority over the order. This bull also confirmed the Rule of the Order as declared at the Council of Troyes in 1128, which allowed the Templars to elect their own Grandmaster without outside interference. The Templars were also permitted to receive tithes from both laity and clergy, on condition that they were given freely as gifts, but were themselves exempted from the payment of tithes, an exemption that up until then had applied only to the Cistercian Order, furthermore they were permitted to keep all the spoils of war that they captured from the Muslims.

In 1144, Pope Celestine II issued the papal bull *Milites Templi* in which donors were encouraged to form confraternities in support of the order, giving them the right to be buried in Templar churches unless they had been excommunicated. In 1145, another bull, *Militia Dei* was issued by Pope Eugenius III, who had been a monk at Clairvaux. This gave the Templars even more privileges, and allowed them to admit priests to the order who could collect tithes and burial offerings, thus swelling the order's coffers still further. These three bulls legitimized the Templars and put them above reproach and for the next 150 years they seemed almost invincible.

LIFE IN THE HOLY LAND

As the years went by, the Europeans resident in the Holy Land succumbed to a slow process of orientalization. Most of the knights abandoned Western fashions altogether, and on returning from battle they would remove their armour and wear a silk burnous in summer and sumptuous furs in winter.[3] To newly-arrived crusaders or pilgrims, life in the Crusader States often seemed shocking because of its luxury and licence. However, it must be remembered that numerically the Europeans were few and lived as a tiny minority both racially and socially in the lands they ruled.[4] However the standards of living they were able to sustain in their new lands were much higher than those they had experienced in Europe and, furthermore, they enjoyed far higher standards of medical care. The skills of the Arab physicians exceeded those of doctors in Europe, so in the crusader kingdoms Christians consulted Arab or Jewish physicians in preference to those of their own culture. William of Tyre recounts that his contemporaries 'scorned the medicines and practices of our Latin physicians and believed only in the Jews, Samaritans, Syrians and Saracens.'[5]

The ongoing hostility that existed between the Christian occupiers and their Muslim subjects and adversaries constituted a relationship of sorts that had its own rhythms and routines that necessitated interaction between the belligerent parties.[6] Slowly a degree of grudging diplomatic contact began to be established as the Europeans in general, and the Templars in particular, entered into guarded relationships with their Islamic neighbours. There had to be dealings with the enemy for, from time to time, there were embassies to be exchanged, alliances to be negotiated against mutual enemies, truces to be arranged and, as a consequence of battle, for all except the Templars there were prisoners to be ransomed.[7] One 12th-century Muslim commentator, Usāmah ibn Munqidh, left us an account of his views of the Christians whom he regarded as worthy enemies, when he referred to them as 'the Franks – may God confound them'.[8] He was contemptuous of their ignorance of medicine, and baffled by the social freedom permitted to Christian women. On the other hand, during periods of truce he was friendly with the Franks and found shared interests with many of them.[9]

Despite the harsh reality of intermittent warfare, each side learned to appreciate the gestures of gallantry and chivalry made by the other. Indeed, the principles of honour and chivalry were concepts that the Christians learned from their Muslim opponents. In times of peace, nobles from each community often joined together for hunting expeditions, and Christian and Muslim lords were sometimes honourably received at the court of the rival faith.[10]

Thus, as Christian dominion came and went in Syria and Palestine, and eventually spread throughout most of Spain, this era became one of permanent hostility rather than perpetual war between the Christian and Islamic worlds. This did not mean that there was an impermeable wall of intolerance between the Christian and the Muslim,[11] for while there could never be lasting peace between the Europeans and their Muslim neighbours, there was considerable contact. A large proportion of the revenues of the Crusader States, for example, came from tolls levied on the trade between the Muslim interior and the coast; this, of necessity, demanded that Muslim merchants had to be allowed full access to Christian ports and be treated honourably.[12] Indeed, there were many Italian communes in the Crusader States, made up of merchants from Genoa, Pisa and Venice who carried almost as much influence as the military orders. Some lived permanently or semipermanently in the East, others came each year in the spring and autumn to buy and sell their merchandise. The merchants carried the trade that brought wealth to the Crusader States, transporting pilgrims, colonists and supplies from Europe, and giving them a definite advantage over the Muslims with the sea power that their ships gave them. In the ports such as Acre and Tyre the merchants had their own quarters and were granted various privileges including the right to hold their own courts and deal with their own legal matters.

It was, indeed, the new immigrants, who had come to fight for the cause of Christianity, whose crudity continually ruined any peaceful policy in Outremer. Furthermore, the policy of Holy Mother the Church seldom favoured any understanding with the infidel, for in the eyes of the hierarchy, no agreement made with an unbeliever could be binding.[13] The Arab diplomat and chronicler Usāmah ibn Munqidh described one incident that demonstrates the problems caused by the intolerance of new arrivals and which also displays close contact between senior Templars and their Muslim adversaries:

When I was visiting Jerusalem I used to go to the al-Aqsa mosque where my Templar friends were staying. Along one side of the building was a small oratory in which the Franji had set up a church. The Templars placed this spot at my disposal that I might say my prayers. One day I entered, said *Allah akbar* and was about to begin my prayer when a man, a Franji, threw himself upon me, grabbed me and turned me towards the East saying 'Thus do we pray.' The Templars rushed forward and led him away. I set myself to prayer once more, but this same man, seizing on a moment of inattention, threw himself upon me yet again, turned my face to the East and repeated once more, 'Thus do we pray.' Once again the Templars intervened, led him away and apologised to me saying 'He is a foreigner. He has just arrived from the land of the Franji and has never seen anyone pray without turning his face to the East.'[14]

Thus we can see from Usāmah's account how he regarded the Templars as his friends and how tolerant they were of the faith of Islam. Indeed, this is only one incident among many that demonstrates the closeness that existed between these two apparently hostile belief systems.

Templar Castles and Fortresses

To convey an accurate and succinct overview of Templar activities in the Holy Land, I shall have to describe each area of influence in turn and therefore weave backwards and forwards in time, for the facts of history, interwoven as they are, rarely conform to the needs of the chronicler.

The Templars were involved in building projects from the time of their inception. They were given free rein by King Baldwin II to develop the land around their headquarters at the al-Aqsa Mosque as they wished. These developments were vast and complex and were described in the 1170s by Theodorich, a German monk on pilgrimage:

… houses, dwellings and outbuildings for every kind of purpose, and it is full of walking places, lawns, council-chambers, porches, consistories and supplies of water in splendid cisterns… On the other side of the palace, that is on the west, the Templars have built a new house, whose height, length and breadth and all its cellars and refectories, staircase and roof are far beyond the customs of this land… There indeed they have constructed a new Palace, just on the other side they have the old one. There too they have founded on the edge of the outer court a new church of magnificent size and workmanship.[15]

The English historian Piers Paul Read states that the Templars were major participants in 'the extraordinary boom in building that took place in the Holy Land under the crusaders.'[16] He elaborated on this, describing the fact that they built fortresses, palaces and, above all, churches. Indeed, another historian, Joshua Prawer claims that 'Not even Herod built as much.'[17] Among their major architectural projects was the construction of a new Church of the Holy Sepulchre in Jerusalem, which was dedicated in 1149, the renovation of the Church of the Nativity in Bethlehem, and the provision of an elaborately decorated tomb for King Baldwin IV on his death in 1185.[18] However, as a warrior order, it is, understandably, for their castles that they are remembered.

In the 1130s the Templars were made responsible for patrolling and protecting the frontier region between Cilician Armenia and the principality of Antioch. Thus, their first major fortresses were actually situated north of the Crusader States in the Amanus Mountains.[19] The stronghold of Barghas, for example, was built on an impenetrable summit on the eastern side of the range and gave them a clear view over the plain of Aleppo below. Other fortresses in this general area included those of Darbsaq, Roche Ruoussel, Port Bonnel and Roche Guillaume.

These guarded the passes in the Amanus range against incursions from the Cilician Armenians and Byzantine Greek Christians.[20]

Templar castles in the Crusader States discharged a wide variety of functions. They provided a safe haven for the members of the order, their allies and their tenants whenever Muslim raiders swept across the countryside.[21] Castles were also used as administrative centres from which estates were governed and, for the military orders, were also the principal centres for their religious and monastic life. It has been noted by many scholars that the concentric castle plan, which developed from the 12th century onwards, was also perfectly suited to the religious needs of the warrior monks in that it allowed the monks to occupy the inner enclosure while the outer circles housed lay people, mercenaries and others. However, this type of building was designed primarily to withstand the siege engines of their Muslim adversaries.

The castle of Latrūn, also known as Torn des Chevaliers, was built by Count Rodrigo Gonzalez of Toledo and he gave this imposing fortress to the Templars in 1141.[22] In 1149 the order received the fortress of Gaza which they used as a base from which to mount raids against the Muslims and to protect the southern frontier of the Kingdom of Jerusalem against Egyptian incursions. William of Tyre, not noted for his support of the Templars, records that the warrior knights discharged their duties at Gaza extremely well.[23] A few years later, in 1152, the Bishop of Tortosa handed responsibility for the castle of Tortosa over to the Templars, exempting their chapels from his authority and reducing the tithes they had to pay. The Templars built a new castle for the protection of the townspeople and the bishop.[24] They successfully defended this castle under the leadership of Grandmaster Gerard de Ridefort when it was besieged by Saladin in 1188.

In the late 1160s the Templars acquired the castle of Safed, but lost it to Saladin in 1188 after a bitterly contested siege. When Saladin's forces swept over the land earlier, in 1180, this provoked a complaint from William of Tyre that neither the Knights Templar nor the Knights Hospitaller had sallied forth to engage him in battle but had remained in their castles. Rather than attack against overwhelming odds, the knights obviously considered that it was more prudent to keep their forces safe. Yet, in wartime, Safed housed over 2,000 people, both non-military and military.

From the 1250s the secular nobility gave or sold many castles to the Templars because they could no longer afford to garrison or maintain them, bringing additional power and influence to the already powerful order. However, this largesse also stretched their resources to the limit.[25] In 1260, after the Mongols had sacked Sidon, the lord of Sidon gave the Templars the castle of Beaufort.[26] In addition to renovating or receiving gifts of old castles, the Templars built many new ones. Between 1217 and 1221, the Templars constructed one on a headland to replace their watch-tower at Atlīt, between Haifa and Caesarea, and named it Castle Pilgrim in honour of the pilgrims who helped with the construction. Stones from a previous wall built by the Phoenicians were used and, in the process, a hoard of ancient coins was discovered. Castle building was expensive, so this fortuitous find was put to good use and helped to finance the construction. Like many castles built by the Templars on the coast, Castle Pilgrim had a sea gate and could be supplied by sea when besieged.

Muslim leaders regarded the military orders in general and the Templars in particular, as a terrible menace to Islam. Imād al-Dīn, Saladin's secretary, described the Templars as rebels, demons, evil men with their castles built on inaccessible crags which were the lairs of wild beasts.[27] Thus the Templars and the Hospitallers were viewed as a serious threat by the military leaders of Islam, and the Muslims rejoiced in every victory that they had over the military orders, turning the event into a cause for celebration.

The Templar actions against the Muslims were not restricted to a purely land-grabbing or defensive role, for many of their raids were made to capture livestock, people and good old-fashioned loot which could be converted into wealth. The fortress of Gaza, for example, enabled the Templars to raid the city of Ascalon and attack caravans sent by the caliph of Egypt with supplies for the city.[28]

THE SECOND CRUSADE

When news of the fall of the city of Edessa in 1144 reached Pope Eugenius III in the autumn of 1145, he wrote immediately to King Louis VII of France begging him to lead a new crusade and retrieve Edessa from the infidels. However, recovering from a virtual civil war, his barons were disinclined to mount an expedition to the Holy Land, and even his own chief advisor, Abbot Suger of St Denis, advised against it. Louis and his barons agreed that the matter would be settled at Vézelay in Burgundy on 31 March 1146. Louis then turned to the greatest orator of the 12th century, Bernard of Clairvaux, for help in raising a crusading army.

The crowd that gathered to hear Bernard preach the crusade was too large to fit in the small church at Vézelay, so Bernard delivered his sermon from a specially constructed platform at the edge of the town. When Bernard finished speaking, King Louis immediately signed up for the crusade, followed by many of his nobles and his brother Robert, the Count of Dreux. Bernard continued his recruitment drive in the north of France and Flanders, and then wrote letters to potential crusaders in England, stressing their good fortune at being given the chance to save their souls.

The Second Crusade was almost a complete disaster from the start to the finish. King Conrad III of Germany, who set out for the Holy

Land ahead of the French, suffered an early defeat, when his army was cut to pieces by the Seljuk Turks.[29] Demoralized at the news of the Germans' defeat, the French came under attack in the Cadmus Mountains, where their heavy cavalry was useless, and were subjected to continuous attacks by the Turkish light cavalry, who were adept at firing from the saddle. As the French army was in danger of falling apart, Louis sought the advice of the Templar Grandmaster, Everard des Barres, and handed over command of the army to him.[30] The army was then divided into units of 50 men, each with a Templar at its head, which enabled them to reach the port of Attalia. Louis took his best troops to Antioch by boat, leaving the remainder to find their own way by whatever means they could. Odo of Deuil, the chronicler who wrote an account of the journey made by Louis VII to Jerusalem during the crusade, praised the Templars' discipline and the military aid they gave the army as it travelled through Asia Minor.[31]

Everard de Barres had joined the crusade in France along with a detachment of more than 300 Spanish Templars who, for the first time, wore a red *croix patté* on their mantles. Though thousands had been killed, the remnants of the army, French German and Spanish, regrouped at Acre in June 1148. Louis was now desperately short of money and turned to the Templars for help. The Grandmaster managed to raise sufficient funds for the king's needs from the Templar treasury and by using the order's possessions as security to raise loans. The king was now in debt to the Templars for 2,000 silver marks, half the annual income from his royal estates in France.

At a council of war it was decided that the crusaders would make for Damascus, with the attack planned for July. The siege began from the west but the crusaders made an ill-advised decision to move to the east of the city, a position that not only had no water but also faced the most heavily fortified area of the walls in an area where they could not deploy their heavy cavalry. When rumours of an advancing Muslim army reached the crusaders, they lost their nerve and retreated, signalling the ignominious end of the Second Crusade.

THE SIEGE OF ASCALON

As I have mentioned above, in 1149, King Baldwin III of Jerusalem gave the city of Gaza to the Templar Order, the first important fortress that the order received in the Kingdom of Jerusalem. The Templars immediately began to rebuild the castle, thus ensuring that the ring of fortresses encircling Ascalon, that were built earlier by King Fulk, was now complete. Ascalon was now completely cut off and so Muslim armies from Egypt attempted to retake Gaza almost as soon as the Templars had acquired it, but they were unsuccessful.[32]

The Christians laid siege to the heavily fortified city of Ascalon on 25 January 1153. In August, the crusaders' mobile siege tower was set alight by the defenders but, unfortunately for them, the wind then changed direction blowing the flames against the city walls, causing the masonry to crack and part of the wall to collapse. A unit of 40 Templars rushed forward under the leadership of the Grandmaster, Bernard de Tremelay. The Templars' greed for booty, according to William of Tyre, was such that the Grandmaster forbade any non-Templars from entering the city. They made a stand in the city themselves, which was unsuccessful as they were annihilated and their beheaded bodies were hung over the city walls the following day. The city fell three days later.[33] The Egyptians were allowed to leave taking their portable belongings with them, but were forced to leave behind large quantities of treasure and arms. Following the death of the Grandmaster during the siege, André de Montbard, the uncle of Bernard of Clairvaux, was then elected as Grandmaster but only lived to hold the post for three years. He was succeeded in 1156 by Bertrand de Blanchfort.[34]

The rest of the 1150s saw no major battles between the Christians and the Muslims, but this relatively peaceful situation changed with the accession of King Almaric who in 1163 launched a campaign against Cairo in which the Templars took part under the leadership of Bertrand de Blanchfort. During Almaric's absence from the Kingdom of Jerusalem, Antioch was attacked by a large force of Muslims. Acting against the advice of the Templars, Prince Bohemond III of Antioch attacked this overwhelming force; his army was routed and all but 7 of the 60 Templar knights who took part were killed. Almaric died in 1174, having dissipated the strength of the Kingdom of Jerusalem with his repeated campaigns in Egypt. He was succeeded by his 13-year-old son, Baldwin IV who was a leper. As Baldwin was too young to rule, his cousin Count Raymond III of Tripoli, acted as regent. In the course of his time as a prisoner of the Muslims the count had learnt to speak Arabic, studied their culture and learnt something of the psychology of his enemies. He was an experienced crusader and a cautious man, supported by the Knights Hospitaller and the families who had established themselves in the Kingdom of Jerusalem over a long period of time, but opposed by the Knights Templar and the more recently arrived settlers, led by Reynald of Chatillon, who were only interested in acquiring new land and were impatient for war. It was at this time that the crusaders greatest adversary emerged – Salah-al-Din Yusuf ibn Ayyub, better known as Saladin.

CHAPTER 10

Saladin & the Decline of the Crusader States

Significant events rarely arise out of a vacuum, unheralded or out of the blue. They are the result of the culmination of a series of apparently unrelated circumstances that have laid the foundations for the future. With the benefit of hindsight, it is possible to discern a cumulative chain of events that weakened the power of the Knights Templar, deprived them of their bases in the Holy Land, which were the very reason for their existence, and ultimately made the order vulnerable to apparently inferior forces.

There was one common problem that plagued both sides in the state of perpetual hostility between Christianity and Islam, and that was a lack of unity. The Christian forces were divided between several autonomous states whose relationships with each other were beset by bitter personal rivalries and the inevitable struggles for power that flowed from them. Even the Knights Templar and the Knights Hospitaller were prone to come to blows and even outright warfare. A series of battles occurred in Acre between the two knightly orders in a dispute over land. The Knights Templar sided with their Venetian allies and fought the Knights Hospitaller, Philipe de Montfort and their allies the Genoese in the streets of Acre and in a large naval engagement off the coast.[1] Similar situations were replicated among the forces of Islam, for not only were the Muslim forces also divided by local rivalries and tribal conflicts, but the majority of the empire was Sunni and the caliphate of Egypt was Shia. Thus, outbreaks of violence between the Christians and Muslim were generally localized because neither side could unite around a common purpose. To complicate matters still further, temporary alliances between Christian and Muslim local lords against their coreligionists were not unknown. All this was soon to change.

Salah-al-Din Yusuf ibn Ayyub, or Saladin, was born in 1138 and he was the man who was eventually to unite the armies of Islam and lead them to a series of resounding victories over the crusaders. His father, Najm-al-Din Ayyub, was a highly skilled general, yet Saladin excelled in learning before he took up arms in the service of the Saracen leader, Nur el-Din.

Christian forces led by King Baldwin III (1130–62) laid siege to the Arab city of Ascalon in 1153 and, after a prolonged siege, when surrender terms were agreed, the Egyptian garrison and the civilian population were allowed to march out of the city unmolested, and Baldwin III of Jerusalem strode in as its conqueror at the age of 23. The English historian Anthony Bridge remarked with some surprise that 'unlike many of the Crusaders before him, he (Baldwin) kept his word.'[2] Such trustworthiness in keeping treaties was rare indeed among the Christian forces. Sadly, Baldwin III took sick and died on 10 February 1162. To the Christians, he was irreplaceable, for he had the makings of a great king and his people mourned him bitterly; even the Muslim peasants of the country lined the road to pay their respects as his body was carried to Jerusalem.

When Nur el-Din was urged to grasp this opportunity to attack the Franks, that chivalrous leader refused saying 'it would have been wrong to take advantage of a nation mourning the death of so great a prince.'[3]

However, with Baldwin dead and gone, the usual brutal and unchivalrous attitude of the Christians manifested itself once again at the capture of Bilbeis in Egypt in October 1168; even many among the Europeans were shocked at the bloody and revolting massacre that followed. Muslims and Coptic Christians, women and children, old men and babies in arms were slaughtered with religious fervour and all of Egypt recoiled in horror. Worse was to come. When newly arrived crusaders from Europe captured the Coptic Christian port of Tanis a few days later, there was another barbaric massacre. The majority of the ordinary Egyptian people, who could easily have sided with the crusaders, fell into the arms of Nur el-Din. Shortly afterwards the caliph died and, as a result of a coup d'état, Nur el-Din's general, Saladin, became ruler of Egypt.[4]

Saladin's skilled diplomacy, patience, political realism and military prowess united the disparate factions within the Muslim world, and by 1185 he was ready to act on his lifelong ambition, to wage *jihad,* or holy war, against the Christian forces of the Kingdom of Jerusalem and recapture the Holy City itself. The patient Saladin bided his time and used the period of a truce signed with the Christians in 1185 to further unify his command of the forces of Islam. The truce between King Guy of Jerusalem and Saladin held firm, but they both reckoned without Reynald of Châtillon who is described as irresponsible and barbarous[5] or as an archetypical robber baron.[6]

The great caravans which travelled between Damascus and Egypt had once more been passing without hindrance through Frankish lands under the truce agreed between Saladin and the king of Jerusalem. In May 1187 an enormous caravan set out from Cairo and was accompanied through Frankish territory by a small troop of Egyptian soldiers as protection against Bedouin raiders. In defiance of the truce, Reynald of Châtillon attacked it without warning, killing the small band of soldiers and taking the merchants and their families with all their possessions to his nearby castle at Kerak.[7] The booty was vast, much larger than he had ever seen before. News of this attack soon reached the ears of Saladin who sent a request to Reynald demanding the immediate release of the Muslim prisoners and full compensation for their losses. Reynald haughtily refused to receive Saladin's envoys who then travelled to Jerusalem and complained to the king. King Guy listened to them with the utmost courtesy and ordered Reynald to make due recompense. Reynald refused. Guy, who had gained his throne through Reynald's support, could not, or would not force his vassal's obedience.[8]

THE BATTLE OF THE HORNS OF HATTIN

Saladin began to gather the largest army he had ever commanded, just across the frontier in the Hauran. When this became common knowledge, the king of Jerusalem summoned his tenants-in-chief to bring their men to Acre, and both the Templars and Hospitallers assembled all their available knights with the exception of those left to garrison their castles. By the end of June 1187, the Christians had assembled 1,200 fully armed knights, a large number of light native cavalry or Turcopoles, and 10,000 infantry outside the walls of Acre. When the news arrived that Saladin and his army had crossed the Jordan, the king went into council with his advisors. The majority of those present advised the king to use a purely defensive strategy, arguing that Saladin could not keep his army in the field for long in that arid climate and would eventually be forced to retire. But they reckoned without Reynald of Châtillion and the hot-headed Gerard de Ridefort, Grandmaster of the Templars, who accused the other nobles of cowardice. In consequence, the army moved to Sephoria, yet another defensible base where the same argument broke out, and this time the wavering king resolved to stay put. Later that night, again under pressure from the bullying and inept Templar leader, he changed his mind again and the scene was set for disaster.[9]

The king ordered the army to march at dawn and set out over the arid hills towards Tiberias. Constantly harassed throughout the day by Muslim archers and debilitated by thirst, they reached the village of Lubiya. There, acting on a request from the Templars who were bringing up the rear, the king ordered the army to camp for the night. The wells at the village were dry, and the army camped on the waterless plain overlooking the village of Hattin where Saladin's army waited for them. The Muslims set fire to the scrub on the hills and Saladin's forces attacked at dawn. The Christian cavalry withstood repeated attacks by their Muslim adversaries, but each onslaught reduced their numbers. Count Raymond and a small force broke through the Muslim ranks and fled to Tripoli. The infantry tried to break through the Muslim ranks to the lake, but were all either killed or taken prisoner[10] and the remaining Christian knights formed a defensive circle around the king, but when the relic of the True Cross was captured, the battle was over and the surviving knights collapsed from exhaustion.

The leading Christian prisoners were taken to Saladin where the Muslim leader offered a glass of rose water, cooled with ice, to the king. After drinking from it, the king passed it to Reynald de Châtillion. The glass was promptly taken from him. He was offered the chance to convert to Islam, and on his refusal he was executed by Saladin himself for what we would now call war crimes[11]. Few shed any tears for Reynald, for he was a violent and unscrupulous man, a violator of truces and an attacker of pilgrims making their way peacefully to Mecca. On his headless shoulders must lie the responsibility for the breach of the truce that led to the Battle of Hattin.

Saladin's defeat of the largest Christian army ever assembled in the

Holy Land heralded the final decline of Crusader States. The fact that this debacle for the Christians was caused as much by the strategic incompetence of Gerard de Ridefort, the Templar Grandmaster, as it was by Saladin's military genius, does not diminish the enormity of the defeat. After the battle, Saladin ordered the execution of all 230 surviving knights of the Templar and the Hospitaller Orders saying: 'I wish to purify the land of these two monstrous orders, whose practices are of no use, who will never renounce their hostility and will render no service as slaves.'[12] Saladin knew that ransom was forbidden to the warrior monks by the rules of both orders. Each of the knights was given the chance to convert to Islam, an offer that was predictably rejected, before being handed over to the Sufis for beheading. The Sufis obeyed their orders in the certain knowledge that their victims' immediate entry to paradise as men who had died for their faith was a far more merciful fate than a lifetime of slavery.

The author of the *Gesta Francorum*, who had fought the Saracens himself, described them in the following words: 'you could not find a stronger or braver or more skilful soldier than they.'[13] The Christians, for all their faults, held the moral worth and the military ability of their opponents in deep respect and Saladin was the principal, but not the sole recipient of this type of admiration. He was a man of his word, pious, wise, clement and just, and was only harsh and terrible to those who, like Reynald of Châtillion, had flouted the laws of war. The Christian chronicler, John de Joinville, quoted Saladin's maxims with unqualified approval: 'Saladin said that you should never kill a man once you had shared your bread and salt with him.'[14]

Saladin achieved his life's ambition when he conquered the Holy City of Jerusalem later the same year, and his treatment of the city's inhabitants stands in marked contrast to that bloody day when the Holy City was captured by the Christians in 1099; then, the fanatical crusaders had killed everyone in sight, Christian, Jew and Muslim, until the horses of the conquering knights waded up to their knees in blood. When the forces of Islam took the city, Saladin negotiated a peaceful surrender, and its inhabitants were offered the chance to be ransomed and not massacred;[15] many were ransomed by Saladin himself or by members of his family. Not one building was looted and no one was injured[16] and, in keeping with Islam's innate tolerance for the People of the Book, Jews were encouraged to settle in Jerusalem once more.[17] Orthodox Christians and members of the Syrian Jacobite Churches remained in the city, assured of their safety by their own earlier history under the benevolent rule of Islam.

Saladin continued to triumph over the Christians. The fortress of Kerak was besieged for more than a year and was only forced to surrender because the inhabitants were starving. The Templar castle of Safed was bombarded for a month before it too was forced to capitulate.[18] Many other castles were lost but the coastal cities of Antioch, Tripoli and Tyre remained in Christian hands. The arrival of a fleet of Sicilian galleys reinforced the garrison at Antioch and the siege of Tyre was relieved by a force under the command of Conrad of Montferrat when, on 1 January 1188, his ships defeated the Egyptian fleet and forced Saladin to abandon the siege.[19]

Showing a hitherto unseen determination, King Guy marched south to Acre in August 1189 accompanied by a force of Templars led by Gerard de Ridefort. The city had been taken by Saladin's forces after the disastrous Battle of the Horns of Hattin. Guy encircled the city and put it under siege, despite the fact that a large part of Saladin's army was still in the area, following an audacious plan that was probably the earlier suggestion of Gerard de Ridefort[20] who died in battle near Acre on 4 October 1189. The Christian siege of Acre was described as 'the only example in 12th-century Syrian warfare of a major siege conducted in the presence of a field army able to harass the besiegers and aid the besieged.'[21] Acre was finally retaken on 12 July 1191 and the Templars continued to lead the campaign to keep the remaining Christian possessions out of the hands of Saladin.

The Crusader States were now reduced to a few cities and ports on the coast along with the surrounding lands that they defended. When King Richard I of England heard the news of the fall of Jerusalem, he vowed to liberate the Holy City once more and landed at Acre, a major fortified port in the truncated remnant of the Kingdom of Jerusalem, on 7 June.[22] It was in the Holy Land that Richard, who was probably the worst king that ever ruled England, set the seal on his reputation as both a fearsome and chivalrous warrior. The battles between Richard the Lionheart and Saladin are truly the stuff of legend. The Christian forces now had a leader they could respect and who was to earn the admiration of his opponent, Saladin.

Saladin personally led an attack on Jaffa in 1192 and had virtually captured it after three days of heavy fighting. Indeed the garrison, which had retreated into the citadel, was on the point of surrender when King Richard of England arrived from Acre with 50 Pisan and Genoese galleys. Accompanied by an advance guard of 80 knights, 400 archers and about 2,000 Italian marines who had disembarked hurriedly, Richard soon had Saladin's army on the run. However, before any reinforcements could reach Richard, Saladin counterattacked displaying his own skill and ingenuity in battle. Nonetheless, Richard's small force was able to repel repeated Muslim assaults.

Saladin watched Richard in admiration[23] and was so moved by Richard's dauntless spirit that, when the English king's mount was killed under him, Saladin instructed one of his grooms to lead a pair of horses through the battle under a flag of truce and give them to the English king with his compliments.[24] It is also alleged that on one occasion when Richard lay ill, Saladin dispatched his own personal physicians to tend to his worthy adversary. True or not, this was widely believed by men on both sides of the conflict at that time, which gives some measure of the affection and respect accorded to these two true giants of chivalry by their opponents.

This battle showed both leaders that neither could win outright, and that they would have to make a truce. Both had other matters that needed their attention so Richard agreed that Ascalon should be demolished, and in return Saladin guaranteed that the Christians would remain in possession of the coastal cities from Antioch to Jaffa; Muslim and Christian pilgrims were free to cross each others' territory, and the latter were free to visit their sacred sites in the Holy Land. The peace was to be kept for the next five years with the aid of the Templars and the Hospitallers.[25]

The customs of that time dictated that any leader of note could exploit his position for financial gain. Saladin, however, was of such a devout character that he refused such opportunities and, uniquely for an Islamic sultan, he died in almost total poverty and his brother even had to pay for his burial shroud.[26] Saladin had avenged the dreadful defeats inflicted on Islam by the crusaders, but in a manner that tempered courage with justice and humanity and thus he undoubtedly won the moral victory. He was renowned by both sides as a leader who had never been known to break his word to either friend or foe.[27]

After the capture of Jerusalem in 1187, the remaining Crusader States in the Holy Land were whittled away little by little, despite several crusades being mounted to regain the Holy City. The Templars took no part in the Fourth Crusade which brutally sacked the Christian city of Constantinople and brought no relief whatever to the truncated Crusader States.

1 **Previous page:** Departing for the Crusades. Illustration from *Histoire de France* by Jules Michelet. Colour litho by Louis Bombled c1900.

2 **Left:** St Bernard of Clairvaux, the founder of the Knights Templar. Mosaic detail from the Crypt of St Peter, 15th century.

3 **Below:** The Chapter of the Order of the Templars held at Paris, 22nd April 1147. Painting by Francois-Marius Granet 1844.

4 Right: Early 12th Century Masonic symbolism in the Church at Utelle, Les Alpes Maritimes.

5 Below: Templar Cross on the wall of the Church at Roquebilliere, Les Alpes Maritimes.

6 Above: The Ark of the Covenant being carried on a cart, carved on a pillar at the Portal of the Initiates, Chartres Cathedral.

7 Left: Rex Deus symbolism within the church at Roquebilliere, Les Alpes Maritimes.

8 Above: Pilgrims under escort of Knights Templar in front of Jerusalem in the 12th century. Engraving, English School, 19th century.

9 Below: Remains of the citadel in the Templar village of Les-Arcs-sur-Argens, Provence.

10 Above: Templar church near Castellane, Provence.

11. Right: Templar church, La Luade, Provence.

12 Below: Templar Castle at Trigance near the Gorges du Verdon, Provence.

13 Above left: Templar Seal showing the Temple of Solomon.

14 Above: Templar Seal of two brothers on one horse.

15 Left: Crusaders surrounded by Saladin's army, illustration from *Bibliotheque des Croisades* by J-F. Michaud, 1877, litho by Gustave Dore 1876.

16 Above: Saladin I in Jerusalem. Painting by Alexandre Evariste Fragonard. c1830-50.

17 Below: Decorated tile with roundels of Richard I and Saladin, from the Benedictine Abbey at Chertsey, Surrey, 13th century.

18 Left: Guillaume de Clermont defending Ptolemais (Acre) in 1291. Painting by Dominique Louis Papety 1845.

19 Right: Jacques de Molay, the last Templar Grandmaster. Engraving, French School.

20 Below: Burning of Templar leaders. Illustration from *L'Histoire de France* by Jules Michelet. Engraving by Daniel Vierge c1900.

21 Above: The Templars before Philippe IV and Pope Clement V, from *The Chronicles of France* (vellum) by Boucicaut Master, 14th century.

22 Above: The Black Virgin in the Chadaraita, French School, 17th century.

23 Right: The Black Madonna, Notre Dame-sous-Terre, Chartres Cathedral.

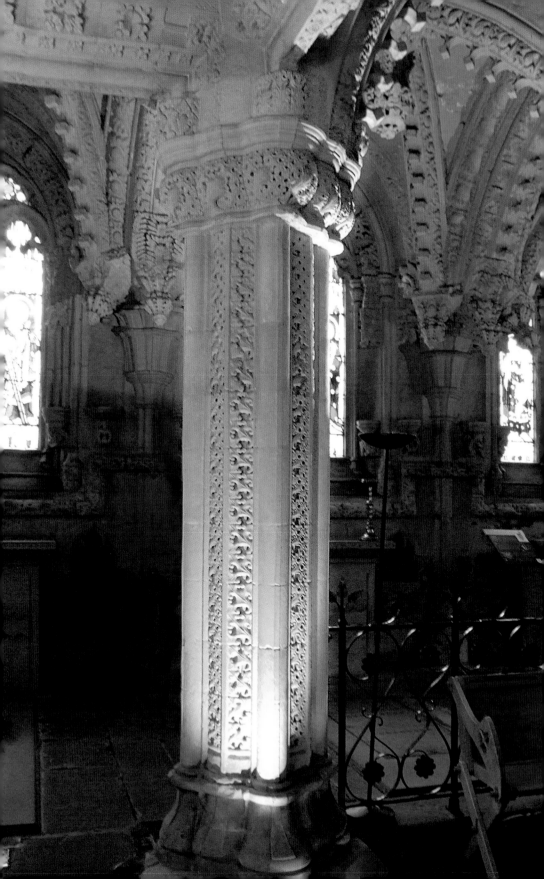

24 Above: Intricate basket-work carving on the capital of the Journeyman's Pillar, Rosslyn Chapel.

25 Left: The sublime carving on the Mason's Pillar, Rosslyn Chapel.

26 Right: Rex Deus symbolism of the Staffordshire Knot on the Apprentice Pillar, Rosslyn Chapel.

27 Above: Lintel carved with a quotation from Esdras, 'Wine is Strong, Women are stronger, Kings are stronger still, but Truth Conquers all.' Rosslyn Chapel.

28 Below: Carving of the head of the 'Murdered Apprentice', Rosslyn Chapel.

29 Below right: Carving of the Head of the 'Grieving Widow', Rosslyn Chapel.

30 Above: Carving of a Green Man on the String Course in Rosslyn Chapel.

31 Left: Badly weathered carving of a Templar Initiation on the South Wall of Rosslyn Chapel.

32 Below left: Carving of Melchizedek with a Grail Cup, Rosslyn Chapel.

33 Below right: Carving of the Hungarian Knight, Ladislaus Leslyn and Princess Margaret on one horse, South Wall, Rosslyn Chapel.

34 Overleaf: The famous Apprentice Pillar, Rosslyn Chapel.

THE FIFTH CRUSADE

Pope Honorius III called for a new crusade which took place in 1218. The Templars, who had played no part in the previous crusade, the Fourth, were heavily involved in the Fifth Crusade. King Andrew of Hungary and Duke Leopold of Austria arrived separately in the East with their armies and attacked the key city of Damietta in Egypt. The crusaders, with reinforcements led by the King of Jerusalem, including Templars, landed at Damietta in June 1218. The city was quickly taken, despite the Christian forces being heavily outnumbered, and it was the quick and decisive action by the Templar Master that brought victory to the crusaders.[28] The Templars had rapidly adapted their methods of fighting to cope with the waterlogged Nile Delta. They used a fleet of ships and pontoons and, coping with the swamps, once again proved their capability as strategists and engineers of genius.

After the capture of Damietta the Egyptian sultan offered them Jerusalem if they would return the city to his control. The papal legate, Pelagius, refused, for unless the lands surrounding Jerusalem were also returned it would be impossible to hold the Holy City. After the imperial army under Emperor Frederick II failed to arrive, Pelagius ordered the army to advance up the Nile, an action that was taken against strong advice from the Templars[29] who believed that the Christian resources were already overstretched. When the crusaders reached the town of Mansurah, the Muslim army trapped them by cutting off their retreat and halting their advance by opening the sluice gates on the river, flooding the crusaders into submission. As the Templar Grandmaster later wrote in a letter to the Templar Preceptor in England, they were 'trapped like a fish in a net.'[30] A truce that was to last for eight years was agreed and Damietta was surrendered.

The Holy Roman Emperor, Frederick II, with his army belatedly reached Acre in September 1228 after a delay at Otranto where many of his forces had fallen ill. This tardy progress so enraged the pope, Gregory IX, that he immediately excommunicated the emperor. Frederick was excommunicated a second time the following spring when he eventually did set sail for Acre, because he had continued the crusade while excommunicated. So, by the time he reached Acre, he was barred from leading the crusade.[31] The Templars and Hospitallers supported the pope but the Teutonic Knights supported the emperor.

Frederick's wife, the Queen of Jerusalem, died in childbirth, and thus he lost any claim to the throne of Jerusalem, except as regent for his infant son, Conrad. Thus, having lost both his crown and any authority that might have flowed from his position as leader of the crusade, he marched to Atlīt and demanded that the Templars hand over the castle to him to be garrisoned by his forces. The Templars refused and he then marched to Jaffa. The Templars and Hospitallers followed a day behind, having refused point blank to accept his command. Frederick eventually handed command over to his generals, and the two military orders rejoined the crusaders. The Templars were prepared for a fight but Frederick preferred to use negotiation, and in a coup previously deemed impossible he regained possession of the Holy City by striking a deal with the Egyptian sultan.[32] They agreed to a ten-year truce, and Jerusalem was returned to the crusaders, but the Muslims retained control of the Temple Mount. A narrow corridor of land that connected Jerusalem to the coastal cities and the Holy City istelf was to remain undefended.

Frederick crowned himself King of Jerusalem in March 1229, supported only by the Teutonic knights; the principal warrior orders of the Knights Templar and the Knights Hospitaller were conspicuous by their absence.[33] Frederick finally left the Holy Land on 1 May 1229, to the accompaniment of jeering crowds who pelted him with offal.[34]

Defeats and disappointments continued. A force led by Henry of Bar, was decimated at Gaza after he led them in an attack on Egypt. The blame for this defeat fell on the shoulders of the Templars and Hospitallers who, having assessed the danger inherent in attacking a much larger force, had signally refused to support Henry in his attack. A fresh crisis arose in 1244 when war broke out between Egypt and Damascus, and Egyptian forces swept south from Edessa and attacked Jerusalem. A month later the city was no longer in the hands of the Christians, and never would be again.[35] The bones of Godfroi de Bouillon and other kings of Jerusalem were disinterred from the Church of the Holy Sepulchre, and then the church was set alight.

The Egyptian and Turkish forces met at Gaza and were attacked by the Christian forces at La Forbie. It was an unmitigated disaster with the Damascenes deserting the field, leaving the Christian forces to be slaughtered by the Muslims; 800 were taken prisoner and subsequently sold into slavery in Egypt. Among them was the Grandmaster of the Templars.[36] Thirty-three Templar knights survived, having lost between 260 and 300 of their comrades in the battle. Damascus finally fell to the Egyptians the following year. In the 1260s the Templar castle of Safed and the Hospitallers' Krak des Chevaliers fell; Antioch was lost in 1268 and the Templar possessions in the Amanus March were abandoned. The Crusader States were nearing their inevitable end.

CHAPTER 11

The Templars Lose Their *Raison d'être*

In March 1291, Mameluk armies from Egypt led by the Sultan al-Ashraf Khalil[1] converged on the city of Acre equipped with over 100 siege engines, catapults and mangonels, and by 5 April they had completely encircled the city. The Christian defenders, comprising about 1,000 knights and 14,000 infantry aided by every man who could bear arms from the population of about 40,000, took their place on the ramparts to defend the city.[2] The northern suburb of Mountmusard was protected by a moat and a double wall; between it and the main city was a further moat and wall linking a series of fortified towers. The Knights Templar, under the command of their Grandmaster William of Beaujeu, defended the northernmost section where the walls of Mountmusard met the sea. Adjoining them were the Knights Hospitaller, and where the walls of Mountmusard joined the walls of Acre itself were the royal knights under the command of Almaric, the brother of the King of Jerusalem. His force was strengthened by a contingent of Teutonic Knights and the rest of the walls were manned by English, French, Venetian, and Pisan knights assisted by troops from the community of Acre.

Fighting began on 6 April when, under the cover of a storm of arrows, Mameluk engineers began to mine under the walls and towers. On the night of 15 April, the Templar Grandmaster and a body of knights sallied out beyond the walls and attacked the main Muslim camp, but after some success were forced back with the loss of 18 knights.[3] The first of the towers undermined by the Muslims began to collapse on 8 May and had to be evacuated and set on fire to prevent it being used by the enemy. During the next few days other towers began to crumble and on 16 May the Muslim forces made a determined attack on St Anthony's gate which was repulsed by the Templars and Hospitallers. William of Beaujeu rushed out without his armour to help repulse an attack on the Accursed Tower and was mortally wounded. Several commentators on this decisive battle claimed that his death was the final blow that sealed the fate of the Crusader States.[4] The knights carried their Grandmaster to the safety of the Templar fortress at the southwestern part of the city where he died that night. The Grandmaster of the Hospitallers, John of Villiers was also wounded and taken to a galley in the harbour.

The harbourside was a scene of confusion and panic as the stricken citizens tried to leave by whatever means they could. In desperation, many dived into the sea and swam to the galleys lying offshore. Overcrowded small boats capsized and many unfortunates were drowned including the Patriarch, Nicholas of Hanape. One Templar, Roger de Flor, extorted large sums from the rich matrons of Acre for a place on his boat and later used this vast profit to fund his eventual career as a pirate. Eventually the harbour was cut off from the main city as Muslim forces fought their way through the streets, killing everyone in sight. Those who sought refuge within the houses were later captured and sold into slavery and this flood of slaves so depressed the market that the price of a slave girl in Damascus dropped to a drachma.[5]

By dusk on the evening of 18 May the entire city was in the hands of the Muslims with the exception of the Templar fortress at the seaward end of the city. A contemporary report states:

> Also, it is said that a good 7,000 people fled to the house of the Templars (in Acre). Because it was located in a strong part of the city overlooking the sea shore and was surrounded by good walls, they defended it for perhaps twelve days after the capture of the city (by the Muslims). But when the Templars and the others who had fled there realised that they had no supplies and no hope of being supplied by human help, they made a virtue of necessity. With devoted prayer and after confession, they committed their souls to Jesus Christ, rushed out strenuously on the Saracens and strongly threw down many of their adversaries. But at last they were all killed by the Saracens.[6]

The 'good walls' of this Templar house were 28 feet thick and under their protection the surviving Templars, under the command of their Marshall Peter de Sevrey, aided by a motley mixture of citizens, knights from other orders, and infantry, fought on bravely. Galleys from Cyprus brought them supplies. A truce was arranged, but angered at the mishandling of women and children, the Templars killed the Muslim emissaries and withdrew once more into the safety of the fortress. That night, the Templar Marshall Peter de Sevrey ordered the Templar commander to take ship and transport the order's treasure to Sidon. The following day, when invited to parley under a flag of truce, the Templar Marshall and his emissaries were seized and beheaded and on 28 May the Mamaluks undermined one of the walls, poured through the breach and slaughtered all the remaining defenders.[7]

The sacrifice of the Templars who fell in defence of the last citizens of Acre would have been a fitting finale to the history of this great warrior order, but sadly worse was to come. Without any realistic hope of relief from the squabbling kings of Europe, the last Christian strongholds in the Crusader States were whittled away one by one. The city of Tyre surrendered in May, followed by Beirut and Sidon in July, Tortosa and Castle Pilgrim in August.[8] Castle Pilgrim was the only stronghold never to have been defeated and to ensure that the Templars could never reoccupy the site again, it was dismantled stone by stone. The surviving knights regrouped at their bases in Cyprus and began to agitate for a new crusade to liberate the Holy Land once more. When Pope Nicholas IV (1288–92) heard the sad news of the final demise of the Crusader States, he summoned a Church council to investigate whether the Holy Land could be recovered and also began openly to discuss how the two great military orders of the Knights Templar and Knights Hospitaller could be amalgamated, thereby implying that the blame for the loss of the Crusader States should fall on the warrior orders.[9] Indeed, some commentators complained that the Holy Land was only lost because the two principal military orders spent too much time fighting each other when they should have been fighting the Muslims.[10]

THE BLAME GAME

Throughout their history, the Knights Templar and, to a lesser extent, the Knights Hospitaller, had been subjected to waves of criticism by commentators within the ranks of the Church. Regarded by many as forming 'a Church within the Church', they were criticized and resented because of their financial power, their arrogance and because they killed in the name of Christ, offending all those pious churchmen who firmly believed that 'the Church should not shed blood' – *ecclesia non novit sanguinem*. However the most damaging charge against the Templars arose out of their tolerant treatment of Muslims which led to accusations of collusion with the enemy and the betrayal of the Christian states for profit.

Treachery and Treaties

As early as the 1160s one chronicler, John of Würtzburg, claimed that the failure of the Second Crusade was due to Templar treachery. One of his colleagues, known as the Würtzburg Analyst, took this claim one step further and suggested that the failure of the siege of Damascus was because the Templars had been bribed by the Muslims.[11] Yet, William of Tyre who was one of the order's fiercest critics makes no mention of either charge.[12] In one Templar raid in 1154 the Templars ambushed a group of Muslims, travelling from Egypt, that included Rukn al-Dīn Abbas with his son Nāsr al-Din who had been the homosexual lover of the caliph of Egypt. Nāsr had just robbed and murdered his lover then fled, laden down with booty. Abbas was killed in the fight and Nāsr was captured by the Templars. One monk from the diocese of Rheims or Laon, who wrote circa 1155, described these events and claimed that the Templars were the instruments of God's justice. Another chronicler, writing somewhat later in the 1190s, added that the Templars handed over their captive Nāsr to his enemies for due punishment for his crimes.[13] Muslim commentators finished the story by describing how Nāsr was executed and his body hung on a cross at the city gate, the standard punishment for traitors according to Egyptian custom.

Thirty years later, William of Tyre writing in the Holy Land and Walter Map writing in England both claimed that Nāsr had converted to Christianity while he was imprisoned by the Templars, but as the knights preferred money to converts, they had sold him back to the Egyptians for a large sum. Needless to say there is no evidence for this sudden change of faith in any of the chronicles, either Christian or Muslim.[14]

At other times, and again with no evidence, Templars were charged with raising sieges for payment from their Muslim enemies. Furthermore, it was well known that the Templars had advised King Richard the Lionheart against advancing further towards Jerusalem as the city could not have been held by the Christians even if they had captured it.[15] The chronicler Matthew Paris remarked somewhat wryly that the many requests to the West for more resources were not believed as neither the Templars nor the Hospitallers had any real interest in conquering the Muslims, but merely wished to prolong the war in order to extort more money from patrons in Europe.[16] Furthermore, Paris reported, the Templars and the Hospitallers were perceived as hostile to each other and with their thousands of manors in the West were perfectly capable of supporting themselves without further aid.

Another source of more general criticism arose because so many of the crusaders had adopted Eastern habits:

> The Franks employed Syrian doctors, cooks, servants, artisans and labourers. They clothed themselves in Eastern garments, included in their diets the fruits and dishes of the country. They had glass in their windows, mosaics on their floors, fountains in the courtyards of their houses which were planned on the Syrian model. They had dancing girls at their entertainments; professional mourners at their funerals; took baths; used soap; ate sugar.[17]

Templars were, as I have mentioned before, particularly tolerant towards the faith of their adversaries, furthermore, the Grandmaster always had Saracen secretaries and many individual Templars learned Arabic. Yet another cause of discontent was the Templars relationship with the Shiite sect of the Assassins.[18] The hatred of the Assassins for their Sunni enemies made them more than amenable to making alliances with the Christians and they paid the Templars an annual tribute of 2,000 besants in return for the Templars leaving their fortress at Alamut in peace.[19] Commentators in Europe and newcomers to the Holy Land rarely understood the complex politics of that place, nor did they have sufficient appreciation of the local political conditions that led the Templars and others to recognize that on many occasions, diplomacy and treaty-making were far more effective than brute force.[20]

Pope Innocent III wrote to the bishops of the Holy Land complaining that treaties with the Saracens undermined his attempts to persuade European monarchs to go on crusade. Treaties with local Muslim leaders were common, and the Templars were far more likely to keep to their terms than their fellow-Christians. In 1207 the same pope remonstrated with the Templars for disobeying his legates, saying mass in churches under papal interdict and admitting anyone 'willing to pay two or three pence to join a Templar confraternity ... even if he is excommunicate' thereby ensuring that adulterers and usurers gained Christian burial. According to the pope, the Templars were 'exhaling their greed for money'.[21] Another cause for resentment against the order was their perceived power as senior advisors to many European rulers.

TRUSTED AND WELL-BELOVED SERVANTS

Senior Knights Templar were appointed to political positions of the utmost trust and delicacy by popes, kings, nobles and senior prelates. From the time of Pope Alexander III until the fall of the order, Templars were routinely appointed as papal chamberlains who were in constant attendance on the pope in his own chambers. Thus they were constantly in the presence of the most powerful member of the entire Church, able to speak privately to him, privy to his thoughts and intentions and, above all, in a supreme position of influence. Templars also acted as papal messengers, treasurers, judge-delegates and as marshals and porters at the papal court. In July 1220 it was a Templar and a Hospitaller who were entrusted with carrying Pope Honorius III's financial contribution to the Fifth Crusade to Egypt as the pope claimed that there was no one he could trust better.

Kings, dukes and earls also employed Templars in positions of considerable trust. The Earl of Pembroke, William Marshall, employed one Templar, Brother Geoffrey, as his almoner, and in 1177 the English King Henry II appointed another Templar, Brother Roger, in a similar position; Templars continued to be royal almoners in England until 1255.[22] The kings of Scotland also had Templar almoners as did the King of France and King James II of Aragon who had Brother Peter Peyronet in his employ.[23] During the Second Crusade in 1148, the Templars provided the financial support that enabled King Louis VII of France to go on the crusade. Later, in 1250, it was Templar money that was used to ransom King Louis IX from the sultan of Egypt.[24] In England, the treasury always remained as an integral part of the royal household and was run by royal officials and the New Temple was simply used as an additional and secure storage facility. In France however, the Temple became the royal treasury and it was not until 1295 that the King of France established his own separate royal treasury at the Louvre. However, in 1303 many of the functions of the royal treasury reverted back to the Temple indicating that the order's expertise was deemed to be essential for the efficient administration of the national finances.[25]

The discretion of the Templars, their probity, and the fact that they were frequently seen travelling the roads of Europe like members of many other religious orders, made them the perfect messengers for secret correspondence or diplomatic operations for popes, kings and nobles. As members of religious orders they could pass anywhere without question and were far less likely to be stopped, attacked, robbed or questioned than any lay person or civilian. They not only gave financial and military advice to rulers, for King Henry II of England sought their counsel during his dispute with Thomas à Becket. That most suspicious of monarchs, King John of England (1199–1216), stated plainly in his will that the Templar Brother Aimery de St Maur was one of the few men whose advice he trusted and followed. King Louis IX of France was so persistent in his attempts to gain one brother as his advisor, Brother Amaury de la Roche, that he prevailed upon Pope Urban IV to force the order in the Holy Land to send Amaury to him. Templars were also used by a variety of English kings to assist in their administration in Ireland and collect taxes.[26]

Any organization as large and powerful as the Templars, backed by papal prestige, economic success and popular esteem due to its valorous actions in the Holy Land, could not escape exciting the envy of others. Their very power and independence tended to breed arrogance, and the degree of papal privilege they enjoyed caused lasting resentment among the episcopate and the secular clergy.[27]

Nonetheless, despite the loss of the Crusader States, Templar history would indicate that, with estates throughout Europe, influential men well established in positions of power in so many kingdoms, and financial tentacles that touched kings, bishops and even the pope himself, this order should remain in an unassailable position. Sadly, this was not, in fact, the case. The downfall of the Knights Templar was not brought about by resentment at their power or their arrogance, nor through their disputed role in the loss of the Holy Land, but by simple plain greed on the part of one bad king, King Philippe le Bel of France, who is rightly remembered in France as *le Roi Maudit*.

CHAPTER 12

Philippe le Bel, the Templars & the Inquisition

With the benefit of hindsight it is apparent that, for the Order of the Knights Templar, matters had started to come to a head with the election of a new Grandmaster in 1293. There were allegations of irregularities in this election and for some inexplicable reason the Grandmaster of the rival Order of the Knights Hospitaller was invited to guide and advise the chapter of the Knights Templar in this closely fought contest.[1] The outcome of the election was that an elderly, and reputedly illiterate, knight from the north of France, Jacques de Molay, became the 23rd Grandmaster of the Templar Order. Most accounts of this tragic figure agree that he was undoubtedly brave, unimaginatively strict and intellectually none too bright.

Shortly after the fall of Acre, Pope Nicholas IV died in Rome. His death was followed by one of the most unedifying episodes in papal history. A succession of particularly corrupt popes was improperly elected, all tainted by double-dealing and scandal. This, in its turn, resulted in a series of forced abdications and even more elections marred by bribery and violence. To crown this whole cascade of corruption, accusations of murder, idolatry, simony, sodomy and heresy were levelled against Pope Boniface VIII.[2] Then, under the malign influence of the cunning and unscrupulous King Philippe le Bel of France, the Frenchman Bertrand de Goth, who was Archbishop of Bordeaux and not even a cardinal, was elected as Pope Clement V. He was apparently chosen as a neutral candidate, a stopgap pope to prevent civil war between the two major contending families in Rome, namely the Orsinis and the Colunnas. Pope Clement V distanced himself from Rome, the traditional seat of the papacy, by choosing to live at Avignon where he reigned in considerable splendour, ruling his flock while under the thumb of King Philippe.

KING PHILIPPE LE BEL

Philippe IV had succeeded to the French throne in October 1285. Despite being of the Capetian line, the Rex Deus traditions had long since died out within the royal family of France, for Philippe's grandfather, King Louis IX, had been a sincere and zealous Catholic and had, indeed, been canonized by the Church as St Louis. France itself was now a large kingdom having gained Normandy, Anjou, Maine and Touraine at the time of King Philippe II and, more recently, by the addition of the county of Toulouse and the whole of the Languedoc following the Albigensian Crusade. Despite its size, the kingdom was plagued by acute financial difficulties exacerbated by the costly wars Philippe had fought. The king levied a 10 per cent tax on the Church and imposed swingeing financial impositions on the Languedoc in the last decade of the 13th century. Forced loans from rich landowners and the nobility were repeatedly imposed between 1294 and 1297 to finance the war with England. The king debased the coinage several times between 1295 and 1306.[3] Ultimately this provoked riots, and the king sought refuge in the Paris Temple, the headquarters of the Knights Templar in France.[4] Philippe owed over 800,000 livres tournois to the Lombard bankers, so these bankers were targeted in the hope of cancelling his debt and producing income.

Throughout the 1290s, Lombard bankers in France were subject to seizures, fines and expulsions until in 1311 all their assets and debts were appropriated and the remaining Lombard bankers in France were imprisoned.[5] The Jews were the next obvious target, and in 1295 their 'usurious profits' were confiscated and they were forced to reveal details of all their financial affairs giving the king other fields to plunder. In July and August of 1306, all Jewish property throughout France was seized and the dispossessed owners were expelled from the country.[6] Most Jews from the Languedoc fled to Moorish Spain, Jews from other parts of France fled to Alsace, Burgundy and northern Italy but the most sizable contingent emigrated to the Muslim-controlled Holy Land. It was becoming blatantly obvious that no one was safe from the depredations of this desperate, depraved and penniless monarch, particularly those to whom he owed money.

Philippe had extracted a high price from Archbishop de Goth for ensuring this cleric's election to the papacy. The king claimed the right to retain all the tithes collected by the Church in France for a period of five years, and it was he who insisted that the new pope lived in Avignon under Philippe's watchful eye. Twelve of the king's friends among the clergy were made cardinals and, according to some sources, a secret condition was imposed that was never publicly disclosed.[7] In 1306, Clement V wrote letters to the Grandmasters of both the Knights Templar and the Knights Hospitaller, inviting them to France to discuss the possible amalgamation of the two principal military orders. In this invitation, their instructions were to, 'Travel as secretly as possible and with a very small train as you will find plenty of your knights on this side of the sea.'[8] The Grandmaster of the Knights Hospitaller, William de Villaret, respectfully declined this invitation, explaining that he was engaged in an assault on the Turkish stronghold of Rhodes, a matter that both the pope and the king were aware of, as it had long been public knowledge. Sadly the Grandmaster of the Knights Templar, Jacques de Molay, had no such excuse to offer, and defying the explicit instructions from the pope, he sailed for the Templar port of La Rochelle with a fleet of 18 ships carrying his personal entourage and 60 senior knights of the order;[9] also 150,000 gold florins, and silver bullion that needed 12 pack-horses to carry it.[10] Jacques de Molay knew the way of the world and was prepared to employ a massive bribe if reasoned argument against the proposed merger failed. The large train of knights, packhorses and transport arrived at the Temple in Paris watched by King Philippe who was waiting to greet the Grandmaster Jacques de Molay and welcome him to France.[11]

The Grandmaster had prepared his case against amalgamation with some skill and argued that, as both orders had rendered signal service to the Church and the cause of Christianity, there was no rational reason to institute change. He also claimed that as the members had chosen their respective order under the guidance of God, it was tantamount to blasphemy to insist that they now join another. He was ready to argue that, as each order owned considerable properties and wealth, any move to amalgamate them might well bring dispute in its train.

De Molay's preparations were in vain, for the proposed amalgamation of the two military orders was simply a ruse to tempt the Grandmaster to exchange the safety of the Templar headquarters in Cyprus for a position of danger and vulnerability in France. At the funeral of the king's sister-in-law, Catherine de Valois, on Thursday 12 October 1307, Jacques de Molay occupied the seat of honour near the king.[12]

Friday 13th

As dawn broke on Friday 13 October 1307, the king's agents in France opened sealed orders that had been distributed on 14 September.[13] Acting on the instructions within them, soldiers swooped on every Templar property within France, arresting the Templar Grandmaster, the 60 knights of the inner circle and a large number of other knights,[14] indeed Gerard de Villiers, the Preceptor of France, was the only leading Templar to effect an escape.

To justify this massive wave of arrests, charges of heresy and betrayal were levelled against the Templars that were described as: 'A bitter thing, a lamentable thing, a thing which is horrible to contemplate, terrible to hear of, a detestable crime, an execrable evil, an abominable work, a detestable disgrace, a thing almost inhuman, indeed set apart from all humanity.'[15] The Knights Templar were accused of causing Christ, 'Injuries more terrible than those he endured on the cross';[16] another charge claimed that they were more evil than the Saracens.

The King was careful to explain that, of course, he was not acting on his own initiative, or for his own ends, but solely at the request of Guillaume de Paris,[17] the chief Inquisitor of France, a deputy of the pope and the king's confessor. However, with his hold over Clement V and his relationship with Guillaume, it is obvious that the king was the prime mover in the whole affair. Thus, in this instance, the Inquisition was acting as an arm of the state and not at the behest of the pope. It is also apparent that, although Philippe and Clement may have discussed these matters prior to 13 October, the king had neither sought the pope's consent to the arrests nor informed him of them until after the event.[18] After their arrest the imprisoned Templars were handed over to the tender mercies of the Inquisition.

THE HOLY INQUISITION

During the Albigensian Crusade, Pope Gregory IX addressed a letter to the bishops in the south of France in which he announced his intention of employing the teaching friars for the discovery and repression of heresy. In July 1233, he appointed two Dominican friars as full-time Inquisitors. Those they accused of heresy were denied any form of legal representation, and torture was routinely used from the beginning, although it did not receive formal papal sanction until 1252.[19] This despite the fact that there was a tradition, hallowed by three centuries of observance, that the Church was forbidden to shed blood – *ecclesia non novit sanguinem*. To conform with this age-old tradition, drawing blood by lance, sword or dagger, was deemed un-Christian, so techniques of torture were devised that kept actual bloodshed to a minimum but caused the maximum pain and suffering with a minimum of mess. Often the mere sight of the instruments of torture was enough to extract confessions of heresy. Although references to torture are not common in contemporary documents, it seems that its use was as widespread in late 13th-century Italy and France as it was later in Spain.[20] Of all the methods of torture used at that time, the principal one used by the Inquisition was fire.[21] Later, Pope Alexander IV authorized Inquisitors to absolve each other for so-called 'irregularities' such as the premature death of a victim.

Under civil law, certain categories of people were deemed to be immune from torture such as doctors, soldiers, knights and nobles. At first the Inquisitors role was limited to that of instructing the civil executioner and making notes of anything the accused said under duress but, in 1252, Pope Innocent IV formally authorized them to administer torture themselves with this comment, '… with the restriction that such compulsion should not involve injury to limb or danger of death.' The traditional stricture about shedding blood remained in force, so sharp implements were avoided in favour of the rack, thumbscrews and other devices that caused blood to flow only as a secondary consequence. To tear flesh with pincers would undoubtedly shed blood unless the pincers were red-hot, in which case the hot metal cauterized the wound and staunched the bleeding.

The Inquisitors kept meticulous records of their interrogations, which enabled them to continue to harass the descendants of those convicted of heresy. Heresy was considered to be hereditary, so the children of heretics could not inherit and the grandchildren were barred from taking holy orders, unless, of course, they successfully denounced someone else for heresy.[22] The aim was to obtain confessions of heresy at any price and there is no record of an Inquisitor ever losing a case.

The Church used the 'Black Book' or *Libero Nero* written by arch-Inquisitor Bernard Gui as a manuscript of instruction for his colleagues. In it we find:

Either a person confesses and he is proved guilty from his own confession, or he does not confess and is equally guilty on the evidence of witnesses. If a person confesses the whole of what he is accused of, he is unquestionably guilty of the whole; but if he confesses only a part, he still ought to be regarded as guilty of the whole, since what he has confessed proves him to be capable of guilt as to the other points of the accusation... If, notwithstanding all the means (of torture) employed, the unfortunate wretch still denies his guilt, he is to be considered as a victim of the devil: and, as such, deserves no compassion from the servants of God, nor the pity and indulgence of Holy Mother Church: he is a son of perdition. Let him perish among the damned.[23]

As the Inquisitors were paid with the confiscated goods and property of convicted heretics, the rich had more to fear from them than the poor. When the expenses of the scribes and executioners had been paid, half of the remainder went to the pope and the rest to the Inquisitors. While some Inquisitors had a keen eye for profit, others tortured simply out of the love of God and these were known as the incorruptibles.

The staunchly Catholic historian of Christianity, Paul Johnson, condemns the Inquisition vigorously and details its activities with horror.[24] Another noted historian, H C Lea, described its crimes as, 'an infinite series of atrocities'.[25] Lord Acton, a Catholic, penned this condemnation of the Inquisition, and of the Church:

> Nothing short of religious assassination... the principle of the Inquisition was murderous for the popes were not only murderers in the grand style, but they made murder a legal basis of the Christian Church and a condition of salvation.[26]

The Inquisition's intent was to prosecute heretics with such vigour that they would create a perpetual climate of fear within which heresy would not dare to rear its head. Inquisitors now had legal authority to convict suspected heretics without any possibility of appeal and, in effect, to pronounce summary death sentences[27] and their first target at their foundation was the Cathars.[28]

The tender ministrations of the Inquisition in the Languedoc, and throughout Europe, ensured that the pope's new gift was far more terrifying than the horrors of the Albigensian Crusade. He lost no time in spreading the beneficial effects of the new organization to the rest of Europe, for in the same year he appointed Peter of Verona as Inquisitor in Lombardy.[29] In 1246 Pope Innocent IV instructed the

Franciscans to join the Dominicans in the work of the Inquisition, and divided Italy into two inquisitorial provinces[30] with the bull *Super Extirpatione*: the Franciscans were to have responsibility in Tuscany, Umbria and the Veneto, while the Dominicans were to preside over the remainder of the country. Inquisitorial duties in the rest of Christendom were apportioned as follows: the Franciscans were to have eastern France south of the Loire, Poland, Dalmatia, Bohemia, Croatia, Serbia, Hungary, Jerusalem and the Holy Land; the Dominicans were to have northern France, western France south of the Loire, Germany and Austria; and they would operate together in Aragon, Navarre, Burgundy and Italy. Thus the Inquisition was set to work throughout much of Christendom from the mid-13th century onwards.[31]

The Inquisition rode roughshod over the established canons of justice, and ignored all written, state and customary laws that granted some semblance of protection to the accused. Over time it developed a system of jurisprudence that infected not only ecclesiastical practice and canon law but also the criminal law, and made a cruel mockery of the mere idea of papal justice for all time. One historian, H C Lea, was moved to write that:

> The judgement of impartial history must be that the Inquisition was the monstrous offspring of mistaken zeal, utilized by the selfish greed and lust of power to smother the higher aspirations of humanity and stimulate the baser appetites.[32]

Legislation against heresy resulted in the creation of a permanent inquisitorial tribunal endowed with almost limitless authority that worked, from a fixed base in each district, in conjunction with the local bishops and clergy.[33] For example, in 1239, a bishop by the name of Moranis was accused of allowing heretics to live and multiply in his diocese. As a result, a Dominican Inquisitor named Robert de Bougre was sent to the county of Champagne to investigate, and within a week of his arrival virtually the whole town was on trial. The result was predictable, for on 29 May, Bishop Moranis and over 180 of his flock were publicly burnt as Cathar heretics.[34]

Methods of Torture

In the early years there were six main methods of torture: the ordeal by water, the ordeal of fire, the strappado, the wheel, the rack and the *stivaletto*. The ordeal by water consisted in the prisoner being forced to swallow water, either by a funnel or by soaking a piece of silk or linen and jamming it into the throat. Water was dripped continuously into the mouth which often resulted in blood vessels bursting. In an ordeal by fire, the prisoner was manacled so that he could not move and placed before a roaring fire with fat or grease applied to his feet so that they literally fried. A wooden or metal fire screen was used to interrupt the procedure to allow for questioning or to provide respite in the case of fainting. The strappado was one of the favourite forms of torture; the prisoner, male or female, was stripped to their underwear, had their ankles shackled and their hands tied behind the back; then the wrists were tied to another rope that ran over a pulley on the ceiling above. The accused was hoisted over six feet above the floor and, with iron weights attached to the feet, was left hanging there from the tied wrists. In this position the prisoner was whipped and interrogated further and, if he remained silent his body was hoisted higher still, until the torturer suddenly allowed it to drop until the feet almost touched the ground; then the process would be repeated. Severe dislocations were the most common result. Sometimes the prisoner was tied to a large cartwheel and his body was beaten and broken by battering it with hammers, bars or clubs.

The rack was the most notorious form of torture used by the medieval Inquisition; a simple machine made from a wooden frame raised from the ground with planks placed across it like the rungs of a ladder. At each end were rollers to which the victim's ankles and wrists were tied. The Inquisitor would question the victim while he was being positioned, then the rack would be tightened by turning the rollers until the victim's body was stretched to breaking point. The *stivaletto* or *brodequins* was a boot torture where four thick boards were attached, two to each leg, with strong rope tied as tightly as possible. Under questioning, wooden or metal wedges were driven between the two boards and the leg until either the pressure became intolerable and the ropes began to cut into the victim's flesh or the Inquisitor heard the sound of the splintering or crushing of bones. Permanent disability was inevitable.[35]

The accused was tortured until ready to confess which, sooner or later, he would be; then the confession was heard, recorded and read back to him and he would be formally asked if it was true. If he replied yes, the transcript inevitably recorded that his confession had been 'free and spontaneous', without the influence of 'force or fear'. Sentencing would then follow. A death sentence was passed in about 10 per cent of cases only, for Inquisitors preferred to keep a 'saved' soul in a more or less intact body, which, through penances or on pilgrimage, would provide a living testimony to the mercy of the Church or, as one shrewd commentator observed, 'A convert who would betray his friends was more useful than a roasted corpse.'[36]

A Punishment to fit the Crime?

Once an accusation had been made, punishment was inevitable and there was no appeal against conviction or sentence. While death was the mandatory penalty for heresy, no one escaped punishment of one form or another. The punishment of an enforced pilgrimage on foot took several years, during which time a man's family would probably starve. Some penitents were sent to the Holy Land as crusaders, for a term of two to eight years. If they survived and wished to return home they were obliged to seek written confirmation from the Patriarch of Jerusalem testifying that they had completed their penance. Some penances took the form of a fine, so bribery and corruption soon became rife. In 1251, the pope prohibited the imposition of fines, but this restriction was only temporary and the Inquisition again, 'Won the right to inflict pecuniary penances at discretion'. If someone died before completing their penance, this was a sign that their sentence had not been sufficiently severe in the eyes of God, so the victim's corpse would be exhumed and publicly burnt, his property confiscated, and his family made liable for his unexpired penances, just as they would for his debts.[37]

The lightest sentence that could be imposed was that the accused was ordered to wear a yellow cross on their clothes, exact dimensions specified, which effectively debarred him or her from all social contact. Anyone reported for helping, feeding, employing or even speaking to those who wore the yellow cross was interrogated in turn. This 'merciful' punishment was, in effect, a death sentence. This ruthless regime deemed that all suspects were guilty until proven otherwise; guilty as charged simply because they were charged. Executions were performed on public holidays so that the maximum possible number of spectators could attend. The condemned victim was tied to a post high enough to be visible to the crowd before the faggots were lit. When the burning was complete, the remnants of the body would be butchered and the entrails thrown onto a fresh fire. There was, of course, a perfectly logical reason for these obscene last rites; no relics were to be left for any followers of the victims to use for heretical and cultic purposes.[38]

To distance the Church even further from bloodletting, in 1227 Pope

Gregory IX ordered that convicted heretics were to be handed over to 'the secular arm' for punishment. The secular arm was the state; laymen and not priests so the Church did not stain its hands with blood. Needless to say, over the centuries, the Inquisition had a very bad press, although some Catholic apologists still try and defend it today. Even after the full horror of the 'final solution' had been exposed to the world, one commentator, C G Coulson, was still able to claim that the Inquisition was responsible for, 'The most elaborate, widespread and continuous legal barbarities recorded in civilized history.'[39] Rollo Ahmed, the Egyptian scholar of the occult described the Holy Inquisition as:

> The most pitiless and ferocious institution the world has ever known... The atrocities the Inquisition committed constitute the most blasphemous irony in religious history, defiling the Catholic Church with the deaths of innocent victims who were burnt to avoid breaking the maxim, *Ecclesia non novit sanguinem* – the Church has never shed blood.[40]

The Inquisition grew ever more efficient, spreading its tentacles right across Christian Europe, and lasted, under one name or another, until the present day. In the final decades of the 19th century, as the Church was forced to relinquish the last shreds of its political and temporal power, it tried to exercise even more rigorous control over the hearts and minds of the flock. The papacy became more centralized, and the Inquisition became the voice of the papacy.[41] It still exists today under the innocuous name of the Congregation for the Doctrine of the Faith who are responsible for theological discipline within the Church and that, until recently, was headed by Cardinal Ratzinger, now Pope Benedict.

The thinking that lay behind the Inquisition's foundation was certainly alive and well at the beginning of the 20th century when a Jesuit professor of canon law, Dr Marianus de Luca, stated that the Holy Roman Catholic Church, 'Had the right and the duty to kill heretics'.[42] *Plus ça change, plus c'est la même chose!* This was the organization selected by King Philippe in 1307 to interrogate the Templars.

CHAPTER 13

Torture & Suppression

The Inquisitors subjected many of the knights to threats and acts of torture long before their first interrogation. The rack, the strappado, the *stivaletto*, water torture and the ordeal by fire were used freely on these heroes of the crusades. Gerard de Pasagio, a 50-year-old veteran of many campaigns claimed that he was tortured, 'By the hanging of weights on his genitals and other members';[1] Bernard de Vaho, a Templar priest from the city of Albi, was subjected to the ordeal by fire with the result that his feet were so badly burned that the bones dropped out of them, bones that he later carried with him in a box.[2] According to one Templar knight, Jacques de Soci, at least 25 members of the order had been subjected to such brutal tortures that they died as a result. Another anonymous friend of the order wrote in Paris in 1308 that at least 36 brothers in the city had died under torture rather than confess and that many others in different parts of France had also died.[3] After each victim's deposition was taken it was duly recorded that the accused had, 'Told the pure and entire truth for the safety of his soul' and not because he had been subjected to, 'Violence... fear of torture, of imprisonment, or any other reason.'[4]

The regime of torture and intimidation applied with an expertise gained over the previous seven decades had the predictable and desired result, for of the 138 depositions from the hearings in Paris in October

1307, which included those of Jacques de Molay and his leading knights, only four record that men had been able to withstand the horrors to which they had been subjected. The results in other parts of France were comparable. The inquisitorial records disclose that, as usual, the Inquisitors were scrupulous in keeping within their papal policy of *ecclesia non novit sanguinem* – the Church shall not shed blood – and that, therefore, the tortures applied to the Templars were the standard ones that had proved so effective over the years. The absurd allegation by the English authors Knight and Lomas, that the Inquisition crucified Jacques de Molay, is not backed up by the slightest shred of credible evidence that the Inquisition ever crucified any of its victims throughout its long and bloody history. To crucify anyone would have been considered the ultimate blasphemy by the fanatical Dominicans who only used their black arts of torture in the service of the Church they loved and in defence of established dogma.

THE ACCUSATIONS

The list of formal accusations that had been made against the Knights Templar was considerable and included, among others:

1 The denial of Christ
2 They exchanged obscene kisses at their reception into the order
3 Defiling the cross
4 Adoration of an idol's head – Baphomet
5 Ritual murder
6 Wearing a cord of heretical significance
7 Alteration of the ritual of the Mass
8 Use of unorthodox forms of absolution

9   Sodomy

10 Treachery to other Christian forces[5]

As the vast majority of the Templars were devout Christians, these charges were mostly without foundation. For the inner circle of Rex Deus nobles who actually controlled the order, while they were undoubtedly heretics in the true meaning of the word, the accusations were also largely fabricated. Despite the fact that they believed that Jesus had come to reveal rather than redeem, they were under an obligation from their own secret traditions to follow the outward form of the prevailing religion, namely Christianity, so even for them the charges were unfounded. The tenth charge, which may have been laid by their rivals, could only be justified by deliberately misinterpreting Templar treaties with the Muslims. Charges of homosexuality and sexual immorality were almost always levelled against anyone accused of heresy and, furthermore, in any all-male organization including the Templars, there may indeed have been the occasional homosexual act, but that would have been the exception rather than the rule.

The secret beliefs held by the inner nucleus of the order about the nature of Jesus and his mission are displayed in many of the churches and cathedrals that the Templars financed, such as Chartres, where carvings of the Crucifixion are notable by their absence.[6] Nonetheless, as Rex Deus members strictly conformed to the prevailing beliefs of their time, charges of heresy cannot have been founded upon credible evidence. The wearing of a cord of heretical significance is a charge that may just have a ring of truth, for in the initiation ceremonies the Templars used a cable-tow noose just as the modern craft of Freemasonry does today.

The most interesting charge against the order was that of idolatry, adoring the bearded head of the idol Baphomet. The cathedral of

Amiens was founded to house one such object of veneration that was of supreme importance to the Templar Order, namely the reliquary reputed to hold the severed head of St John the Baptist. Other depictions of bearded heads have been found on Templar property, such as the large painting of a head discovered at Templecombe in Somerset. The French scholar J-A Durbec lists another, among the symbols that he claims are diagnostic of Templar influence, namely the 'Mandylion', a depiction of a bearded head on a cloth, such as the Veil of Veronica or the Turin Shroud.[7] The English scholar and historian, Noel Currer-Briggs, suggests that there is a considerable body of evidence that the Shroud of Turin was also used by the Templars and may have been the original used to design the head at Templecombe.[8] The actual provenance of the Turin Shroud is still obscure, particularly since the internationally renowned microbiologist, Dr Leonicio Garza-Valdes, has discredited, on purely scientific grounds, the carbon dating that suggested it was a medieval artefact.[9]

At first glance, the most absurd charge levelled at the Templars was that of ritual murder. However this might have some tenuous basis in Templar ritual. It is highly probable that the initiation ceremonies of the medieval Knights Templar had much in common with those of the Children of Solomon and it is not unreasonable to suggest that they included a re-enactment of the murder of Hiram Abif, much as modern Freemasons use today. This may have led to the making of this otherwise inexplicable charge.

The Templars' innocence of the majority of the charges brought against them was established by the American historian Henry Charles Lea who published his work in 1889. Historians now see the charges for what they really were, an exercise in political propaganda.[10] The charges of heresy were all very carefully constructed and were based upon a clever and deliberately malicious interpretation of some of the practices of the order.[11] They also took the maximum advantage of the prevailing fears of the time, for fear of heresy in the Middle Ages was remarkably similar to the paranoid fear of Communism that prevailed in the USA in the 1950s, or the fear of Satanism in England during the 1990s, or the fear of terrorism in both countries today. In all such cases these fears are often irrational and exaggerated resulting in undue pain, misery and distress to those falsely accused. As it was absolutely impossible for anyone accused of heresy to escape conviction by the Inquisition, making such charges became the perfect way of disposing of political enemies.

It appears that the original charges largely arose from the fertile mind of one man, Esquiu de Floyran of Beziers, Prior of Montfaucon. A year after the arrests he wrote jubilantly to James II of Aragon informing him that the charges against the Templars, that James had refused to believe, had now been taken seriously by King Philippe of France. Modern scholars are now of the opinion that using de Floyran's charges as a basis, the final accusations were worked up by William de Nogaret who had previously planned the king's attack on Pope Boniface VIII and had used similar charges against the Bishop of Troyes.[12]

TROUBLE AT THE TOP?

Pope Clement V was outraged at this apparent usurpation of his responsibilities despite the fact that King Philippe had outwardly conformed to established procedures by using the Inquisition. It was particularly galling for him as, enumerated in several papal bulls, the Templars were responsible to the pope and the pope alone. However, Clement had neither the power nor the will to halt the proceedings that were already well underway. He issued a papal directive, dated 22 November 1307, ordering the Christian rulers of Europe to arrest all the Templars[13] in their domains and to confiscate their properties in the name of the pope,[14] but this proved to be a vain attempt to regain control over the situation. This missive was not received with universal acclaim or agreement, for the King of England had already refused to give 'easy credence' to the charges against the Templars and had written to the pope and said so. He had also written to the kings of Portugal, Castile, Aragon and Naples in terms that left no doubt as to his support of the order. The terms of the new papal directive now left him no choice and he replied that he would initiate action against the order, 'In the quickest and best way.' His interpretation of that phrase, however, was in stark contrast to the actions of the French king, in that very few knights were actually imprisoned; most were allowed to stay in their preceptories and, as torture was forbidden under English law, no one confessed to heresy when interrogated.

Proceedings in England were therefore unproductive until June 1311 when one knight, Stephen de Stapelbrugge confessed to denying Christ and claimed that homosexuality had been encouraged within the order. This confession only came after papal pressure had resulted in the full application of church law and the use of torture had been sanctioned, a situation that understandably resulted in further confessions.[15] In the Kingdom of Portugal the order was tried and a verdict of 'not guilty' was returned. In Scotland the trial of the Templars was conducted by the Bishop of St Andrews, William de Lamberton, and brought in the old Scottish verdict of 'not proven' despite the best efforts of the papal legate and prosecutor John Solario.[16] Lamberton was a close associate of Baron Henry St Clair of Roslin and was also the leader of a shadowy group responsible for organizing support for Robert the Bruce in his struggle to gain the throne of Scotland.

The Archbishop of Compostela wrote to Pope Clement and pleaded that the Templars should be acquitted, as their skills and resources were desperately needed in the ongoing war against the Moorish forces in Spain.[17] The rulers of Lombardy, the Rex Deus family of the House of Savoy, ensured that most of the bishops in their realm supported the Templar cause and those bishops issued a statement claiming that they could find no incriminating evidence against the order; others were less favourable, and did bring in convictions; in Germany and in Greece the results were equally mixed. In France however, the agony of the Templars continued until it reached its fiery finale in 1314.

THE DEATH OF JACQUES DE MOLAY

On 18 March 1314 the Archbishop of Sens, who had already super-vised the burning of 54 Templar knights in 1310,[18] accompanied by three papal commissioners, took their place on a stage erected outside the west front of the cathedral of Notre Dame de Paris. The Bishop of Alba read out the confessions that had been extracted from the tortured knights and sentenced them to perpetual imprisonment. At this point, Jacques de Molay redeemed himself by an act of calculated bravery that will never be forgotten. This tortured wreck of a once great warrior, now over 70 years of age and physically and mentally scarred by seven years in the care of the Inquisition, indicated that he wished to speak. The bishops, assuming that de Molay wished to confess, graciously granted him leave to address the crowd. The Grandmaster then made a speech that ensured his immortality:

> It is just that, in so terrible a day, and in the last moments of my life, I should discover all the iniquity of falsehood, and make the truth triumph. I declare, then, in the face of heaven and earth, and acknowledge, though to my eternal shame, that I have commit-ted the greatest of crimes but... it has been the acknowledging

of those which have been so foully charged on the order. I attest – and truth obliges me to attest – that it is innocent! I made the contrary declaration only to suspend the excessive pains of torture, and to mollify those who made me endure them. I know the punishments which have been inflicted on all the knights who had the courage to revoke a similar confession; but the dreadful spectacle which is presented to me is not able to make me confirm one lie by another. The life offered me on such infamous terms I abandon without regret.[19]

De Molay's courageous and moving speech was greeted with roars of support from the assembled crowd and Geoffroi de Charney moved and stood beside his Grandmaster as a sign of support for his statement, and then spoke in similar terms asserting the sanctity of the Templar Order and finally revoked his previous confession.[20]

The proceedings were immediately suspended and the clergy cleared the square and reported to the king. He solved the problem by sentencing the two courageous knights to a slow and lingering death. The execution took place on the evening of the same day on the Isle des Javiaux where a slow, hot and smokeless fire was prepared to ensure that the Templars' agony would be as prolonged as possible. Both Jacques de Molay and Geoffroi de Charnay were slowly cooked to death but, before being placed on the fire, legend claims that Jacques de Molay cursed Pope Clement V and King Philippe le Bel and called upon them both to appear before God in heaven within the year.[21] If the legend is true, then it must be said that both the accursed king and the pope heeded that prophetic call: Pope Clement, who had suffered from chronic ill-health for many years, died on 20 April and King Philippe IV of France followed him to the grave on 29 November the same year.

SUPPRESSION

Whatever the truth or falsehood of the charges, the Templars were never, as an organization, convicted of any of them. Yet the decision to suppress the order was announced in the papal bull, *vox in excelso* issued on 22 March 1312. The Order of the Knights Templar was dissolved 'not by way of judgement but as a provision and an apostolic decision' – a diplomatic way of announcing to the world that the pope thought he had no choice in the light of recent events. This papal bull was read to the assembled council on 3 April, and a clerk ended the proceedings by stating bluntly that no one was allowed to speak on this issue on pain of excommunication. The assembled delegates were furious for most did not believe the order guilty of anything, yet no debate was allowed by the pope who was in fear of King Philppe's army.[22] The phraseology within the papal bull is revealing:

> … considering, moreover, the grave scandal which has arisen from these things against the Order, which it did not seem could be checked while this Order remained in being… even without blame being attached to the brothers… not by judicial sentence, but by way of provision, or apostolic ordinance, we abolish the aforesaid Order of the Temple… and we subject it to perpetual prohibition… Which if anyone acts against this, he will incur the sentence of excommunication ipso facto.[23]

Thus the pope had suppressed the order without actually condemning it. Furthermore, King Philippe had demonstrated to the entire Christian world that he now effectively controlled the pope.

The next problem was what to do with the order's vast estates, financial assets and other possessions. Clement transferred most of the Templar assets to the Knights Hospitaller, and the only exceptions he allowed were Templar properties in the kingdoms of Castile, Aragon, Portugal and Majorca. In France, however, certain deductions were authorized in favour of King Philippe before any such transfer could take place. These were to cover the costs of the interim administration of these properties since the original arrests and the expenses incurred by the imprisonment and interrogation of the knights of the order. So a situation was created whereby the Templars had to pay for their imprisonment and torture. In fact, the order to transfer the property and assets of the Templars to the Hospitallers was obeyed in a patchy manner. In England many Templar lands had been seized by King Edward II or by the families who had originally donated these estates to the order. A similar situation obtained in Germany. It is perhaps ironic to record that the Order of the Knights Templar, which had always been trusted and used by kings, was not suppressed because it was corrupt, inept or heretical, but was finally destroyed by a king from the royal house of France which the order had served valiantly for centuries.

The Templar Treasure

The fate of the treasure that the King of France had seen during his sanctuary in the Paris Temple, in addition to the considerable sums he had observed being carried into the Temple when Jacques de Molay and his large train arrived from La Rochelle, is still a matter of speculation. When, after the initial arrests, the king's seneschals raided the Temple, the treasure had vanished and by the time his troops reached La Rochelle, the Templar's Atlantic fleet, along with the 18 ships that had carried Jacques de Molay from Cyprus, had disappeared, destination unknown.

There is some evidence that the order received some advance warning of impending trouble, for, shortly before the arrests, Jacques de Molay is said to have recalled all the order's rule books and accounts and had them burnt. Another brother who left the order in 1307 was informed that he was wise as some form of unspecified catastrophe was imminent and, furthermore, a memo was circulated throughout the order's French properties, forbidding the brethren from releasing any information about the order's rites and rituals.[24]

A variety of theories have been proposed to explain the disappearance of both the Templar treasure and fleet. One story, so far uncorroborated, indicates that an unspecified sum was transported northwards to Belgium in a cart covered by hay. The Templar historians Stephen Dafoe and Alan Butler claim that a considerable portion of the Templar treasure was secretly transported eastwards to a country beyond the reach of King Philippe le Bel, where the Templars owned considerable property. They elaborate this theory by proposing that the Templar knights then went underground and used their financial assets and skills to found that country's banking system.[25] It is suggested that the Templars offered their services to the first three Swiss Cantons of Uri, Schwyz and Unterwalden when they signed their pact of mutual assistance in 1291. What is beyond doubt is that Switzerland, once established, suddenly produced one of the best armies in Europe that was not to be defeated for over two centuries. Did Swiss banking and military prowess owe their origins to the Knights Templar? No one can be certain, but it is a line of inquiry worth following.

As both Desmond Seward and myself have remarked in other works, no medieval institution did more to facilitate the rise of capitalism in Europe than the Knights Templar.[26] Neither of the theories put forward to explain the disappearance of the treasure or the Templar fleet is mutually exclusive, nor do they negate the third hypothesis, which at least has the merit of plausibility and, more importantly perhaps, is substantiated by a high degree of circumstantial proof. To delineate this concept we must first of all examine the fate of the surviving members of the newly suppressed order.

THE FATE OF THE SURVIVING KNIGHTS?

After the suppression, individual Templar knights fled throughout Europe. The fate of many of them is hardly mysterious and can easily be established, for they joined other warrior orders such as the Teutonic Knights who were carving out their own fief on the shores of the Baltic; many more joined the Order of Calatrava in the Kingdom of Aragon; others, equally interested in fighting the infidels, joined either the Knights of Alcantara or the Knights of Santiago and continued their service in Spain. The Knights of Santiago, also known as the Knights of the Sword, actually became affiliated to the Knights Hospitaller in order to ensure their survival, proving that they had learnt a lesson from the persecution of the Templars. They too became immensely powerful and, by the end of the 15th century, controlled over 200 commanderies throughout Spain.[27]

In Portugal, the order had its name changed to the Knights of Christ, carried on administering the old Templar properties, changed its previous allegiance and obedience from the pope to the Portuguese king, and carried on much as before. Many fleeing knights joined the renamed order, but soon the rule of the Order of the Knights of Christ was changed so that it could only admit those who were born in Portugal.

In England, some knights were granted a small pension and many simply ended their days in other monastic orders. Some fled for sanctuary to Lombardy, where the Cathars had sought refuge before them. Lombardy was not only renowned for its tolerance, but as a centre of banking that certainly enjoyed a measure of resurgence after the suppression of the Templars. However, it would be wise not to place too much emphasis on Templar recruits as the source of this renewal of activity, for, with the suppression of the Templar Order, the Lombards' main competitor in financial services had been destroyed. Many more brothers simply seemed to vanish.[28]

Templars in Scotland

There was one safe haven in Europe where the pope's writ simply did not run, namely Scotland which was under papal interdict. The Kingdom of the Scots was riven by civil war to gain the crown. The main contender, Robert the Bruce, had been excommunicated for the ritual murder of one of his rivals, John Comyn, on Church premises. The papal decree against Robert the Bruce was ignored by his nobles – they too were excommunicated; that was ignored in turn and so the pope, in an act of total desperation, excommunicated the entire country. Many Templars fled by sea to this Celtic refuge and, along with those who came on foot over the border from England and the Templars who were stationed in Scotland, offered their assistance to Robert the Bruce. At the Battle of Bannockburn that finally secured the throne for the Bruce and completely vanquished the English invader, 432 Templar knights (including Sir Henry St Clair, Baron of Roslin, and his sons William and Henry) took part in the final charge which completely routed the English army and preserved Scottish independence.[29] Rex Deus tradition recounts that after Bannockburn, as an act of gratitude and recognition, King Robert the Bruce became the Sovereign Grandmaster of the Templar Order.[30]

The king was, above all, a pragmatist; he knew that in order for his new realm to survive, he would have to live in the medieval world as it really was and that meant making peace with the pope in Rome. Accordingly, he warned the Templars in Scotland to go underground; a feat that, with the assistance of the many Rex Deus and Templar families, was accomplished in a manner that ensured the long-term survival of Templar traditions. Templar property in Scotland passed to the Knights Hospitaller, but here it is apparent that the manner in which they were administered in Bruce's realm was very different from the rest of Europe. In most countries, Templar holdings were absorbed into the itineraries of the Hospitallers: in Scotland they were accounted for separately, as though they were being 'held in trust' and might be restored to their rightful owners at some time in the future.

What can we say about the vanished treasure of the Templars? Nothing can be proven definitively, but French Masonic tradition recounts that some of it was destined for Scotland. The fortunes of the leading Scottish Templar family, the St Clairs of Roslin, underwent a dramatic improvement from that time forward. The St Clairs, who were already wealthy, suddenly became 'super-rich' to use modern phraseology. A later St Clair Baron of Roslin who became the third Earl of Orkney, William St Clair, was renowned for his incredible wealth.[31] Earl William was the architect and builder of Rosslyn Chapel, a unique library, in stone, of arcane symbolism, a superbly carved reliquary of the Holy Grail, a memorial of Templar beliefs and the core church of Freemasonry. He was also known as 'one of the Illuminati' and had been initiated into some of the leading chivalric orders in Europe.

CHAPTER 14

Did the Order Survive?

The total number of Templars arrested in France on Friday 13 October 1307 was only 620 and not all were knights. Yet, according to most historians, the number of Templar personnel in the country on that day numbered over 3,000. If only one in five was arrested, then what befell the others? One who was detained in Paris in November of 1309[1] admitted that he had fled from his base 15 days before the initial wave of arrests. The proportion of Templars arrested in other countries was far lower than in France. Therefore it is reasonable to assume that some prior warning of the arrests must have leaked out. Following the suppression, the fate of many Templars can be found in the records of the pensions paid to them in various countries, others became involved in scandal or crime and that too is a matter of record. Most, however, joined other orders, and among them were many Rex Deus members. Thus, Rex Deus were able to turn adversity to advantage and spread their tentacles into other military orders where they gained positions of power and influence far greater than their numbers might suggest.

When Robert the Bruce instructed his Templar allies to go underground after the Battle of Bannockburn, the last vestige of the original Templar Order simply ceased to exist. Despite the vociferous and often angry claims made by many of the modern neo-Templar revived orders, not one order actually exists that can honestly claim direct and unbroken continuity with the medieval Order of the Knights Templar. However, Templar tradition and teaching did survive and was preserved, especially in Scotland.

REX DEUS IN SCOTLAND

The tightly knit group of families in Scotland who were linked by Cohenite ties of intermarriage, had long acted as a vibrant repository of Rex Deus tradition and teaching. Some years after the fall of the Templars, they founded a military organization that the English authors Michael Baigent and Richard Leigh describe as, 'Perhaps the most genuinely neo-Templar institution of them all.'[2] This new order fitted neatly into the context of 'the auld alliance', created by a treaty between Robert the Bruce and Charles IV of France in 1326 which played a vital role in the Hundred Years War and is still remembered with affection in the 21st century. Scottish troops played a significant role at the Siege of Orleans during the campaigns led by Joan of Arc, where three Scottish commanders, the two Douglas brothers and Sir John Stewart, distinguished themselves notably. Scotland's ties with France were reinforced by the fact that another Scot, John Kirkmichael, became Bishop of Orleans and the celebrated white banner that was the rallying point for the French army was reputedly painted by a Scot.[3]

After the French victory the new king, Charles VII, created a standing army to restore order and maintain his hold on the kingdom. This was the first standing army in Europe since the suppression of the Knights Templar and the first national one since the fall of the Roman Empire.[4] The elite regiment in this new army was the *compagnie des gendarmes Ecossais*. The outstanding bravery and loyalty of this unit was demonstrated at the Battle of Vermeuil in 1424 where the Scots company (led by John Stewart, the Earl of Buchan, and his senior officers Alexander Lindsay, Sir William Seton and the earls of Douglas, Murray and Mar) was almost annihilated.[5]

The Scots Guard

In recognition of this supreme act of gallantry, a special unit of Scots troops were established and given the honour of rendering personal service to the King of France. This was the king's personal bodyguard and all officers were honoured by initiation into the Order of St Michael; a branch of this prestigious order was later established in Scotland.[6] Unlike purely chivalric orders such as the Knights of the Garter or the Order of the Bath in England or the Order of the Golden Fleece in Burgundy, the Scots Guard was an active military unit that was often tested in battle and thereby earned all the rights and privileges of elite professional soldiers. Despite their small numbers, the Scots Guard was powerful enough to play a decisive part in the wars of that era. Its membership was drawn from the leading families of Scotland; the Setons, St Clairs, Stewarts, Montgomerys, and Hamiltons, who still take pride in their families' association with the Scots Guard. The Guard became, 'A special vehicle whereby they (the young Scots Nobles) were initiated into martial skills, politics, court affairs, foreign manners and mores and, it would appear, some species of ritualistic rite as well.'[7] The Scots Guard enjoyed immense status in France for over 150 years, for their officers were used as emissaries and couriers in matters of importance and delicacy in both the political and diplomatic fields. The commander of the Guard often also discharged the function of the royal chamberlain.

The Scots Guard owed allegiance to the Valois dynasty, whose right to rule was under almost constant threat from the House of Guise, a cadet branch of the House of Lorraine. This was a truly murderous rivalry and no less than five French kings are alleged to have died either by violence or poison and many members of both the Guise and Lorraine families were assassinated. This quarrel placed the Scots Guard in an impossible position, for the family of Guise were Rex Deus and, in 1538, Mary of Guise had married King James V of Scotland, thereby uniting two of the leading families within the secretive group. Despite being granted a considerable increase in salary by Henry II of France in 1547, the Guard often acted on behalf of the House of Guise and matters came to a head in June 1559 when a captain of the Guard, Gabriel Montgomery, caused the death of King Henry II during a jousting tournament by striking the kings head with a broken lance. A splinter from the lance pierced the king's skull above the right eye causing his death from the wounds 11 days later. It has been alleged that this was no accident but was part of a plot to benefit the family of Guise.[8]

Other Chivalric Orders

The Knights of Santiago, who provided such a haven of refuge for fleeing Templars in Spain, carried Templar traditions and practices throughout the Spanish-speaking world for centuries. When the *Reconquistà* ended, it developed a 'chivalric' nature and welcomed into its ranks leading members of Rex Deus from all over Europe, including Earl William St Clair, Earl of Orkney and Baron of Roslin.[9] Having established its 'orthodox' credentials by the crucial role it played in the *Reconquistà*, the Knights of Santiago became an ideal vehicle for Rex Deus purposes. Its mixed membership, where only a select but influential few were members of the secretive family group, was not merely an asset but also a perfect form of disguise for the actions of the dissembling plotters. The members of the Rex Deus dynasty were able to use the order for their own purposes behind the respectable façade of an order whose members were drawn from a wide variety of families committed to the

Church/state establishment. Other orders were also infiltrated by Templar knights such as the Knights of Alcantara and the Knights of Calatrava mentioned earlier.

Founded in 1430 by Philip the Good, Duke of Burgundy,[10] was the Order of the Golden Fleece, whose membership was restricted to 24 knights, all of whom were senior members of Rex Deus carefully chosen from the best families in Europe. They were described by Pope Eugenius IV as 'Maccabeans resurrected',[11] thus unintentionally emphasizing their true Hebraic origins. The membership being restricted to 24 was of immense significance to Rex Deus, as it is the number of hereditary families of the *ma'madot*, the hereditary high priests of the Temple in Jerusalem. It was also the number of knights permitted in a chivalric order founded by the King of Hungary in 1408. When the founder, King Sigismund became Holy Roman Emperor, the order became known as the Imperial and Royal Court of the Dragon.[12]

Another restricted order was the Order of the Crescent, founded at Angers in 1448 by a leading member of Rex Deus, René d'Anjou. René, who had fought bravely for France under the leadership of Joan of Arc, was the titular King of Jerusalem, King of the Two Sicilies, Aragon, Valencia, Majorca, Sardinia and Corsica. He was also Count of Provence, Forcalquier and Piedmont, Prince of Gerona, Duke of Calabria, Lord of Genoa and the Count of Guise.[13] Many strands of Rex Deus ancestry were united in this one man who was not merely highborn, but a most accomplished man in his own right, a scholar of international repute and a regular correspondent with Earl William St Clair. Like Earl William, he collected original manuscripts in Hebrew, Greek, Arabic, Turkish and Latin. He was famous for his organization of jousts and festivals, usually centred on themes drawn from the Grail romances. René d'Anjou's Order of the Crescent (Croissant) merged many years later with another order of Rex Deus creation to form the

Order of the Fleur de Lys that adopted a four-barred cross as its symbol, *La Croix Fleury*, which is still worn with pride by the members of the order in the 21st century. Membership is strictly by invitation only, or by right of birth into certain families, however only members of the families of legitimate descent within the Rex Deus group are allowed to hold office within the order.

According to my first Rex Deus informant, the late Michael Monkton, the Order of the Bath in England might well have been another 'cover' for Rex Deus activities at the time of its original foundation. Therefore it is reasonable to assume that a comparative study of the membership lists of these various orders would give great insight into the identity of members of this proud and secretive tradition that has reached out over the millennia from ancient Egypt to the present. Membership of the families within these various orders also tends to explain certain differences in ritual that exist between one set of Rex Deus tradition and others. We were quite surprised to discover, when we introduced our first informant to another self-declared Rex Deus member (one who holds high rank within the Order of the Fleur de Lys) that while they were each able to fill in gaps within the knowledge and understanding of the other, certain distinct differences in their traditional rituals do exist.

Developing and constantly evolving traditions within the differing chivalric orders the families used, would readily explain this. The use of so many orders also gives us an insight into the wisdom of these families who, after the suppression of the Knights Templar, were not about to risk the failure of their divinely inspired mission by putting all their eggs in one basket: that had nearly led to ruin in the past and was not going to be allowed to happen again.

The Charter of Larmenius

Scotland was not the only country that claims to have preserved Templar traditions, for in Portugal the Templar Order was simply renamed the Knights of Christ, and continued, at first at least, like its parent order. However, it soon changed and restricted membership to Portuguese nationals only and became devotedly Catholic in its beliefs and rituals; thus in its later years it could not honestly claim to be a direct continuation of the original order, and has long since ceased to exist.

France also has claimed to house a direct continuation of the medieval Knights Templar. In 1804 an order founded by a certain Bernard-Raymond Fabré-Palaprat claimed to be a direct continuation of the original Templars and cited a document known as 'The Charter of Larmenius' to substantiate its legitimacy.[14] This charter is allegedly dated 1324, more than ten years later than the ritual burning of Jacques de Molay, yet within the charter is the claim that de Molay had named his successor as Grandmaster, one Jean-Marc Larmenius, and that the order had continued after the suppression. Using this charter as justification, Fabré-Palaprat claimed that a non-masonic neo-chivalric order still existed that was the direct heir to the original Knights Templar. This order, 'the Ancient and Sovereign Military Order of the Temple of Jerusalem' is still in existence today.

There is one strange statement within the Charter of Larmenius which is intriguing to say the least, namely: 'I lastly... will say and order that the Scots Templar deserters of the Order, be blasted by an anathema.' Thus, apparently, confirming the tradition of Templar knights fleeing to Scotland with, or without, a portion of the Templar treasure. However, to put it as politely as possible, the authenticity of the Charter of Larmenius has been repeatedly challenged from the day that Fabré-Palaprat first brought it to the attention of the world. In the opinion of the vast majority of historians who have studied it in depth, it is a blatant 18th- or early 19th-century forgery. However, it is clear that at the time it was first composed, and various dates have been suggested such as 1324, 1705 or 1804, its author, whoever that may have been, was prepared to admit to some form of Templar survival in Scotland after the suppression of the order.

Therefore, there is at present absolutely no undisputed or credible evidence of Templar survival within France and, until the provenance of the Charter of Larmenius is settled beyond all doubt by carbon dating and spectrographic analysis of the ink, for example, this question must remain open. Nor is there any clear evidence that the Templar Order survived unaltered in any country. However, there is one country at least that can legitimately claim an unbroken chain of transmission of Templar teaching and tradition, and that country is Scotland.

SCOTLAND GOES ITS OWN WAY

One modern author who has a reputation for meticulous research, Prince Michael of Albany, claims that after 1326 in Scotland some form of Templar organization continued despite papal suppression. He states categorically that, from that time onwards, Templar properties were administered by the Hospitallers' preceptor of Torphichan where surviving Templar knights were allowed to take up residence in a building that became known as the Templar Tower. Furthermore, Albany claims that in all succeeding charters these knights in the new combined chivalric entity were always separately named. He states that Latin charters of the 15th century refer to the Knights of St John and the Brothers of the Order of the Temple.[15] Sadly he does not cite any sources for these claims, but knowing his work as I do, I person- ally have no doubt as to the veracity of his statements. However, there is a great deal of difference between direct continuity with an order as complex as the medieval Templars and some form of highly modified continuation by the amalgamation of a few survivors with a far stronger rival institution. In the same work Prince Michael goes on to mention the Confreres of the Templars, namely the secretive guilds of their skilled tradesmen and artisans, and their role in preserving Templar tradition, which was considerable, a matter to which we will return in a later chapter.

There is at least one organization that is still operative today which may combine Templar teaching and tradition within its rituals, 'The Most Noble and Ancient and Jacobite Order of St Germain'. This is not a direct continuation of the medieval Templar Order, nor does it claim to be, for it was founded by the exiled King James VII of Scotland, who was also James II of England, on 18 June 1692 and, at its inception, comprised two categories of members, Knights and Companions.[16] Modelled on the earlier Stewart Order of the Thistle, the first knights admitted to its ranks were exiled members of that order, members of the Order of Lorraine and several knights of the Orders of St Louis and St Michael.[17] The primary purpose of this new order was the safety and security of the exiled members of the royal family and the promotion of the Stewart cause. It has been suggested that this body retains the sole rights of leadership of Scottish Freemasonry, but I have yet to see this confirmed. Nonetheless, as we shall see in a later chapter, Scotland undoubtedly became the principal repository of Templar tradition after the suppression of the order. It also became the birthplace of another fraternity, founded to promote Rex Deus spiritual teaching and Templar tradition that was to spread worldwide.

THE WORLDWIDE PROPAGATION OF REX DEUS & TEMPLAR BELIEFS

R ex Deus beliefs were firmly founded on the true teachings of Jesus which can be accurately delineated from the records of the thoughts and actions of James the Just and the original disciples in Jerusalem. The initiatory 'Way' that they followed was one which brought them into closer union with God and the Torah. So it is not surprising to find that the Rex Deus tradition, as it came down to us in the 21st century, was simply an evolved and ritualized form of the 'Way' as practised 2,000 years ago.

If we compare the vast range of the achievements of the Knights

Templar in their brief 180-year history, with those of the other monastic orders that were established long before them and who outlasted them by many centuries, the contrast is truly startling. Yet, the lines of inquiry that could explain these differences are usually ignored or brushed under the academic carpet as irrelevant. The Templars were ignominiously suppressed at the beginning of the 14th century and their internal records were either stolen by the Inquisitors, hidden by the knights themselves or destroyed. The resultant information vacuum has given the fantasists free rein and provides the most academic historians with an apparently sound reason for doing nothing.

Yet all is not quite as it seems. One historian at least had the insight to question the underlying belief system that motivated the Templars and that was the renowned historian of the Crusades, Sir Steven Runciman who believed that there just might have been some substance to the charges of heresy. He claimed that 'it would be unwise to dismiss these rumours (of heresy) as the unfounded invention of (the order's) enemies. There was probably just enough substance to them to suggest the line along which the order could be most convincingly attacked.'[1]

He was far closer to the truth than many of his colleagues would publicly admit. Not only were the members of the inner core of the Templar Order truly heretical in the eyes of the Church, but so was the fraternity later founded by Rex Deus to propagate these beliefs right across the known world, the Freemasons.

CHAPTER 15

The Beliefs of Rex Deus

Pope Pius IX condemned the medieval Order of the Knights Templar as being Gnostics from the beginning and followers of the Johannite Heresy. Now, while it is easy to find definitions of the majority of heresies condemned by Holy Mother the Church, when it comes to the Johannite Heresy, there is a suspiciously deafening silence. What is it about this particular belief system that so terrifies the Church? Is it, as the Masonic scholar A E Waite and the 19th-century mystical writer Magnus Eliphas Lévi have suggested, that Jesus was an initiate of the Egyptian cult of Osiris and a follower of the goddess Isis,[1] which is apparently confirmed by the well-known Templar veneration of Isis in the guise of the Black Madonna?[2]

Throughout European history, Rex Deus nobility demonstrated a consistent and remarkable degree of toleration for people persecuted for their beliefs by the Church, such as the Jews and the Cathars. The overt arm of the hidden Rex Deus group, the Knights Templar, followed ancient Egyptian tradition by sharing the material benefits of their spiritual insight among the communities in which they moved. However, the Templars' written records disappeared after the suppression of the order and we can only glean what we know of their belief system from their actions and from the plentiful iconography which they left behind. To Rex Deus, Jesus was a Jew and an initiatory teacher, not a vicarious human sacrifice to appease an angry God. To all people of Jewish descent brought up in the kosher tradition, the mere idea of 'drinking blood' would have been regarded as blasphemous; as was the idea that Jesus was God.

When I first began to investigate what was then 'the Rex Deus hypothesis' some 15 years ago, I could only speculate about the probably Judaic nature of Rex Deus beliefs. However, several years after my first meeting with Michael Monkton, my first Rex Deus informant, and following the publication of Knight and Lomas's *Second Messiah*, other members of this secretive group of families made themselves known to me. These contacts, further meetings with Michael and a great deal of in-depth research began to bear fruit and I now have a far clearer idea of the beliefs and rituals which motivate these descendants of the 24 high-priestly families of the *ma'madot*.

THE LITURGY OF THE HOLY TWINS

Rex Deus members follow a form of 'New Covenant' Judaism that was proclaimed by Jesus and preached after the Crucifixion by his twin brother Judas Thomas and by the new leader of the original disciples, James the Just. Within a short time after the Crucifixion, Judas Thomas became the Patriarch of Edessa and James the Just was described in the Acts of the Apostles as 'the first Bishop of Jerusalem'. James and the original disciples behaved in a rather strange and odd manner for people who, according to the Church at least, were supposedly founding a 'new' religion, for they continued to worship daily at the Jewish Temple.[3] While these reported actions are in direct conflict with the concept of a 'new religion' as suggested by the Church, they are wholly consistent with James' position as a Jewish high-priest at the Temple and his desire

to follow a form of 'New Covenant' Judaism that became the foundation of Rex Deus belief and practice.[4]

The central beliefs and rituals of Rex Deus religious practice were
recorded in a document known as The Liturgy and Gospel of the Holy
Twins, which incorporates many writings by the original disciples and
other leading figures from the Essenes, especially John the Evangelist and
Judas Thomas. The original version of the Gospel of John, known to
the Cathars as The Gospel of Love was one important source and the
Gospel of Thomas, rediscovered among the Nag-Hammadi scrolls, was
the basis for nearly 50 per cent of the contribution attributed to
Thomas in The Liturgy and Gospel of the Holy Twins. The Church
had, many centuries earlier, declared The Gospel of Thomas as heretical and ordered its suppression; it did not see the light of day for over
1,500 years until its rediscovery in the 20th century.

As there was no written copy of the liturgy I had to rely on
Michael Monkton for the understanding that I have gained of it. It
begins with The Proclamation of the Book, which reads as follows:

The Book of the Old Covenant is sealed with seven seals and is
  locked with seven keys.

The Angel of God holds the Book and it will be opened
  no more.

The Book of the New Covenant is opened at the first page and
  the Messiah has written:
  The Oath
  The Encryption
  The Prayer of Abba Ra Heim
  The Proclamation of the Law

The Proclamation concerning the Poor
The Proclamation of Forgiveness
The Commemoration

Much of this phrasing is familiar to anyone who has read the Revelation of St John where the concept of the seven seals occurs repeatedly.[5] After The Proclamation of the Book and preceding the statements of belief, law, commandments, prayers and ritual in the liturgy, the Oath of the Messiah is read:

> If the words that I spoke are not the words of God, but were my own words and if those who heard my words believed that they were the words of God, and trusted in them (i.e. believed in the revised Law, the first two commandments... and relied upon the relaxing of the dietary laws, circumcision and travelling) then the sin of breaking the Law is not theirs but mine – may the blood of their sin be upon my hands as I will answer for that sin when I stand before God at mine end. Therefore you can believe and trust in my words as being the words of God.

Jesus was telling his flock that, as the Messiah, he was taking the sole and entire responsibility for the massive change that he was enunciating in the Law and for any sin that may be committed arising from belief in his words.

This apparently startling change in the Law, instigated by Jesus, had its origins very early on in Jewish history, for the prophet Abraham had received his initiation from his teacher Melchizedek,[6] and, not surprisingly, this Gnostic early form of Judaism spoke of a much more loving and less demanding God than the one described in the rather legalistic version of the Law that was developed during the Babylonian Exile.

After the Babylonian revision and rewriting of the scriptures, Judaism became a strictly conformist and legalistic religion that placed demands upon its people that they could not be reasonably expected to meet. Indeed, the Law now became so demanding that it made any man, however pious, into a sinner. However, this was moderated to a certain extent by the actions of the high priest who, on Yom Kippur, acted as the spokesperson for his people atoning for their sins and pleading for forgiveness.[7]

Following the Oath, came the Encryption which listed some of the aspects of God and defined Jesus' relationship to him. It insists on the humanity of Jesus, in stark contrast to the blasphemous Christian idea that he was God Incarnate.

The Encryption

God is God.

God is the Great God of the Universe.

God is the Alpha and the Omega.

God is the Creator.

God is the Destroyer.

God is Life.

God is the Lawgiver.

God is the Judge.

God is Mercy.

God is Love.

God is Knowledge.

God is Wisdom.

A man was sent from God.

He was the Star.

He was the Teacher.

> He was of the House of David.
>
> He was of the line of Aaron.
>
> He is the Prince of Peace.
>
> He is the Learned Lamb.
>
> He is Our King.
>
> He is Our High Priest.
>
> He is the Prince of the West.
>
> He is the Messiah.
>
> His name is Jesus.

When I read this list, particularly as I have studied comparative religion, I find little or no difficulty whatsoever in accepting the basic thesis put forward by Michael Baigent, Richard Leigh and Henry Lincoln, that high on the hidden agenda of the Templars was the desire to reinstate true monotheism by uniting Judaism, Christianity and Islam.[8] Certainly no devout Muslim would have any difficulty in accepting any of the statements within the Encryption; few Jews at the time of Jesus would have had any disagreement with the descriptions of God or the statements about the Messiah, although it must be accepted that modern Jews would be aghast at the idea that Jesus was the Messiah. However, there is one section of the Liturgy and Gospel of the Holy Twins that is absolutely guaranteed to upset adherents of all three of the world's great monotheistic faiths, its emphasis on the polytheistic origins of early Judaism.

Despite the feelings of the devout, it needs to be recognized that much of the Old Testament teaching derives from ancient Egyptian and Mesopotamian roots. The Ten Commandments derive from the Judgements of the Soul made before the court of Osiris as recounted in the Egyptian Book of the Dead;[9] furthermore, the renowned Psalms of David bear an uncanny resemblance to certain hymns of Egyptian origin. Proverbs attributed to King Solomon are simply a verbatim translation from the work of the Egyptian sage Amenemope and other Egyptian sources, including The Pyramid Texts and the Coffin Texts were used in the Old Testament by simply substituting Jehovah for the Egyptian Sun God Ra. The definition of the name Abba Ra Heim, which appears above the prayer ascribed to him, is: 'The children who are the followers of their father, the god Ra' which again demonstrates the Egyptian initiatory origins of much of both Judaic and Christian mysticism. Indeed, there is a clear distinction between the loving nature of this prayer and the demanding, legalistic anachronisms of Judaism at the time of Jesus.

The Prayer of Abba Ra Heim

Our Heavenly Father
Allelujah
May Your Heavenly Kingdom come upon the earth.
Allelujah
May Your Heavenly laws be obeyed upon the earth.
Allelujah
May you protect us from chaos and grant us our needs.
Allelujah
Amen.

The Lord's Prayer in the New Testament has many similarities with the Prayer of Abba Ra Heim and both clearly display the Egyptian roots of Jesus' teaching.

By the time of Jesus, the 613 strictures of the Law had become almost impossible to apply in everyday life. Furthermore, understanding of the Law was complicated by the innumerable and almost impenetrable commentaries that constantly proliferated, all written with the best of intentions to try and make the Law comprehensible to ordinary people. Jesus had come to create order out of this legalistic chaos, and with his teaching the Law was swept away and replaced with two simple, yet demanding commandments known as The Proclamation of the Law:

1

You will love God, your Heavenly Father.

You will obey His Heavenly Commandments.

You will serve the Lord Your God all the days of your life.

2

You will love your brother as you love yourself.

You will love all the people of the earth.

As you love your brother you will bring heaven on earth.

The Proclamation of the Law is one of the true teachings of Jesus which was included within Christianity:

Master, what is the greatest commandment in the Law?

Jesus said unto him, Thou shalt love the Lord thy God with all
  thy heart,

And with all thy soul, and with all thy mind.

That is the first and greatest commandment.

And the second is like unto it, Thou shalt love thy neighbour as
  thyself.

On these two commandments hang all the Law and the
  prophets.[10]

The responsibilities of all Jews to the poor were detailed separately and in such a manner that there could be no excuse for anyone being in doubt as to their obligations. This matter was deemed to be of such importance that Jesus made it the central theme of a proclamation he made from the steps of the Temple after his triumphal entry into Jerusalem as the rightful heir to the throne of Judah. As the heir, Jesus was regarded as a high priest, with all the obligations that went with that position. Standing on the Temple steps in the position reserved for the high priest who was known as The Melchizedek, he said:

> You shall not eat
> If the poor do not eat.
>
> You shall have no clothing
> If the poor have no clothing.
>
> You shall not have a habitation
> If the poor have no habitation.
>
> You shall not have warmth or a fire in your grate
> If the poor do not have warmth or a fire in theirs.
>
> You shall not be cured of your illness
> If the poor are not cured of theirs.

Forgiveness

When it comes to the forgiveness of sin, the words of Jesus, as reported in the liturgy of Rex Deus, are somewhat different from those promulgated by Holy Mother the Church. Jesus' teaching in this regard can be found within the liturgy under the title of The Proclamation of Forgiveness:

If a man sins against another, he shall seek forgiveness from
that man.

If that man will not forgive the sinner, the sinner will turn to God,
trusting in the words of the Messiah and being sincere in his
desire to be forgiven, ask God to forgive him his sins.

God has spoken through the Messiah and said that a man who
sincerely desires to be forgiven, will be forgiven.

In Christianity, having confessed his sins and done penance, the sinner
is at liberty to sin again and again. Nowhere in canon law is the sinner
encouraged to ask forgiveness from those he has offended or make
amends to them. The Proclamation of Forgiveness seems far more in
accord with both natural justice and the law of God than any of the
guilt–inducing doctrines of the Church.

THE FOLLOWERS OF JESUS

The sect that Jesus led throughout his ministry on earth was known as
the Nazorean or the Nazarene. Later, after the Crucifixion, it became
known as the *Ebionim*, or 'the poor'. The Ebionim continued with the
principle of hereditary leadership for over a century after the
Crucifixion, with its leaders always being descendants of the family of
Jesus.[11] 'The Way' they all followed was designed to eventually bring
about the creation of heaven upon earth by strict adherence to the law
of the New Covenant and the true teachings of Jesus. The medieval followers of 'The Way', the Knights Templar were not, as is popularly
believed, sworn to vows of poverty but took a solemn oath to hold all
their goods in common so that they could amass wealth to benefit the
order, Rex Deus and the communities in which they operated. This
resulted in an enrichment of ordinary people by the encouragement of

trade and industry and the raising of the standards of living of the peasantry, skilled craftsmen and the newly emerging merchant classes. The key phrases that display Rex Deus beliefs are contained within the last two attributes of God listed in The Encryption: *God is Knowledge* and *God is Wisdom*. Concepts repeated many centuries later by Vincent de Beauvais who wrote: 'Man can encompass his salvation by means of knowledge.'[12]

The terms 'The Way', the 'Vineyard' and the 'Garden' had a deep esoteric meaning to the original followers of Jesus. The followers of the Way, the labourers in the Vineyard or the Garden, were seemingly interchangeable terms used to describe the disciples of Jesus and their later spiritual heirs, the members of Rex Deus. As we have demonstrated, the efforts of the medieval Order of the Knights Templar had transformed the economic face of Europe and brought about a change in the balance of power so that the previous domination by petty feudal lords was slowly, but irreversibly, challenged by the rising economic power of the emerging trading classes. This rather indicates to me that the Templars' ultimate goal of creating heaven on earth was becoming a real possibility. Furthermore, in a successful attempt to spread their message further, the Templars left a series of permanent signposts to the true nature of their spiritual path encoded within the carvings and iconography of their greatest gift to the European cultural heritage – Gothic architecture.

CHAPTER 16

An Indelible Mark on the Landscape

The medieval Gothic cathedrals that still adorn the European landscape today, act as visible hymns to Gnostic initiatory spirituality. They are melodic symphonies in stone celebrating a concept of divine harmony envisioned by gifted initiates. These sublime buildings, the cathedrals of Chartres, Amiens and Rheims, still attract devout pilgrims, New Age seekers, students of architecture and simple tourists in their thousands. These are the true, lasting and most visible legacies of the Templars, for the order was inextricably and intimately involved in that sudden outburst of cathedral construction in the 12th to 14th centuries that the gifted English architectural historian William Anderson called 'The Rise of the Gothic'.

Fred Gettings, another English architectural historian, was explicit about this involvement of the warrior knights when he wrote:

> The Knights Templar who were founded ostensibly to protect the pilgrimage routes to the Holy Land, were almost openly involved in financing and lending moral support to the building of Cathedrals throughout Europe.[1]

The early 20th-century initiate, Fulcanelli, and his biographer Kenneth Rayner Johnson, both claim that Gothic architecture, which arose from Templar knowledge of sacred geometry, not merely gave rise to extraordinary buildings of great architectural beauty but acted as a three-dimensional code that passed a hidden message in an architectural form of *la langue verte*, the language of initiation. As I have written elsewhere:

> *La langue verte* arose from an understandable desire of initiates to mask the details of their conversations from casual eavesdroppers such as the Church hierarchy. Thus heretics could communicate using a verbal code, without putting either their lives or their freedom in jeopardy. This useful defence against persecution became the language not only of the initiates but also of all the poor and oppressed. It was the direct medieval ancestor of cockney rhyming slang and the 'hip-talk' or 'rap' of the American inner-city ghettos.[2]

Towards the end of the 19th century another historian, J F Colfs wrote in a similar vein: 'The language of stones spoken by this new art, (Gothic architecture) is at the same time clear and sublime, speaking alike to the humblest and to the most cultured heart.'[3]

SACRED GEOMETRY

Sacred geometry is a divinely inspired art form that encompasses many skills including those of engineering, building and design. Its practitioners invariably claim that it was handed down from master to novice in an unbroken chain from the earliest times until the fall of Jerusalem in 70 CE, thus transmitting, preserving and enhancing the secret knowledge used by the ancient Egyptians and biblical Israelites to construct their sacred buildings. After the fall of Jerusalem, much of this knowledge was apparently lost until the Knights Templar returned to Europe from Jerusalem in 1128 after completing their excavations under the Temple Mount. Did the Templars find the keys to this new form of building under the Temple Mount or were other influences at play? Searching through the architectural heritage of Europe from the fall of the Roman Empire until the 12th century, we can find no transitional period between Romanesque and Gothic architecture. The Gothic style was a startlingly new development that came after 1127, but what were its true origins?

The Rise of the Gothic

In earlier works, one possible source for Gothic architecture has been suggested in the documentation allegedly discovered under the Temple Mount. However, both Egyptian and Hebraic architectural forms were based on transverse lintels not arches, and the only influence that might have stimulated the creation of an arch in that era was Roman. Two learned historians, the Englishman William Anderson, and the French scholar Jean Boney, each independently claim that the Gothic arch was introduced from Islamic culture[4] and my good friend and colleague, Gordon Strachan of Edinburgh, has now developed this theory further. Gordon is a longtime associate of Keith Critchlow whose research knows no boundaries of faith or culture and who has devoted most of his life to an in-depth study of sacred geometry. Furthermore, Gordon's theory is completely consistent with what we know of the cultural interchange occurring at the time of the First Crusade and thereafter.

Like William Anderson and Jean Boney, Gordon is absolutely convinced that the origin of the pointed arch lies outside Europe and is not merely Islamic but that it came specifically from the Holy Land.

Gordon claims that the Gothic arch resulted from: 'A unique blending of indigenous building skills with the architectural genius of Islam.'[5]

During their first nine years in Jerusalem, the Knights Templar met many Sufis. Within Islam at that time, Sufism itself was undergoing a revival[6] and the Sufis were initiates who espoused a devout belief in interfaith pluralism immortalized by the words of the Mevlana Jalaluddin Rumi: 'The religion of love is apart from all religions. The lovers of God have no religion but God alone.' Furthermore, like their Rex Deus counterparts in Europe, they too followed an initiatory spiritual pathway that had much in common with the secret teachings of Jesus.

It was from contact with the Sufis, Strachan claims, that the Templars first became aware of the geometry required to design the Islamic *mukhammas* pointed arch. Indeed, before bringing this knowledge back to Europe, the Templars used it in the Holy Land to build a three-bayed doorway with pointed arches on the Temple Mount which can still be seen today.[7] Thus, contact between the initiatory orders of both faiths, namely the Templars and the Sufis, gave an immense boost to European knowledge of sacred geometry. If Strachan is correct, the interfaith architectural legacy bequeathed to us by the Templars can still be appreciated in the medieval Gothic cathedrals.

Two other mystical writers of the last century also noted the importance of Templar influence on the Gothic cathedrals. Ouspensky claimed that:

> The building of cathedrals was part of a colossal and cleverly devised plan which permitted the existence of entirely free philosophical and psychological schools in the rude, absurd, cruel, superstitious, bigoted and scholastic Middle Ages. These schools have left us an immense heritage, almost all of which we have already wasted without understanding its meaning and value.[8]

Fulcanelli wrote in *Le Mystère des Cathédrales*, that a church or cathedral was not merely a place of worship or a sanctuary, but also a place of commercial activity, public theatre and secular beliefs.

> The Gothic cathedral, that sanctuary of the Tradition, Science and Art, should not be regarded as a work dedicated solely to the glory of Christianity, but rather as a vast concretion of ideas, of tendencies, of popular beliefs; a perfect whole to which we can refer without fear, whenever we would penetrate the religious, secular, philosophic or social thoughts of our ancestors.[9]

Furthermore he went on to say that the Gothic cathedrals were a form of philosophical 'stock exchange' *where lingering pockets of arcana and heresy were flouted under the noses of an unsuspecting clergy.*[10] (my emphasis)

THE MEDIEVAL CRAFTMASONS

The Knights Templar financed and envisioned many of the great Gothic cathedrals, but employed skilled craftsmen to build them. Initiatory orders had existed for centuries among the craftmasons who built the churches, cathedrals and castles of Europe. Initiated masons gained qualification into a hierarchy of three ascending degrees – apprentice, companion and master mason – that are replicated in the modern, worldwide craft of Freemasonry by those of Entered Apprentice, Fellow Craft and Master Mason. In medieval times, apprentices learnt their trade in a peripatetic manner, moving from yard to yard throughout the country, described as a *Tour de France*, receiving instruction from skilled initiated men known as *companions*. When they attained the required degree of skill, they were initiated by their masters in secret conclaves known as *cayennes*.

In France these initiatory orders went by a variety of names: *The Children of Father Soubise, The Children of Master Jacques* and *The Children of Solomon*. Their spiritual heirs are known today as *Les Compagnons des Devoirs du Tour de France*, or, more simply, as *The Compagnonnage*. These three brotherhoods all observed a moral tradition of chivalry within their craft, a humility towards the work that must be done and, above all, they were men who knew how to use a pair of compasses.[11] Furthermore, according to Raoul Vergez, a Companion-carpenter of the Duties who rebuilt most of the church spires in Brittany and Normandy after the Second World War,[12] they all shared the same bread. He claims that sharing the same bread is the hallmark of a true fraternity, and that those who know how to use a pair of compasses are all men who have been initiated into the secret knowledge of 'sacred geometry'. These indeed were the qualifications that admitted them to the status of 'mason'. The allegedly divine origins of their skills was emphasized by the English author Ian Dunlop when he wrote: 'It is not uncommon in medieval illumination to find God the Father represented as the "*elegans architectus*" holding a large pair of compasses.'[13]

The three medieval fraternities that, many centuries later, merged into one, had different duties, skills and traditions. The Children of Father Soubise, who mainly built in the Romanesque style, could be found at the very heart of the Benedictine monastic system and also built the vast array of churches and cathedrals in the Romanesque style that still stand to this day. Their masons marks differ greatly from those of their brethren who built in the Gothic style.

It is claimed that the *Compagnons Passants du Devoir*, or the Children of Master Jacques, founded by a certain Master Jacques, the son of Jacquin who, according to tradition, was made a master craftmason after an apprenticeship served in Greece, Egypt and Jerusalem. The same tradition claims that it was he who made the two pillars of the Temple of Solomon, namely Boaz and the one that is actually called Jacquin.

The Children of Solomon

The third fraternity, the Children of Solomon, is the most important in our investigations into Templar involvement within the great Gothic cathedrals. They built most of the great Gothic Notre Dames, such as those at Chartres, Rheims and Amiens. These beautiful buildings are all marked with their signature, the *chrisme à l'epée*, a Celtic cross enclosed in a circle. The Children of Solomon were named after King Solomon, the prime mover behind the construction of the first Temple in Jerusalem, and learned the principles of sacred geometry from Cistercian monks. Another branch of The Compagnonnage that built many of the smaller Templar churches in the South of France, in both Occitania and Provence, were known as *The Compagnonnage Tuscana*. Their secret traditions and rituals trace their sacred mysteries back to Egypt and biblical Israel via Roman and Greek roots and record that they were part of a *collegia* of constructors known as *Les Tignarii*, which was reputedly founded by the Roman king and initiate, Numa Pompilius.[14]

The true nature of the relationship between the Children of Solomon and the Order of the Templars is impossible to establish with any precision. It is simply not possible to discern whether this guild of craftsmen was an integral part of the knightly order, affiliated with it in some mysterious and intangible way, or just associated with it by usage. What can be proved beyond all doubt is that, with the encouragement of Bernard of Clairvaux, the Knights Templar gave a rule to this fraternity in March 1145 that was prefaced by the words:

> We the Knights of Christ and of the Temple follow the destiny that prepares us to die for Christ. We have the wish to give this rule of living, of work and of honour to the constructors of churches so that Christianity can spread throughout the earth not so that our name should be remembered, Oh Lord, but that Your Name should live.[15]

Indeed it is highly probable that this fraternity of masons, who worked solely in the new Gothic style, was affiliated in some way with the Order of the Templars, however no documents have yet been discovered that can substantiate this. They were granted great privileges by the establishment of that time, including freedom from all taxes and protection against any form of prosecution by the constructors of other buildings; but, it is highly indicative that at the time of the suppression of the Knights Templar, the Children of Solomon lost all their privileges and immunities. Some degree of guilt by association has been at work here.

CHARTRES CATHEDRAL

Perhaps the most powerful example of the architectural insight that flows from the vision of true initiates can be found at Chartres Cathedral. This sublime building is a superb statement in stone of the truths that lead man closer to God. Each tourist or pilgrim leaves this mystical building spiritually uplifted, inspired and transformed. This is the true measure of the enduring magic and sense of mysticism that pervades this cathedral. Chartres has been described by one modern mystical writer, Louis Charpentier, as the Golden Book, in which inspired sages have inscribed their wisdom as a lasting legacy to all who seek spiritual truth.[16]

The west front of Chartres Cathedral, built as an addition to Fulbert's 11th-century Romanesque structure, is sometimes described as either 'transitional' or Gothic, and contains the three main doors. Thirty-eight scenes from the life of Jesus are carved in detail along a narrow frieze that runs just above the capital figures that flank and also separate the doors. These scenes do not include any representation of the Crucifixion, indeed, there is not one 12th-century carving of the Crucifixion in the entire cathedral.[17] This startling omission of any commemoration of the central tenet of Christian dogma – that Christ died to redeem us from sin – is quite deliberate: it reflects the Templar belief that Jesus came to reveal and not to redeem.

The central door is described by Louis Charpentier as the door of Mystical Faith[18] and the tympanum above it is dominated by the figure of Jesus enthroned in Glory, barefoot with his right hand raised in blessing and his left clasping a bible. To denote his divine status, Jesus' head is surrounded by a nimbus, or halo, containing a cross. Here we find another clue that some heresy that contradicts Christian dogma is being indicated here, for the cross behind the head of Jesus is a specific Templar cross, *La Croix Céleste*, the Cross of Universal Knowledge or Gnosis, and Gnosticism in any shape or form was always deemed heretical by the Church.

On entering the cathedral, the magnificent stained-glass windows transform the natural daylight into a shimmering haze of subtle blue colour that pervades the interior. The stained glass of Chartres was made using scientific knowledge, true gnosis, brought back by the Templars after their excavations in Jerusalem.[19] It does not react like ordinary glass. Mystical scholars claim that this type of glass was deliberately manufactured to filter out specific wavelengths of light that were deemed harmful to man's innate capacity for spiritual activity. Thus, this selective filtering of the cosmic rays deliberately creates a wavelength that harmonizes with the natural vibrations of human cellular tissue and maximizes the effect of initiatory energy.[20]

Immediately below the huge rose window in the north transept is a row of stained-glass lancet windows. In the central lancet, St Anne, the mother of the Virgin, is depicted wearing a halo that, according to one knowledgeable priest at least, is usually associated with the Magdalene in devotional pictures of the 17th and 18th centuries. The two lancets flanking it on either side depict initiates: Melchizedek, the King of Righteousness, whose teaching inspired the Essenes; Aaron, the brother of Moses and a priest of the Egyptian temple mysteries; King David the founder of the Royal House of Israel; and lastly, King Solomon who was 'wiser than Moses and full of the wisdom of Egypt'.

There are three Black Madonnas in Chartres: a modern replica of the medieval copy, based upon the Druidic figure *Virginibus Pariturae*, in the crypt which the official guide states was used as an initiation chamber; another in the ambulatory of the cathedral, the Virgin of the Pillar, clothed according to tradition in heavy, ornate robes formally shaped in a triangle;[21] the third is depicted in stained glass, *Notre Dame de la Belle Verrière*, which miraculously survived not only the fire that destroyed Fulbert's Romanesque cathedral but centuries of strife, the French Revolution and two World Wars. Immediately in front of the Virgin of the Pillar is a tangible level of energy, a place of God-given power where the vibration is especially low and induces a fainting feeling indicating that this is a point of spiritual transformation.

There are many other points of telluric power within the cathedral which have the capacity to raise one to a point of etheric enhancement. A true 'state of grace' induced by natural earth energies that were recognized, used and enhanced by the craftsmen who created this magnificent building.

The spiritual pathway of initiation is commemorated by figures flanking the entrance to the main door in the north portal which is known as the Portal of the Initiates. On the extreme left-hand side is a carving of Melchizedek holding a chalice from which the Grail stone protrudes. Abraham stands beside him with his son Isaac, bound and ready for sacrifice, but Abraham is transfixed by the gaze of an angel above Melchizedek's head: an angel who carries the message that human sacrifice is forbidden to all Jews. Next comes Moses who received the two tablets of the Law, that some scholars claim also symbolize the twin pillars of the Temple of Solomon, Jacquin and Boaz.

One of the most intriguing aspects of Chartres Cathedral is the labyrinth, a circular design made of black and white flagstones, that occupies over a third of the floor of the nave. Labyrinths are not just a Christian practice as several Neolithic labyrinths of an identical pattern have been found. One day after visiting Chartres, I visited a folk festival in Brittany and watched a dance that indicated the initiatory nature of the labyrinth. The music was pure North African Arab music, slow, reedy, rhythmic and entrancing. The entire village, led by the mayor and his wife, danced with their arms linked so closely that their sides seemed to touch, shuffling sideways in a curving formal design that replicated the exact pattern of the labyrinth. I was watching a variation of a Sufi dance deliberately designed to bring about a shift in consciousness. Thus, aspects of Chartres Cathedral are mementoes and symbols of the Gnostic streams of spirituality, constructed in such a manner that the building is an instruction book to the pathway of initiation, carved in stone and masked by an outward display of Christian worship.

AMIENS CATHEDRAL

The Cathedral of Amiens, the largest in France, has a vault that soars 140 feet heavenwards. The west front is dominated by a statue of Jesus known as the *Beau Dieu* of Amiens, depicted with his feet resting on a lion and a dragon.[22] So here, in pride of place, is a symbolic representation of Jesus and the *Wouivre*, the initiatory telluric energy of the Druids. Immediately below this is a statue of that supreme adept of the Old Testament, King Solomon. The walls flanking the doors are, like those at Notre Dame de Paris, decorated with quatrefoils depicting alchemical symbolism; representing not the transmutation of base metals into gold but the initiatory principle of the spiritual transformation of base humanity into the pure gold of spiritual enlightenment.[23]

In travelling from Chartres to Amiens, according to the French mystical writer François Cali, one makes an almost imperceptible transition, 'from the love of God to the love of Wisdom, which is in order, number and harmony, which can be equated with God, but which need not be.'[24] Order, number and harmony are all attributes of divine gnosis. This cathedral, a wondrous, symphonic blend of space, stone and light, was deliberately designed and constructed to celebrate the Gnostic principle of Sophia or sacred wisdom. This temple of wisdom was rebuilt after yet another fire, to house the most precious relic of the Knights Templar: the reliquary containing the severed head of John the Baptist. According to the Templar scholar and mythologist, the late Guy Jordan of Bargemon in Provence, this object of veneration is nothing less than *la vrai tête Baphometique Templier* – the true Baphometic head of the Templars.

On the wall of the south transept there is a series of carved panels depicting the biblical story of John the Baptist, all coloured in the medieval fashion. To reinforce the point, the outer wall of the choir is decorated with superbly sculpted bas-reliefs that depict his life and death, including one where the top of his severed head is being pierced by a knife. The significance of this piercing is not known, but its importance to the Templars can be seen in their burial practices for in the Templar church in Bargemon, Provence, part of the floor has been replaced with a transparent perspex sheet that allows a clear view of the human remains in the crypt beneath. A row of skulls and long bones can be seen and each skull is pierced in the manner depicted at Amiens.

John the Baptist was not merely of importance to the Knights Templar, but is celebrated in the Gospel of Thomas where Jesus is quoted as saying:

Among those born of women, from Adam until John the Baptist, there is no one so superior to John the Baptist that his eyes should not be lowered [before him].[25]

Throughout the lands once subject to Templar rule, churches dedicated to St John the Baptist abound. In one, near Trigance in the Var, an ingenious arrangement allows a beam of light to illuminate the altar with a golden glow at dawn on the Baptist's feast day. Carvings of John the Baptist take precedence in most of these churches and chapels, but contemporary carvings of the Crucifixion are notable by their absence. A large number of these buildings are noted not only for their alchemical symbolism, but also as homes to the Black Madonna which I describe in the next chapter.

CHAPTER 17

Tracing the Beliefs of the Knights Templar

T he Templars have left us a considerable legacy of symbols and iconography that can guide us to an understanding of their beliefs. One important area of study is that of a form of veneration that is almost invariably associated with Templar activity, namely the cult of the Black Madonna. The warrior monks also left us an indelible and lasting guide to their main principles of belief, carved as three-dimensional teaching boards within the great Gothic cathedrals they built or financed.

THE CULT OF THE BLACK MADONNA

The cult of Mariolatry received its main impetus from Chartres although its true origins derive from a variety of forms of the pagan worship of mother goddesses. Notre Dame Sous-Terre at Chartres Cathedral, for example, is simply a Christianized variation on the ancient Druidic practice of worshipping the fire-blackened figure of a virgin about to give birth, *Virginibus pariturae*, as described by Julius Caesar in *de Bello Gallico*. Adoptionist techniques such as this were often employed by the Church to incorporate older forms of pagan worship into Catholic practice. While veneration of the Black Madonna started in a similar manner, and several sites of importance predate the foundation of the Templar Order or are situated far beyond the order's realm of activity, nonetheless, the peak years of the development of this strange cult coincide with the time of the order's power, and the majority of her effigies are located in areas of Templar influence. This cult is also intimately entwined with the veneration of Mary Magdalene and, as a result, the Church, while it has always been happy to rake in the financial benefits of pilgrimage to these sites, has consistently felt uncomfortable with the cult of the Black Madonna. What on earth can this effigy represent that causes the hierarchy so much embarrassment?

One clue to the acute discomfort felt by the Church in this matter originates with Bernard of Clairvaux who, at the time of the Council of Troyes, required all the members of the new knighthood to make, 'Obedience to Bethany and the House of Mary and Martha'. In other words, render obedience and loyalty to the dynasty founded by Mary Magdalene and Jesus. Many scholars have concluded from this that many of the great Notre Dame cathedrals built or financed by the Templars were dedicated not to Mary the mother of Jesus, but to Mary Magdalene and the son of Jesus: an idea which, in the eyes of the Church is outrageously heretical.

Templar veneration of the Magdalene in the guise of the Black Madonna was widespread throughout the lands they controlled and the perceptive Scottish author, Ean Begg, lists over 50 effigies of this strangely coloured Madonna that can be found within churches dedicated to Mary Magdalene.[1] In the Western esoteric tradition, the Magdalene is described as 'the symbol of divine wisdom' and, according to the Nazorean tradition, she was to be depicted garbed in black like the priestess Isis, surmounted by Sophia's crown of stars, and her infant was to wear the golden crown of royalty.[2] The 20th-century initiate, Rudolf Steiner, claims that symbolism can be interpreted at up to at least nine different levels depending on the perception and initiatory status of the viewer. At the first, exoteric, level the Black Madonna is simply the mother of Jesus with her only child; at the second level it is Mary, the seat of wisdom that is depicted. At the esoteric level, the symbolism represents the Magdalene and the child of Jesus; at a deeper level, as in ancient Egyptian symbolism, the colour black indicates wisdom, so the Templars were venerating the goddess of wisdom, Sophia in the form of the goddess Isis and the Horus child, which is then given a Christian gloss.[3] At yet another level of understanding, Isis was venerated as 'the Initiate of Light'.[4] In the tradition of the Christianization of pagan deities, the Black Virgin represents the Earth Mother, the Egyptian goddess Anna, who was represented in Egyptian tradition as being black.[5] Ean Begg, who has dedicated several years to the study of the Black Madonna and the hidden streams of spirituality within Christian Europe, claims that the study of the history and legends of the Black Virgin may reveal a heretical sect with the power to shock and astonish even current post-Christian attitudes, and a secret involving political forces still influential in modern Europe. A comment which, when judged in the light of the Rex Deus tradition, is right on the button!

THE TAROT

Rex Deus rulers in northern Italy knew their people and understood and catered for their needs. One indication of the tolerant and heretical nature of one of the Visconti rulers' thinking manifested itself in the tarot trumps. The origins of the tarot are disputed; most scholars now believe that it originated in medieval times from the areas of Provence and northern Italy. Others suggest that they came to the West via the crusaders and that the original Eastern packs were transformed by influences traceable to the Cathars, the Gypsies, the Knights Templar, the kabbala and ancient Greek hermetic thought.[6]

The English grail scholar, Malcolm Godwin has written that: 'It is possible that the Templars learnt their use from their Saracen rivals.'[7] He is also of the opinion that the overt references to the Holy Grail and the obvious Gnostic content of the tarot was the principal reason for the Church's hostile attitude towards it. Indeed, according to the theologian Margaret Starbird, the tarot was, 'a virtual catechism for the suppressed beliefs of the alternative Christian Church, the "Church of the Holy Grail", whose articles of faith included the partnership of Christ and his bride, the woman whom the Gospels called the Magdalene.'[8]

The Church viewed these cards with grave suspicion, branding them as both dangerous and heretical and, according to one monk, the tarot trumps were, 'rungs on a ladder that leads straight to hell'.[9] Other priests described the cards as the Devil's breviary.[10] Margaret Starbird interprets them using scriptural references to the dynasty of Israel's rulers, the House of David and the medieval heresy of the blood royal – the *sang real* – which, she claims, leads us to their secret meaning. The Church has good cause to be uneasy, for the use of the tarot as a system of visual teaching, either as 'flash cards' or as a pocket-sized teaching board, was very much in the Templar tradition that was continued into the 21st century by the worldwide fraternity of Freemasonry and the modern Templar Orders.

Margaret Starbird's astute analysis is based on the historical evidence within the designs on the cards. She correctly claims that their origin is late medieval and bases this on the fashions of costumes and symbolism used within the early packs that she claims, 'are directly and irrefutably related to the Church of Amor and the medieval heresy of the Holy Grail.'[11] Despite being completely unaware of the Rex Deus

tradition at the time she wrote her book, she states without fear of contradiction that all four suits of the handsome, vividly hand-painted
15th-century decks produced in Provence and northern Italy, were
clearly associated with the medieval heresy surrounding surviving
descendants of the Holy Grail.[12] She again unknowingly reinforces the
validity of the Rex Deus tradition by stating:

> The very elaborate cup symbol found on some of the early fif-
> teenth-century decks – the Visconti-Sforza (usually dated between
> 1440–1480) packs named for the artist's patrons – is very similar
> to numerous medieval images of the Holy Grail. And it is pre-
> cisely the noble families of Provence and Northern Italy, the allied
> ducal families of Anjou and Milan, who were connected by ties
> of friendship and even related by blood and marriage to the *sang
> real*. The trump cards in the fifteenth-century tarot decks belong-
> ing to the Visconti family of Milan appear to be among the earliest
> in existence…[13]

Certainly the tarot teaches a very different form of spirituality to that
of the Church, one including distinctly heretical themes such as rein-
carnation, spiritual renewal, spiritual rebirth and transformation.[14] In the
tarot, the goddess Isis, the seat of wisdom venerated by the Templars as
the Black Madonna, is depicted in the card known as Temperance.
Perceval, the hero of Wolfram von Eschenbach's Grail saga, is represented
symbolically on the bottom left of this card as a valley between two
peaks, Perce a Val. The pack is a symbolic depiction of a form of Grail
quest where an innocent pilgrim undergoes initiatory trials, including
a symbolic death to this world and resurrection to spiritual gnosis, before
he meets the goddess. The card known as the Fool is Parzival; the Hermit
represents the Grail hermit; the Fisher King is depicted by the Hanged

Man, although this is also a reference to the tortured Templars; the Tower is a symbolic representation of the Magdalene and the Moon is the Grail bearer.[15] One suit is held to represent the House of Pendragon, a reference to the Arthurian legends; another, the South or the House of the Spear, refers to the St Clair family as the House of Lothian and Orkney, for the St Clairs were Lords of Roslin in Lothian and also the Earls of Orkney.

MYTH AND ALLEGORY

The use of myth and legend to carry spiritual allegories and uncomfortable truths into the public consciousness in an acceptable manner is as old as speech and memory. Those who dismiss these cultural vehicles as some form of 'inspired fiction' suitable only for children or the credulous, ignore the fact that every meaningful part of life – heroic deeds, family and national traditions and all religions, including Christianity, have always developed a colourful mythology of their own. Thanks to the great work of Professor Joseph Campbell and others, the value that is attached to mythology has undergone significant change.[16]

Myths, like symbolism, have to be understood at many levels and when viewed with discernment, can be a signpost to hidden truths. Campbell himself claimed that: 'Mythology is the penultimate truth, because the ultimate cannot be put into words.'[17] Ananda Coomeraswamy, that great Indian scholar wrote: 'Myth embodies the nearest approach to absolute truth that can be stated in words.'[18] The poet Kathleen Raine made a similar point when she said: 'Fact is not the truth of myth; myth is the truth of fact.'[19]

The Holy Grail

Despite the existence of the Rex Deus families being a closely guarded secret that was not revealed until the later decades of the 20th century, Rex Deus beliefs, legends and stories had been widely known for more than nine centuries without anyone being aware of their true origins. The masterstroke that immortalized the Rex Deus traditions was the creation and dissemination of the stories of the search for the Holy Grail. The first epics within this literary genre were deliberately created to serve the purposes of the descendants of Jesus and are a clever amalgam of pre-Christian traditions with a Christian gloss and contain a coded guide to the true teachings of Jesus.

Described variously as a chalice, a cup, a stone that fell from heaven, a stone within the cup or a magical bowl,[20] the Holy Grail is deemed to be capable of restoring life to the dead or good health to the wounded or infirm. Many pre-Christian and Celtic legends describe the Grail as a cauldron with similar qualities.[21] I have already described how the Grail is carved as the 'stone within the cup' carried by Melchizedek in the carving of this priest-king of Jerusalem that has place of honour by the north door of Chartres Cathedral, in the porch known as the Portal of the Initiates.[22]

The Grail sagas acquired their 'Christian' gloss through the inspired genius of two remarkable men, Wolfram von Eschenbach,[23] who spent some years in the Holy Land and is believed by many to have been a Templar himself, and Chrétien de Troyes. Their stories are a clever mixture of pagan legend, Celtic folklore, Jewish mystical symbolism, and Rex Deus tradition with alchemical and kabbalistic nuances, all enclosed within a thin veneer of mainstream Christian veneration for the holiest relic in the Christian tradition – the cup used at the Last Supper, that was also reputedly used by Joseph of Arimathea to catch the blood of Jesus after the Crucifixion.

The first Grail romance appeared on the European literary scene around 1190, in the form of an unfinished epic, *Perceval*, or *Le Conte del Graal*, written by Chrétien de Troyes[24] a relative of Hugues de Payen,[25] who had trained for the priesthood and became a translator and a writer of considerable repute. He dedicated three of his early works to Marie, countess of Champagne and the daughter of King Louis VII of France and Eleanor of Aquitaine.[26] It is believed that he originally intended to dedicate *Le Conte del Graal* to Marie, however, when her husband, Count Henry of Champagne, died shortly after returning from the Holy land, she retired from public life. At this juncture, Chrétien sought a new Rex Deus patron, Philippe d'Alsace the Count of Flanders, the son of a cofounder of the Knights Templar, Payen de Montdidier and a close relative of the early Christian kings of Jerusalem.[27]

The collection of legends that Geoffrey of Monmouth composed concerning King Arthur, which came to public notice in 1136 (18 years after the foundation of the Knights Templar) and those concerning the search for the Holy Grail, while separate and distinct to begin with, soon became inextricably mixed. Both genres share ideals of chivalry and speak of a spiritual search for perfection played out against the backdrop of brutal reality that was all too familiar to the enthralled listeners and readers.

It is ironic that both the Arthurian and Grail traditions are believed to share a common source that has long since been lost. Comparisons have been made between this alleged 'common source' and its relationship to the resulting sagas, and the relationship between the 'Q' document and the Synoptic Gospels. I am not in a position to dispute the theory that there may indeed have been some common written source linking these two chivalric legends, one that was perhaps known to both Chrétien and Wolfram. However, both Chrétien de Troyes' work and that of Wolfram von Eschenbach are linked by a lasting common source, the teachings and traditions of Rex Deus. One Grail scholar, Malcolm Godwin, came remarkably close to identifying this linkage when he wrote:

> The Legend of the Grail, more than any other Western myth, has retained the vital magic that marks it as a living legend capable of touching both imagination and the spirit. No other myth is so rich in symbolism, so diverse and often contradictory in meaning. And at its core there exists a secret which has sustained the mystical appeal of the Grail for the last nine hundred years, while other myths and legends have slipped into oblivion and been forgotten.[28]

The most common description of the Holy Grail describes it as a holy relic, the cup used by Joseph of Arimathea to collect the blood of Jesus after the Crucifixion. This story was certainly concocted by someone with no knowledge whatsoever of Jewish burial practice at the time, for any men who handled a corpse would be obliged to immediately undergo a prolonged period of purification, which is hardly likely on the eve of Passover. The Jewish aversion to men handling corpses, much less blood, in biblical times renders this story absolutely incredible. Also, the orthodox Jewish burial traditions of that era demand that the corpse be interred with the entire body and blood together in order to guarantee life in the hereafter, and would be an absolute bar against the taking of blood from any corpse.

When the first Grail romance was written, Europe closely resembled a police state where anyone who was perceived as spiritually or religiously different was liable to be burned at the stake. The Rex Deus families had learned the art of dissembling simply in order to survive. Thus while the Grail sagas purport to describe a long and dangerous quest for that most holy of all relics, the cup of Jesus, encoded within it is another, very different message.

They describe a long, arduous search by a knight who is subjected to many temptations and physical dangers, a romanticized tale based on the known perils of pilgrimage. Set, as it is, during the supreme age of the veneration of holy relics, what is so different about the story of the quest for the Holy Grail? The standard description of the Grail quest was perfectly acceptable to the hierarchy of the time, but hidden within it is another story, it is an allegory for an alchemical quest,[29] a heretical guide to a spiritual pathway to enlightenment.

Any 12th-century devout knight sincerely seeking salvation simply volunteered for duty in the Holy Land. The indulgence gained for this crusading activity was unconditional absolution for all sins, both those already committed and any that might be committed in the future. Service in the Templars, for example, ensured that, when killed in battle, the knight would go immediately to heaven, so why seek the Grail? Another reason to question the basic overt message of the Grail sagas is that by going to any church or cathedral anyone could, by the miracle of transubstantiation, get direct access to the actual body and blood of Jesus through the simple act of communion without great trials or dangers, merely the mild embarrassment of making an act of confession.

In another interpretation, the words 'Holy Grail' are claimed to be a corruption of the term 'Holy Gradual', gradual in the sense of a gradual spiritual ascent or ascending initiatory way leading to eventual enlight-enment. In a best-selling book published over 25 years ago, yet another meaning has been ascribed to the term. *Sangraal*, as it is written in French, is claimed to be a disguised version of *Sang Real*, or Holy Blood.[30] This was first brought to the notice of the English-speaking world in 1981 with the publication of *The Holy Blood and the Holy Grail* which claimed that Jesus, supposedly the celibate Son of God, was in fact as mortal as we and had married and founded a dynasty. This concept has now literally become commonplace after the unbelievable success of Dan Brown's *The Da Vinci Code* which worked the same concept into a best-selling novel and film.

The two principal Grail romances carry coded clues to a heretical belief system embedded within them that contradict the dogma of the Church. The King of the Grail castle, the wounded Fisher King, imperfectly serves his impoverished realm just as the usurpers of the true teachings of Jesus, those who lead the Christian Church, despoil the spiritual lives of the flock they claim to serve. When someone pure enough to see the Grail restores the Fisher King to full health, his wasted kingdom will be restored. Likewise, when the true teachings of Jesus triumph over greed, lies, and distortion, the dream of heaven on earth will become a reality.

My first literary collaborator, the late Trevor Ravenscroft, composed his masterwork, *The Cup of Destiny*,[31] around just these themes, for he wished to reveal to the younger generation that within their drama and symbolism, these sagas veil signposts to a unique path of initiation into the deepest mysteries of the true message of Jesus. He was not alone in this conclusion, for the world's leading mythologist, the late Professor Joseph Campbell, writing of the importance of the Grail, cites a passage from the Gospel of Thomas, where Jesus is reported as saying 'He who drinks from my mouth will become as I am, and I shall be he.'[32] For Professor Campbell this represents the ultimate form of enlightenment that can arise from a successful Grail quest.[33]

It was just these beliefs that sustained the Templars and which the Rex Deus families passed on to a vast congregation by founding a fraternity in Scotland that now spans the globe and is even more hated and distrusted by the Church than the Knights Templar.

CHAPTER 18

Rosslyn Chapel & Earl William St Clair

Cathars fleeing from the bloody, inquisitorial aftermath of the Albigensian Crusade and the Knights Templar who fled some years later to Scotland found their principal refuge in the lands owned by the St Clairs of Roslin. The first member of this Norman family to arrive in Scotland was William 'the Seemly' St Clair, who came along with the knight Bartholemew Ladislaus Leslyn when they acted as the escort to the Saxon Princess Margaret, who later married King Malcolm Canmore.[1] William 'the Seemly' St Clair was granted the lordship of Roslin. The first St Clair to be born in Scotland, Henri de St Clair, fought under Godfroi de Bouillon in the Holy Land in 1096 and was present at the siege of Jerusalem.[2] On the First Crusade he was accompanied by members of 11 other leading Scottish aristocratic families.

Representatives of all these 12 families met regularly before the crusade and continued to meet at Roslin until the late 18th century. They included the Stuarts, the Montgomerys, the Setons, the Douglases, the Dalhousies, the Ramseys, the Leslies, and the Lindsays, as well as the St Clairs; all linked by marriage and shared beliefs. All 12 families were involved with the Templar Order and continued to propagate the order's traditions after the suppression. They were also intimately involved in the foundation of Freemasonry in Scotland.

EARL WILLIAM ST CLAIR

The figure who did the most to preserve and propagate Rex Deus traditions was Earl William St Clair who lived in the 15th century and whom I have mentioned in earlier chapters. He was not only the Lord of Roslin but also the third St Clair Earl of Orkney. He was described as 'a man of exceptional talents much given to policy, such as buildings of Castles, Palaces and Churches'[3] and as 'a Grandmaster and an adept of the highest degree'.[4] He was appointed as the patron of craftmasonry in Scotland and the Scottish archival records confirm that he was not only hereditary Grandmaster of the craftmasons but also of all the hard and soft guilds in Scotland,[5] such as the shipwrights, papermakers, tanners and foresters.[6]

Earl William St Clair, René d'Anjou and Cosimo de' Medici were all obsessive collectors of original manuscripts and William amassed a vast library that he housed at Roslin Castle. The respect accorded to this collection by the earl is recorded by one family historian in the following terms:

About this time (1447) there was a fire in the square keep by occasion of which the occupants were forced to flee the building. The Prince's chaplain seeing this, and remembering all of his masters writings, passed to the head of the dungeon where they all were, and threw out four great trunks where they were. The news of the fire coming to the Prince through the lamentable cries of the ladies and gentlewomen, and the sight thereof coming to his view in the place where he stood upon Colledge Hill, he was sorry for nothing but the loss of his Charters and other writings; but when the chaplain who had saved himself by coming down the bell rope tied to a beam, declared how his Charters and Writts were all saved, he became cheerful and went to … recomfort his Princess and the Ladys.[7]

The importance of these documents reinforces the fact that spiritual insight and respect for ancient knowledge were of the highest importance to William. Indeed his description as 'one of the Illuminati' marks the respect in which he was held for his deep and abiding spiritual knowledge and perception. Indeed, according to Tessa Ransford, a director of the Scottish Poetry Library, the name Roslin translates from Scottish Gaelic as 'ancient knowledge passed down the generations'.[8] The St Clairs of Roslin were the principal guardians of the divinely inspired gnosis that was the true treasure of the Knights Templar and Earl William preserved this heritage for all time within Rosslyn Chapel.

ROSSLYN CHAPEL

Earl William is mainly remembered for his lasting and enigmatic legacy, the mystical shrine of Rosslyn Chapel. Originally planned as a large collegiate church, the chapel's foundations were laid between 1446 and 1450 and Earl William brought skilled and experienced master masons from every part of Europe to construct it.[9] He had to enlarge Roslin village in order to accommodate these skilled workmen and the village grew at such a pace that it began to rival nearby Haddington and even Edinburgh in size and was granted a royal charter in 1456 by King James II.

The architect, patron and designer of the chapel was Earl William himself, who exercised total control over every aspect of its construction.

Before any carving was made in stone, a model was carved in wood and submitted to the Earl for approval. Only then did the stone carving begin. Thus, the essential symphonic harmony of design in the chapel is due to the cumulative result of several factors: a plan drawn up by a supremely gifted man who exerted absolute control over design, quality and construction; a comparatively rapid rate of build that left no time for contamination of the original conception; and a band of highly skilled masons who worked continuously and without a break on the same project, a rare occurrence in church building in that era.

My first literary collaborator and teacher, Trevor Ravenscroft, once wrote that: 'The sculptures in Rosslyn are magnificent manifestations of spiritual insight or vision, given substance in stone.' In 1982, Douglas Sutherland described the chapel as: 'A medieval masterpiece of masonry, containing some of the most exquisite carvings ever fashioned in stone, Rosslyn Chapel may now be half-forgotten but it is still very memorable.'[10]

No realistic analysis of the spiritual and artistic content of the carvings within the chapel can be made unless it is conducted in the light of the family history and complex character of its founder. Considered on their own, the carvings are simply beautiful and mysterious manifestations of Masonic art that are open to varied and gross misinterpretation. Within this late-medieval, supposedly Christian church, we find symbolic references in stone to every known initiatory spiritual tradition that can be found in the history of mankind before its construction. For example, there is a carving of the head of Hermes Trismegistos, the reputed author of the Emerald Tablets who is so often equated with the Egyptian god Thoth and over 120 carvings of the Green Man commemorate the principle of spiritual death and rebirth central to all initiatory paths. There are depictions of rosettes and five-pointed stars that once decorated the temples dedicated to Ishtar and Tammuz in ancient Babylonia, 2,500 years before the birth of Jesus and, above all, symbolism of supreme significance to the heretical Knights Templar.

Templar Symbolism in Rosslyn Chapel

Symbolism directly associated with the Templars is found throughout the chapel. The early 20th-century French Templar scholar J-A Durbec lists the signs and seals that can validate the Templar attribution of any building as follows:

1 Carvings of a five-pointed star, L'étoile

2 Two brothers on one horse, *deux frères sur un seule cheval*

3 The seal known as the Agnus Dei, also known as the Templar seal, *un agneau pascal (nimbé ou non) tenant une croix patté au-dessus de lui*

4 A stylized representation of the head of Jesus such as that represented in the Shroud of Turin or on the Veil of Veronica, known as the Mandylion

5 A dove in flight carrying an olive branch. *Une colombe tenant en son bec une branche d'olivier*

6 A form of oriental cross known as the floriated cross[11]

Throughout Europe, in making an attribution of any building to the Templars, we must procceed with extreme caution for most of their buildings are remarkably plain and devoid of decoration. Furthermore, the symbols listed by Durbec are all individual items of standard Christian iconography, but whenever we find two or more of them in combination within the same building, this suggests strong Templar influence. When they all occur together prior to the suppression of the order, we know we have a genuine Templar edifice.[12] In the case of Rosslyn

Chapel, which was founded over a century after the suppression of the Templars, we have another mystery to unravel, why were they placed there? The sacred geometry of the architecture shows all the signs of Templar construction and, moreover, within the vast array of iconography carved within the chapel, Templar influence is not just restricted to the diagnostic symbols already listed, they occur in one form or another at almost every turn.

In the vault of each bay in the aisles and arching across the roof of the crypt are carvings of the *engrailed cross* of the St Clairs, and at the junction of the arms of each of these crosses, is a distinctly delineated variation of the *croix patté* of the Knights Templar known as the *cross of universal knowledge*. Furthermore, it is no coincidence that the heraldic colours of the St Clair family are argent and sable, the same as those sported by the Rex Deus family of the Sforzas of Milan and also displayed on the battle flag of the Templar Order, the Beauseant.

Two Templar burial stones from local graveyards reside in the chapel, one in the crypt, adjoining a 17th-century guild stone depicting the King of Terrors, the other in the north aisle of the chapel, engraved with the name William de Sinncler, and surmounted by a floriated cross. Both of these, however, were found in churchyards on the St Clair estate and have only recently been brought into the chapel for safekeeping. The Templar seal of the Agnus Dei appears on a pillar on the north wall; a similar pillar on the south wall bears the veil of Veronica, a carving of a cloth adorned with a bearded head. The superb carving of the dove in flight carrying an olive branch in its beak adorns the western section of the roof in a sea of five-pointed stars.

In the clerestory is a stained-glass window depicting St George, a warrior saint who was of some importance to the Knights Templar. According to Pope Gelasius (494 AD), St George 'was a Saint, venerated by man, but whose acts were known only to God.' The legends surrounding St George link him closely to St Michael and the resurrecting Babylonian god Tammuz. I have mentioned some of the bizarre connections between the Sufis and the Templars, this depiction of Tammuz provides further evidence of this, for most modern authorities now believe that *El Khidir*, the mystical teacher of the Sufis, Tammuz and St George are simply one and the same person portrayed in a varying mythological guise. Tammuz, described as the spouse, son or brother of the goddess Ishtar, is also known as 'the Lord of Life and Death,' a title with deep Masonic overtones, yet it predates the known history of the Masonic movement by several millennia.

The St Clair family of Roslin were members of the Rex Deus group who founded the Order of the Knights Templar and Roslin Castle was the ultimate destination of Hugues de Payen when he visited Scotland in 1127. The grave-marker within the chapel that is so beautifully decorated with Templar symbolism, a sword and the floriated cross, is the memorial to the commander of the Templar charge at Bannockburn in 1314 that preserved the independence of Scotland and secured the crown for Robert the Bruce, namely Sir William St Clair.[13]

When one evaluates the vast array of symbolism encoded within the carvings at Rosslyn Chapel in the light of St Clair family history, there can only be one valid conclusion: this chapel and all its carvings whose design was so strictly supervised by Earl William, was deliberately created as a lasting memorial to the much-maligned Order of the Knights Templar and as a means of transmission of their ideals and spiritual beliefs to future generations. Earl William had used the skills of his Masonic colleagues to good effect and celebrated every known initiatory spiritual pathway that had contributed in one way or another to the sacred gnosis preserved at such cost by the descendants of the 24 *ma'madot* of Israel.

This form of lasting celebration was not the only means used by Earl William to ensure the preservation of these initiatory rites. In fact, there are more clues and signposts in the chapel to his plans for the future. These symbolic representations of sacred principles central to the Rex Deus tradition have been used for over 500 years by a fraternity founded by Earl William, for he used the construction of this holy shrine as the first step in creating an organization that would treasure and guard these secrets, and pass them on to future generations throughout the world – the craft of Freemasonry. This organization's members have used their spiritual insight to transcend the geographic, cultural, and religious barriers that normally impede the progress of man.

Earl William's position as hereditary Grandmaster of all the hard and soft guilds in Scotland, his authority over the Masonic court at Kilwinning, his Templar antecedents, the Masonic symbolism within Rosslyn Chapel, and his position as a scholar of esotericism all combine to demonstrate that he had the means, the motive, and the opportunity to play an active role in transforming the ancient craft guilds into the modern speculative fraternity. The new Freemasonry recognized no barriers of class and eventually included King James VI of Scotland, who was initiated into the craft at the Lodge of Perth and Scone in 1601.[14] When he became King James I of England two years later, he needed influential allies as a counterweight to the greed of the self-serving British aristocracy. He found them among the members of the trade and craft guilds of England and introduced them on an informal basis to Freemasonry.[15] The first documentary proof of inductions into English Freemasonry dates from 1640, during the reign of James' son, Charles I. In this era of repression, bloodshed and war fought in the name of religion, the new fraternity wisely decided to be secretive from the start.

The secrecy and an absence of documentation obscure any study of the early years of Freemasonry making it extremely difficult to demonstrate the connections that could relate the Freemasons with the other esoteric movements that first came to public notice at the time of the

Renaissance. However, the carvings within Rosslyn Chapel give indications of some of these possible links, with the Rosicrucians for example, and there is a wealth of Masonic symbolism that belies the 'official' history of Freemasonry that declares, rather dogmatically, that the craft was only founded in the 17th century.

After the suppression of the Templars, initiation continued within the Rex Deus families and they soon began to pass on their initiatory teachings to carefully selected novices from outside the ranks of the families. This ultimately led to the creation of Freemasonry, Rosicrucianism, the Invisible College, and the Royal Society in England. This relatively small group of spiritual initiates transformed the thinking, art, commerce, social and religious systems of a continent, and made a significant contribution to the creation of an intellectual climate within which science, democracy and intellectual freedom could flourish.

> Nearly all the major intellectual figures of the period – including many of the founding fathers of modern science down to Newton's day – were deeply invested in… esoteric traditions, as if they believed there might lay hidden in these buried sources, secrets of human nature and the universe that were nowhere else to be found.[16]

Many of the intellectuals, artists and philosophers of the Renaissance were members of organizations that were the true heirs of the Knights Templar. These men initiated great advances in European culture, in art, religion, architecture, philosophy, literature, democracy, freedom and science. They were all deeply influenced by the hidden streams of spirituality which operated at horrendous risk under the ever-watchful gaze of repressive Church authorities.[17] In reconciling the ideals of spirituality and intellectual endeavour, we need to remember that, unlike the

Church who attempted to limit and control all access to knowledge, to the Gnostics and medieval craftmasons *Ars sina scienta nihil est* which translates as 'Art without knowledge is nothing'. In this context, 'gnosis', or spiritual knowledge is the quality to which they refer.

The mystery that surrounds the foundation of Freemasonry is complicated still further by the fact that the craft guilds of medieval masons throughout Europe each had their own different foundation myths, traditions, and rituals. Somehow and somewhere, the craftmasons were transformed into the precursors of modern Freemasonry, but the debate as to how, where, and when this happened has been prolonged and bitter. Debate over Masonic origins, even within Freemasonry itself, often degenerates into a modern version of *odium theologicum*, in which the character of the proponent is questioned more vigorously than their theories. However, open-minded researchers from both sides of the argument are pursuing their various theories in a manner that will eventually resolve the issue. I would submit that one family above all others had the means, the motive, and the opportunity to exert a transformative effect on the medieval craft guilds of operative masons, and used it to such good effect that they eventually developed into the craft of Speculative Freemasonry.

CHAPTER 19

The Craft of Freemasonry

T he English poet and mythologist Robert Graves, claims that Freemasonry began as a Sufi society and describes the Sufis as:

An ancient spiritual freemasonry whose origins have never been traced or dated although the characteristic Sufic signature is found in widely dispersed literature from at least the second millennium BCE.[1]

Graves goes on to recount how their hidden wisdom was passed down through the generations, from master to pupil as in so many other initiatory orders.[2] He then stated that Fremasonry first reached England during the reign of King Athelstan (924–39) and was then introduced into Scotland as a craft guild. In his Introduction to the first edition of Idris Shah's *The Sufis*, he not only describes the Sufic origins of the craftmasons and the important role played by the Templars in preserving their traditions, but also the much later transformation of the operative craft guilds into Freemasonry.

In stressing the role played by Sufi masters in the building of Solomon's Temple in ancient Israel, Graves echoes another Sufi tradition, for the Sufi's legendary mystical teacher, *el Khidir*, or the Verdant

One, is an amalgam of two prophetic figures of that time, namely Elijah and John the Baptist. The question thus arises: From where did these ancient Sufi Masons obtain their ancient knowledge?

The ancient Egyptian Pyramid Texts give us a clue. In ancient Egypt, the first initiates that are described in the Pyramid Texts are the *Shemsa-Hor*, the followers of Horus.[3] These were priestly initiates who transmitted an extraordinary body of knowledge from master to pupil down through the generations. The origin of this knowledge lay in the mysterious 'time of the Neteru', when the gods supposedly ruled Egypt immediately prior to the time of the earliest Pharaohs. These initiates were not necessarily kings, but immensely powerful and enlightened individuals carefully selected by an elite academy that established itself at the sacred site of Heliopolis-Giza in the era of Egyptian prehistory.[4] These initiates preserved the body of mystical knowledge, or gnosis, that was the foundation of Jewish mysticism in biblical times that was later transmitted into Europe by the Rex Deus families.

I have already described the level of sophistication and insight achieved by the three main branches of the Compagnonnage in medieval France and similar craft guilds operated in Germany, Spain and Italy – those who built in the Gothic style had a particularly close relationship with the Templar Order. Thus when the historian John Robinson suggests that fleeing Templar knights were aided in their escape by lodges of craftmasons, our only unresolved question is: Were these particular lodges that gave shelter and passage in this manner the Children of Master Jacques, who later gained the name of *les Compagnons Passants*? In Scotland, when the knights were instructed to go underground by King Robert the Bruce, Templar tradition was kept very much alive. Then, under the protection of the St Clairs of Roslin, these two mystical traditions arising from the Templars and the craftmasons were merged into one.

The gifted and insightful master masons who created Rosslyn Chapel took it for granted that their artwork should be beautiful. Mere beauty, however, was not enough. There had to be meaning, a deep spiritual meaning. For the medieval craftmasons who built Rosslyn Chapel, *ars sina scienta nihil est* – art without knowledge is nothing. In this context, the knowledge they referred to is gnosis, spiritual knowledge or mystical insight. Earl William laid the foundations for an organization of like-minded men who, from its inception, were taught through the means of time-honoured ritual, symbolism and allegory. This led the new initiates by progressive involvement in the spiritual world through the ascending degrees of initiation and thus brought the gnosis preserved by the Rex Deus families to a far wider audience. It is their symbolism that takes pride of place within Rosslyn Chapel.

THE APPRENTICE PILLAR

Few of the mysteries and legends that envelop Rosslyn Chapel are as well known as that surrounding the Apprentice Pillar. The story of the murdered apprentice, with its obvious reference to the initiation rituals of both the medieval guilds of craftmasons and the far older legend of Hiram Abif, master mason at the building of King Solomon's Temple, has developed immense symbolic and spiritual resonance for the worldwide brotherhood of Freemasonry. The legend of the murdered apprentice is summarised in these words:

> The master mason having received from his patron the model of a pillar of exquisite workmanship and design, hesitated to carry it out until he had been to Rome or some such foreign part, and seen the original. He went abroad, and in his absence, an apprentice, having dreamed the finished pillar, at once set to work and

carried out the design as it now stands, a perfect marvel of workmanship. The master mason on his return was so stung with envy that he asked who had dared to do it in his absence. On being told it was his own apprentice, he was so inflamed with rage and passion, that he struck him with his mallet, killed him on the spot, and paid the penalty for his rash and cruel act.[5]

This allegorical reference to the Hiram Abif legend is reinforced by the maul-marked face of the murdered apprentice who gazes fixedly across the chapel at the contorted features of the master mason who reputedly killed him. Another Masonic reference can be found on the south wall of the clerestory where one can see the carved face of the apprentice's widowed mother. The phrase: 'Who will come to the aid of the son of the widow', is one that has held particular resonance for members of the Masonic crafts and guilds from the times of ancient Egypt down to the present.

The Apprentice Pillar is one of three that separate the retro choir from the main body of the chapel. Next to it is the Journeyman's Pillar and then the sublime Master Mason's Pillar. According to Masonic tradition, every true lodge must to be supported by three grand pillars of deep symbolic significance. The Master Mason's Pillar represents wisdom or sacred gnosis; the Journeyman's Pillar symbolizes strength; the Apprentice Pillar signifies beauty. In the architectural terms pertinent to Masonic tradition, wisdom constructs, strength supports and beauty is designed to adorn. Furthermore, wisdom is ordained to discover, strength is made to bear and sustain, while beauty is made to attract. Yet, according to that tradition, all is for naught unless these pillars are erected upon the same rock or foundation that is named truth and justice. The qualities symbolized by these three pilars reflect the aspirations of every humble initiate of the spiritual path:

He who is as wise as a Perfect Master will not be easily injured by his own actions. Hath a person the strength which a Senior Warden represents he will bear and overcome every obstacle in life. He who is adorned like a Junior Warden with humility of spirit approaches nearer to the similitude of God than any other.[6]

Rosslyn Chapel was founded in 1446 and Freemasonry some centuries later. Yet, within the confines of the chapel, symbolic references to Masonic ritual, belief and practice abound and, as a result, there are few Masons today who do not regard Rosslyn Chapel as the unofficial core church of the worldwide Craft. In creating the arcane library in stone that is Rosslyn Chapel and in stimulating and strengthening the new speculative 'free' Masonic orders, Earl William has left us a lasting and vitally important spiritual legacy.

REX DEUS IN MASONIC RITUAL

Public knowledge of Freemasonry and its workings is limited to what has been published by the Craft, and circumscribed by vows of secrecy taken by individual members. Therefore, what I can reveal here only represents the tip of an iceberg. But even with these restrictions it is still possible to identify the Rex Deus origins of the Craft. The charge of idolatry, in the form of the worship of a head, that was levelled at the Knights Templar, as well as their ritual use of skulls, finds echoes within Freemasonry, for the Masonic historians Knight and Lomas informed their readers that 'Freemasonry around the world probably possesses some 50,000 skulls!'

The eventual support of English Freemasonry for the Hanoverian dynasty after the Stuarts were deposed has led to some strange anomalies. The United Grand Lodge of England actively discourages serious investigation into the origins of the Craft, as they wish to expunge from the record any reference to its Scottish origins and its alliance with the Stuart cause. Thus there was a thorough purging of Scottish rituals from English Masonic practice. Nonetheless, the dedicated work of the Masonic scholar Dimitrije Mitrinovic in the early years of the 20th century disclosed a high level of Rex Deus influence in some of these purged rituals.

Mitrinovic's library contains one book that records that the fourth degree, that of the Secret Master, is concerned with mourning someone who remains anonymous.[7] The ritual of this degree commemorates a time when the building of the Temple in Jerusalem was brought to a halt due to a tragedy. For this ritual the lodge is draped in black and white and illuminated by the light of 81 candles, and the jewel of the degree is inscribed with the letter 'Z', which refers to Zadok.[8] The Dead Sea Scrolls record that the sons of Zadok were the descendants of the high priests of the Temple who were known as the Righteous Seed and the Sons of Dawn. This ritual commemorates James the Just, who succeeded Jesus in the position of the Zadok, or Teacher of Righteousness, and is obviously a celebration of the ancient Jewish tradition of the hereditary transmission of holiness preserved by the Rex Deus families.

HIRAM ABIF

Freemasonic rituals claim that the Craft arose at the time of Hiram Abif, who was killed by a blow to the temple for his refusal to betray a secret, and this is an allegorical reference to the death of James the Just. Hiram was killed immediately prior to the completion of Solomon's Temple and, almost 1,000 years later, when work on the Herodian Temple was nearing completion, building was brought to a temporary standstill as a mark of respect for James, the brother of Jesus, who had just been ritually murdered. Thus, when Freemasons celebrate the ritual death of Hiram Abif, they are commemorating one of the founders of Rex Deus.[9]

Another suppressed degree of the Perfect Master, supposedly commemorates the reburial of the corpse of Hiram Abif. In this ritual, the lodge is lit by four groups of four candles, each placed at the cardinal points of the compass. The ritual recounts that King Solomon ordered Adoniram to build a tomb for Hiram Abif in the form of an obelisk of black-and-white marble. The entrance to the tomb was set between two pillars supporting a square lintel engraved with the letter 'J'. Thus the association between this degree and the death of James the Just is made explicit. For this ritual the lodge is draped in green; green and gold are the heraldic colours of the royal house of David. Green and gold are used again in the 15th degree, that of the Knight of the Sword and the Knight of the East, which celebrates the building of Zerubbabel's Temple.

Not surprisingly, the founding of the Knights Templar is also recorded in one suppressed ritual, that of 'The Knight of the East and West'. This ritual claims that this degree was created in 1118, when 11 knights took vows of secrecy, fraternity and discretion under the eagle of the Patriarch of Jerusalem. These knights include all nine founders of the Knights Templar, with the addition of Count Fulk d'Anjou and Count Hughes I of Champagne. In this rite, the presiding officer is known as the Most Equitable Most Sovereign Prince Master, and the High Priest supports him. Knight and Lomas claim that the Most Equitable Sovereign Prince Master was originally King Baldwin II of Jerusalem, and that the High Priest was most probably the Grandmaster of the Templar Order. I would suggest that it is far more likely that the High Priest represents the Patriarch of Jerusalem.

Among the suppressed degrees is the 20th degree, that of 'The

Grandmaster', which describes the destruction of the second Temple in Jerusalem by the Romans in 70 CE. Its ritual tells of the grief experienced by the brethren who were in the Holy Land and how they had to flee from their homeland with the intention of erecting a third temple that would be a spiritual rather than a physical edifice, which is a direct reference to the spiritual obligations of the Rex Deus families for whom the creation of this new 'Temple of God on Earth' is a sacred duty.

Enshrining Rex Deus secrets in a variety of degrees within the complex symbolism of Freemasonry is akin to a man on the run seeking refuge in a large and crowded city. It is similar to the device used by Earl William in randomly hiding a plethora of Templar and Rex Deus symbolism amongst the crowded and apparently confused collection of carvings in Rosslyn Chapel. Despite the vigorous attempts of the Hanoverian censors, the rituals used in these degrees have been recorded for posterity and may well still be in use in France and America.

The spiritual inspiration of Freemasonry gave the world the gift of the American Constitution and made a significant contribution to the establishment of the principles of *liberté, égalité and fraternité* that inspired the French Revolution and, ultimately, the transformation of despotism into democracy. Freemasonry played a major role in the campaign for the reunification of Italy through its influence on the Carbonari; both of the principal leaders of this revolutionary movement, Garibaldi and Mazzini, were active Freemasons. When their armies liberated Rome from the tyranny of the papacy, and gave a vibrant new reality to the old Visconti dream of a united kingdom of Italy, Pope Pius IX, stripped of all temporal power, began his lifelong exile in his self-imposed prison of the Vatican.

Pope Pius openly acknowledged that the Freemasons were the authors of his debasement and fulminated furiously against them in a series of encyclicals, papal bulls, and allocutions. Unlike many Masonic historians within the craft today, this aged pope was under no illusions as to the origins of the organization that had stripped him of all earthly power. For him, Freemasonry derived directly from the heretical Order of the Knights Templar whom he describes as being Gnostic from their inception and followers of the Johannite Heresy. Nor was Pius under any illusions as to the true purpose of the Masonic fraternity, for according to him, their aim was to destroy Holy Mother the Church. For him there was little difference between the true aim of the Rex Deus families, that of reforming the Church by bringing back the true teachings of Jesus, and the destruction of the Church that had propelled him to the dizzy heights of the papacy. Can we honestly doubt his views? It was Pius IX who first promulgated the doctrine of Papal Infallibility.

FREEMASONRY TODAY

Mention the word Freemasonry in any conversation and stand by for a jaundiced response, for Freemasonry has long been viewed with suspicion by the Church/state establishment throughout Europe; it is frequently targeted by the tabloid press with accusations of corruption; has been linked with worldwide Jewry as the source of all the world's evils by conspiracy theorists galore; and has been subject to condemnation by the Catholic Church for centuries. What is the true nature of Freemasonry? Is it an evil or dangerous vehicle of power and corruption, or an organization that, teaching through allegory and ritual, strives to 'make good men better'?

The manner of instruction used in Masonic allegory and ritual employs the symbolism of the tools of the earlier craftmasons, such as the square, compasses, rule, plumb line, mallet and chisels. Each new initiate is encouraged to apply these tools and work on the rough stone of his own being to reshape himself into the perfect Ashlar of enlightenment so that he can build the temple of God on earth in spiritual form. Thus these tools are used to knock off the rough edges of the 'stone' and create an improved and highly moral human being; in this manner the process of initiation through the ascending degrees of Freemasonry replicates the alchemical process of transmuting the base metal of humanity into the pure gold of spiritual enlightenment. It is one of the world's oldest secular fraternities, yet it is concerned with moral and spiritual values. Founded on the three great principles of Brotherly Love, Relief and Truth, it aims to bring together men of goodwill, regardless of background and differences, and make these good men better.

That these aims can be achieved is apparent when we study the formative political and social developments of the 18th and 19th centuries and discover that many leading members of the various movements for change were either Freemasons or men who had been influenced by Freemasonic thought. It is for these reasons that the emerging Craft, despite its strictly enforced ban on political and religious discussion within its lodges, acquired a reputation as being political in nature. Even more controversially, the overt participation of many Masons in the march of progress towards greater democratic involvement and representative government, ultimately led to the illusion that membership of the Freemasons was one of the essential keys to political power and commercial success in life.

This led to the conspiracy theorist's fantasy that Freemasonry, acting in concert with politicians of right, left and centre, and allied with the Jews, of course, were trying to establish a 'New World Order'. Some spurious credence was given to these fantasies by the illicit takeover of the Italian Lodge P2 that came to light in the 1980s. The P2 affair was an obscene example of political and financial corruption on a massive scale that allegedly involved the Mafia, the Vatican and the Banco

Ambrosiana, and led to the murder of the banker, Roberto Calvi in London. This unsavoury episode had absolutely nothing to do with the true spirit of Freemasonry, but simply illustrated the dangers that can arise when unscrupulous individuals take over a branch of a society with closed membership that routinely shrouds its affairs in secrecy.

RELIEF OR CHARITY

When Freemasonry first appeared in Scotland it created benevolent societies which were the first charitable institutions in Europe outside the direct control of the Church. In 1846, the Grand Lodge of Scotland established a body known as the Grand Lodge Charity Fund to administer relief among the membership. Another body, the Annuity Fund was established in 1888 to take care of the widows and elderly members. A more specific organization, the Orphan Annuity Fund was founded in 1917 and in 1957 the Grand Lodge of Scotland began purchasing a number of buildings that now act as old people's homes.

When the Grand Lodge was first established in London it set up its first charity fund. Charity, or relief, is one of the three great principles of Freemasonry and the various British Grand Lodges have practised it from their inception. In the early 19th century, that great Grandmaster of the United Grand Lodge of England, the Duke of Sussex, did not simply restrict himself to being active within Masonic charities he also became involved in various Jewish charitable organizations. The educational charities eventually evolved into the Royal Masonic Institution for Girls and the Royal Masonic Institution for Boys. The Royal Masonic Benevolent Institution was created in 1842 to provide annuities or residential care for elderly Freemasons, their widows and dependants. During the First World War, Freemasons founded a hospital in London and after the war this led to the building of the Royal

Masonic Hospital at Ravenscourt Park. Various trusts have been established to meet the needs of Masons, their widows and their children.

Freemasonry has often been accused of restricting its charitable activities solely to benefit its own membership yet, by as early as 1731, English lodges were raising money to assist poor emigrant families to settle the colony of Georgia. They also funded the apprenticeship of the orphaned sons of a number of operative Masons. All three of the Grand Lodges in the British Isles contributed funds to assist British prisoners of war in Europe and to help relieve the misery of French prisoners of war in England. In 1967, a trust with a capital sum of over £600,000 was established by the United Grand Lodge of England to fund medical research into both cancer and heart disease. British Masonic charities have purchased lifeboats for the Royal National Lifeboat Institute; founded a Chair of Gerontology at Cambridge University; funded research and welfare projects in the field of drug abuse; and given countless grants to a wide variety of medical charities as well as subscribing generously to disaster appeals.

In the United States of America, Freemasons have founded charitable institutions that provide scholarships, educational grants for young people in higher education and vocational grants, irrespective of whether or not the parents of such children have Masonic backgrounds. The track record of Masonic charities in the US when it comes to funding medical research, especially those branches of science investigating diseases of childhood, is truly exceptional. Vast sums have been raised to support children's hospitals that treat all children and not just those with a Masonic father; also funded are specialist burns units; clinics dealing with children affected by language disorders and handicapped children. American Freemasonry has funded research into children's illness, cancer, schizophrenia and both alcohol and drug abuse. In 1985, for example, Masonic charities of all jurisdictions contributed over 300 million dollars to support research, medical assistance and other community projects in which the vast majority of beneficiaries were ordinary citizens with no Masonic affiliation whatsoever.

While Freemasonry's charitable record is truly exemplary, that is but one of its main aims and objectives which are Brotherly Love, Relief and Truth. Just as charitable Relief is not restricted to Freemasons but instead extends the majority of its generosity horizontally and outwards into the wider communities that Freemasons serve, Brotherly Love and Truth are also lovingly dispersed far beyond the boundaries of the Craft, sometimes with an intensely personal effect.

As to those who claim that Freemasonry is allied to the Jews to create a new world order, I have yet to read of either a Freemason or a Jew being elected pope, emerging as the leader of any African nation, becoming head of state in any republic arising from the ashes of the Soviet Union or becoming president of an Islamic country anywhere in the world.

THE FRUITS OF INITIATION

The achievements of many individual Freemasons are viewed with pride, not merely by Freemasons but by humanity as a whole. The poetry and spiritual insight of Goethe, the musical genius of Mozart, the works of Jean Sibelius, Rudyard Kipling, Jonathan Swift (the author of *Gulliver's Travels*), W S Gilbert of Gilbert and Sullivan, Duke Ellington, Winston Spencer Churchill, Robbie Burns and Irving Berlin are just a small sample of the fruits of Freemasonry made manifest in the creative world.

What are the benefits of being a Freemason today? Companionship, conviviality and a heightened sense of purpose in life within a worldwide fraternity that brings together people of every class, race, creed and colour. The opportunity to gain spiritual insight from the constant repetition of age-old rituals and teachings imparted with solemnity and grace. Truly Freemasonry does make good men better. It makes them better people, more responsible citizens and more devout in their religious practices. Can you visualize any other organization that can bring this about with a mixed membership that is composed of Christians, Jews, Muslims, Hindus, Zoroastrians and Buddhists?

In a world assailed by fundamentalist terrorism and wars that are perceived as being religious in nature, have we not a deep-seated need for the principles of true Brotherhood, Tolerance, Justice and Peace? When fundamentalism, of either the Christian or Muslim variety, preaches hatred, intolerance, violence and death, do we not need some sanity? Freemasonry has created a tried and tested way to inspire men of goodwill to live in peace with one another, and serve their communities with true generosity of spirit. Masons have learned to ignore the differences that tend to divide mankind and both enhance and treasure the common humanity and spirituality that unites us all. In the Sufi tradition, men learn how to recognize the divine unity that exsists within all the diverse aspects of God's creation and, by serving that, they serve God. Freemasonry, like the Sufi path, is a true Brotherhood that is founded firmly on the one foundation of Truth and Justice. It exsists to serve humanity, irrespective of apparent divisions brought about by race, creed, sex or colour and perhaps that is the ultimate result of the search for the Holy Grail.

NOTES

Section 1 Gnosticism, Judaism, Christianity and Islam

Chapter 1 **The Parting of the Ways – Conflict Between Truth & Church Dogma**

1 Bauval, Robert & Hancock, Graham, *Keeper of Genesis*, William Heineman, London, 1996, p.203

2 Wilson, Colin, *From Atlantis to the Sphinx*, Virgin Books, London 1997, p.21

3 Freud, S, *Moses and Monotheism*, London, 1939

4 Sellin, E, *Moses and His Significance for Israelite-Jewish History*

5 *Encyclopaedia Brittannica*, London, 1956, Vol.5, p.721

6 Vermes, *Jesus the Jew*, p.79

7 Armstrong, Karen, *A History of Jerusalem*, p.116

8 Eisenman, Robert, *James the Brother of Jesus*, p.200

9 *Ibid* p133

10 Ezekiel 18,17–21

11 Zohar 59b on 'Noah'

12 Sanmell, S, *Judaism and Christian Beginnings*, OUP, New York, 1978, p.22

13 Josephus, *Antiquities*, book XVIII, Ch.1, 2–6.

14 Armstrong, Karen, *A History of Jerusalem*, p.121

15 Josephus, *Antiquities,* Book XVIII, Ch.1, v.5

16 Epiphanius Haeres, lxxviii

17 The Gospel According to St Mark, Ch.5 v.3

18 The Gospel According to St Matthew, Ch.13 v.55

19 *Homilies Clementines*

20 From The Gospel of Thomas as translated in *The Nag Hammadi Library* (revised edition), James Robinson ed.

21 St Paul's Epistle to the Galatians, Ch.2, v.9

22 Ranke-Heinemann, Ute, *Putting Away Childish Things*, p.173

23 In a series on St Paul on BBC Radio 4 broadcast

24 Wilson, A N *Jesus*, p.101

25 Hassnain, Fida, *A Search for the Historical Jesus*, p.84
26 The Gospel according to St John 2:1–5.
27 Hassnain, Fida, *A Search for the Historical Jesus*, p.84
28 The Gospel according to St John Ch.11, vs. 20, 28–9
29 The Gospel according to St Luke Ch.10, v.39
30 Published by Bear & Co.
31 The Gospels according to Matthew 26:7 & Mark 14:3.
32 Starbird, Margaret, *The Lady with the Alabaster Jar*, p.36
33 From The Gospel of Thomas as translated in *The Nag Hammadi Library* (revised edition), James Robinson ed.
34 Schonfield, Hugh, *Those Incredible Christians*, p.48
35 The Acts of the Apostles, Ch.2, v.22
36 St Paul's 1st Epistle to Timothy, Ch.1, vs.15–17
37 St Paul's Epistle to Titus, Ch.2, v.13
38 Gardner, Laurence, *The Bloodline of the Holy Grail*, p.154
39 Eusebius, *Ecclesiastical History*, III, xxvii, LCL, p.261
40 Eusebius, *Ecclesiastical History* II, xvii, LCL, p.53

Chapter 2 **St Paul, the Gospels & Emerging Christianity**

1 Acts of the Apostles, Ch.7, v.59, Ch.8 vs. 1–8, Ch.9, vs.1–2
2 Galatians, Ch.1, v.17
3 The Acts of the Apostles, Ch.24, v.14
4 *Ibid*, Ch.11
5 Eisenman, Robert, *The Dead Sea Scrolls and the First Christians*, p.146
6 The Community Rule, viii, 20ff
7 St Paul's Epistle to the Galatians, Ch.2, vs.11–13
8 St Paul's Epistle to Titus, Ch.2, v.13
9 St Paul's Epistle to the Romans, Ch.5, vs.6 & 8, Ch.14, v.9 & St Paul's Epistle to the Corinthians, Ch.15, v.3
10 Johnson, Paul, *A History of Christianity*, p.41
11 St Paul's First Epistle to the Corinthians, Ch.9, vs.24–26
12 Robert Eisenman devotes an entire chapter to Paul's attack on James citing a variety of sources – Chapter 16, *James the Brother of Jesus*. See also the *Pseudo-Clementine Recognitions*.
13 St Paul's Epistle to the Galatians, Ch. 5 vs. 1–4

14 I Corinthians, Ch 9, vs.24–26

15 An entire chapter in *James the Brother of Jesus* is devoted to this subject

16 Acts of the Apostles, Ch. 23 v.10

17 *Ibid*, vs.20–21

18 *Ibid*, Ch.23 vs. 23-24

19 St Paul's Epistle to the Romans, Ch. 16 vs 10-11

20 Wilson, A N, *Paul, the Mind of the Apostle,* p. 54

21 Acts of the Apostles, Ch. 24 vs.1-27

22 Josephus, *The Antiquities of the Jews*, Book XIV, Ch.8, v.3

23 Eisenman, Robert, *The Dead Sea Scrolls and the First Christians*, p.230

24 St Paul's Epistle to the Philippians, Ch.4, vs. 8-18

25 *Ibid*, v.21

26 Johnson, Paul, *A History of Christianity*, pp.3–4

27 St Paul's 1st Epistle to the Corinthians, Ch.9, vs.1–6

28 Burton, Mack, *The Lost Gospel*, p.4

29 Cited by Douglas Lockhart in *Jesus the Heretic*, p.230

30 Origen, vir ill 2 cited by Eisenman in *James the Brother of Jesus*, p.365

31 *History of the Church*, Hubert Jedin Ed.Vol I p.416

32 Johnson, Paul, *A History of Christianity*, p.76 & *A History of Heresy* by David Christie-Murray, p.1

33 Moore, David L, *The Christian Conspiracy*, pp. 45 & 62

34 Johnson, Paul, *A History of Christianity*, p.88

35 Moore, R I, *The Rise of a Persecuting Society,* p.12

36 Fox, Robin Lane, *Pagans and Christians*, p.656

37 Johnson, Paul, *A History of Christianity*, p.85

38 Fox, Matthew, *The Coming of the Cosmic Christ*, pp.31–2

39 Moore, R I, *The Formation of a Persecuting Society*, p.12

40 Ravenscroft & Wallace-Murphy, *The Mark of the Beast,* p.124

41 Christie-Murray, David, *A History of Heresy*, p.1

42 Johnson, Paul, *A History of Christianity*, pp.116–17

43 Cardinal Ratzinger speaking in 1990, cited in Baigent & Leigh's *The Dead Sea Scrolls Deception*, p.191

44 Gardner, Laurence, *Bloodline of the Holy Grail*, p.159

45 Wallace-Murphy, Hopkins & Simmans, *Rex Deus*, p.97
46 Albany, HRH Prince Michael of, & Salhab, Wakid Amine, *The Knights Templar of the Middle East*, p.7
47 Wallace-Murphy & Hopkins, *Custodians of Truth*, p.85
48 Hopkins, Simmans & Wallace-Murphy, *Rex Deus*, p.100
49 Ravenscroft & Wallace-Murphy, *The Mark of the Beast*, p.79
50 Wallace-Murphy, Tim, *The Templar Legacy and the Masonic Inheritance within Rosslyn Chapel*, p.12

Chapter 3 The Rise of Islam & its Empire

1 Armstrong, Karen, *A History of God*, pp.156–7
2 The Preliminary Discourse by George Sale used as an introduction to his translation of the Koran
3 Armstrong, Karen, *A History of God*, p.159
4 *Larouse Encyclopaedia of Ancient and Medieval History*, p.260
5 Hattstein, Marcus, & Delius, Peter (eds) *Islam Art & Architecture*, p.12
6 Armstrong, Karen, *A History of God*, p.159
7 Hattstein, Marcus, & Delius, Peter (eds) *Islam Art & Architecture*, p.12
8 Armstrong, Karen, *A History of God*, p.159
9 Beinhart, Chaim, *Atlas of Medieval Jewish History*, p.19
10 *Ibid*
11 Armstrong, Karen, *A History of God*, p.155
12 *Ibid*, pp.158–9
13 *Ibid*, pp.160–1
14 The Holy Koran 96:1 (Muhammed Asad trans who added the words in square brackets for clarity in English)
15 Ibn Ishak, Sira 153, in *A Life of Muhammed*, (Guillaume trans)
16 Armstrong, Karen, *A History of God*, p.162
17 Hattstein, Marcus & Delius, Peter (eds) *Islam Art & Architecture*, p.14
18 Wallace-Murphy & Hopkins, *Custodians of Truth*
19 *Ibid*
20 Albany, HRH Prince Michael of & Salhab, Walid Amine, *The Knights Templar of the Middle East*, p.12

21 Hattstein, Marcus, & Delius, Peter (eds) *Islam Art & Architecture*, p.23

22 *Ibid*, p.14

23 *Larouse Encyclopaedia of Ancient and Medieval History*, p.261

24 Cited by Karen Armstrong in *A History of God*, p.176

25 Armstrong, Karen, *A History of God*, p.180

26 *Ibid*, pp.177–8

27 Hattstein, Marcus, & Delius, Peter (eds) *Islam Art & Architecture*, p.27

28 Barnavi, Eli (ed) *A Historical Atlas of the Jewish People*, p.80

29 *Ibid*, p.81

30 *Ibid*, p.82

31 *Ibid*, p.82

32 De Lange, Nicholas, *Atlas of the Jewish World*, p.39

33 Fossier, Robert (ed) *The Cambridge Illustrated History of the Middle Ages*, p.204

34 *Ibid*, p.246

35 Hattstein, Marcus, & Delius, Peter (eds) *Islam Art & Architecture*, p.92

36 *Ibid*, p.90

37 *Larouse Enclyclopedia of Medieval History*, p.271

38 Holmes, George (ed) *The Oxford Illustrated History of Medieval Europe*, p.4

39 *Ibid*

40 Hattstein, Marcus, & Delius, Peter (eds) *Islam Art & Architecture*, p.208

41 Fossier, Robert (ed) *The Cambridge Illustrated History of the Middle Ages*, p.200

42 Ravenscroft & Wallace-Murphy, *The Mark of the Beast*, p.24

43 Hattstein, Marcus, & Delius, Peter (eds) *Islam Art & Architecture*, p.209

44 Beinhart, Chaim, *Atlas of Medieval Jewry*, p.36

45 Hattstein, Marcus, & Delius, Peter (eds) *Islam Art & Architecture*, p.214

46 Goodwin, Geoffrey, *Islamic Spain*, p.10

47 *Ibid*, p.5

48   Albany, HRH Prince Michael of & Salhab, Walid Amine,
     The Knights Templar of the Middle East, p.45
49   Goodwin, Geoffrey, *Islamic Spain*, p.12
50   *Ibid*, pp.42–3
51   Albany, HRH Prince Michael of & Salhab, Walid Amine,
     The Knights Templar of the Middle East,
52   Holmes, George, (ed) *The Oxford Illustrated History of Medieval
     Europe*, p.61
53   Ravenscroft & Wallace-Murphy, *The Mark of the Beast*, p.125
54   Hattstein, Marcus, & Delius, Peter (eds) *Islam Art & Architecture*,
     p.216
55   Armstrong, Karen, *Muhammad*, pp.23–4.
56   *Ibid*, p.22
57   Holmes, George (ed) *The Oxford Illustrated History of Medieval
     Europe*, p.15
58   Barnavi, Eli, *A Historical Atlas of the Jewish People*, p.100
59   Akbar, S W Ahmed, *Discovering Islam*, p.4
60   Goodwin, Geoffrey, *Islamic Spain*, p.43
61   Barnavi, Eli, *A Historical Atlas of the Jewish People*, p.96
62   Eisenman, Robert, *James the Brother of Jesus*, p.200
63   Wallace-Murphy, Tim, *The Templar Legacy and the Masonic
     Inheritance within Rosslyn Chapel*, p.16
64   Wallace-Murphy & Hopkins, *Rosslyn: Guardian of the Secrets of the
     Holy Grail*, p.83
65   Robert Graves in his Introduction to the first English Edition of
     The Sufis by Idries Shah
66   Maimonides, Obedyah, *The Treatise of the Pool*, Octagon Press,
     1981, p.ix
67   Holmes, George, (ed) *The Oxford Illustrated History of Medieval
     Europe*, p.208
68   Ward, Colin, *Chartres the Making of a Miracle*, p.8
69   Wallace-Murphy & Hopkins, *Custodians of Truth*, pp.113–14

Chapter 4 **The Dark Ages in Christian Europe – From the Fall of the Roman Empire to the First Crusade**

1   Johnson, Paul, *A History of Christianity*, p.135–8
2   Wallace-Murphy, Tim, *The Templar Legacy and Masonic Inheritance within Rosslyn Chapel*, p.13
3   Bede, *A History of the English Church and People*, p.66
4   *Trias Thermaturga*, p.156b
5   Malmes, *History of the Kings*, pp.19–20
6   Elder, Isabel Hill, *Celt, Druid & Culdee*
7   Albany, HRH Prince Michael of, *The Forgotten Monarchy of Scotland*, p.30
8   *Ibid*, p.19
9   Elder, Iasabel Hill, *Celt, Druid & Culdee*, pp.131–132 & 134
10 Dunford, Barry, *The Holy Land of Scotland*
11 Hopkins, Simmans & Wallace-Murphy, *Rex Deus*, p.105
12 *Ibid*
13 Stein, Walter, Johannes, *The Ninth Century, World History in the Light of the Holy Grail*, p.28 see also Ravenscroft, Trevor, *The Spear of Destiny*, pp.206–7
14 Ravenscroft, Trevor, *The Spear of Destiny*, p.45
15 Zuckerman, A J, *A Jewish Princedom in Feudal France 768-900*, Columbia University Press, 1972, p.37
16 *Ibid*, p.49
17 Roth, Cecil, *A Short History of the Jewish People,* p.165
18 Zuckerman, A J, *A Jewish Princedom in Feudal France 768-900,* Columbia University Press, 1972, p.60
19 Beinhart, Haim, *Atlas of Medieval Jewish History*, p.23
20 Zuckerman, A J, *A Jewish Princedom in Feudal France 768-900,* Columbia University Press, 1972, p.34
21 *Ibid*, p.112
22 *Tractatus adversus Judaeorum inveteratam duritiem*, PL CLXXXIX col.560
23 Adler, M N, *The Itinerary of Benjamin of Tudela*, 459–467
24 Saige, G, *Les Juifs du Languedoc*, pp.272–93 & Regne, *Juifs de Narbonne,* pp.127–32

25 Hodgekin, T, *The Barbarian Invasion of the Roman Empire*, Vol. VIII, *The Frankish Empire*, p.127

26 Gibbon, Edward, *The Decline and Fall of the Roman Empire*, Vol. VI, p.170

27 Fossier, Robert (ed) *The Middle Ages*, p.484

28 *Ibid*, pp.426–7

29 Bridge, Anthony, *The Crusades*, p.16

30 *Ibid*, p.17

31 Fletcher, Richard, *The Cross and the Crescent*, p.50

32 Runciman, Stephen, *A History of the Crusades*, vol I, p.88

33 Fletcher, Richard, *The Cross and the Crescent*, pp.42–4

34 *Ibid*, p.44

35 *Ibid*, p.82

36 Bridge, Anthony, *The Crusades*, p.18

37 Mansi, *Concilia*, vol.xix, pp.89–90

38 *Ibid*, pp.483–8

39 Bridge, Anthony, *The Crusades*, p.18

40 Mansi, *Concilia*, vol.xix, pp.827–8

41 Runciman, Stephen, *A History of the Crusades*, vol I, p.87

Section 2 The Knights Templar

Chapter 5 **A Family Affair – the Conspiracy that Led to the Foundation of the Knights Templar**

1 Ward, Colin, *Chartres the Making of a Miracle*, p.7

2 Ravenscroft & Wallace-Murphy, *The Mark of the Beast*, p.75

3 Article entitled '*Une Vie par réforme l'église*' by Michel Kluber published in the journal *Bernard de Clairvaux*, les editions de l'Argonante

4 Wallace-Murphy & Hopkins, *Rosslyn: Guardian of the Secrets of the Holy Grail*, p.95

5 Knowles, D, *Christian Monasticism*, p.78

6 Querido, Renée, *The Golden Age of Chartres*, Floris Books, Edinburgh, 1987, p.84

7   Article entitled '*Une Vie par réforme l'église*' by Michel Kluber published in the journal *Bernard de Clairvaux*, les editions de l'Argonante

8   St Clair, L-A de, *Histoire Généalogique de la Famille de St Clair*

9   Barnavi, Levi, *A Historical Atlas of the Jewish People*, p.78

10 *Ibid.* pp.98–9

11 Wallace-Murphy, Tim, *The Templar Legacy and the Masonic Inheritance within Rosslyn Chapel*, p.18

12 Albany, HRH Prince Michael of & Salhab, Walid Amine, *The Knights Templar of the Middle East*, p.69

13 Baigent, Leigh & Lincoln, *The Holy Blood and the Holy Grail*, p.61

14 Runciman, Stephen, *A History of the Crusades*, vol.I, pp.90–1

15 Fletcher, Richard, *The Cross and the Crescent*, p.72

16 Runciman, Stephen, *A History of the Crusades*, vol.I, p.37

17 *Ibid*, p.49

18 *Ibid*, p.50

19 *The Chronicles of the Crusades*, p.20

20 Bridge, Anthony, *The Crusades*, p.44

21 *Ibid*, pp.39–41

22 Fulcher of Chartres, 1, iii, pp.130–8; & Robert the Monk, 1, i-ii, pp.727–9

23 Bridge, Anthony, *The Crusades*, p.45–5

24 *Ibid*, p.27

25 Fulcher of Chartres, 1, iii, pp.130–8; & Robert the Monk, 1, i-ii, pp.727–9

26 *The Chronicles of the Crusades*, pp.64–5

27 Bridge, Anthony, *The Crusades*, p.33

28 *Ibid*, p.60

29 *Ibid*, p.54

30 *Ibid*, p.71

31 *The Chronicles of the Crusades*, p.60

32 Bridge, Anthony, *The Crusades*, p.95

33 *Gesta Francorum*, x 38 pp.202–4

34 Letter from Daimbert of Pisa and other leaders to the pope

35 Bridge, Anthony, *The Crusades*, p.111

36   Ibn al Qalānisī, *Continuation of the Chronicle of Damascus: the Damascus Chronicle of the Crusades*, (H A R Gibb trans.) London, 1932

37   *Gesta Francorum* xx, p.204–6

38   Runciman, Stephen, *A History of the Crusades*, vol.I, p,287

39   Bridge, Anthony, *The Crusades*, p.115

40   Raymond of Aguillers, xx, p.301

41   Nicholson, Helen, *The Knights Templar, A New History*, p.19

42   Smail, R C, *Crusading Warfare 1097–1193*, CUP, 1956

43   *Ibid*, p.130

44   Seward, Desmond, *The Monks of War*, p.13

45   Riley-Smith, Jonathan, *The First Crusade and the Idea of Crusading*, London, Athlone Press, 1986

46   Nicholson, Helen, *The Knights Templar, a New History*, p.20

47   Cited by Malcolm Barber in *The New Knighthood*, CUP, 1994, p.3

48   *Ibid*, p.6

49   Martin, Sean, *The Knights Templar, The History and Myths of the Legendary Military Order*, p.24

50   Leroy, Thierry, *Hugues de Payns, Chevalier Champenois, Fondateur de L'Ordre des Templiers*, Editions de la Maison du Boulanger, p.34–5

51   Laurent, J (ed), *Cartulaire de Molésme*, 230 Pp 214, & Leroy, Thierry, *Hughues de Payns, Chevalier Champenois, Fondateur de L'Ordre des Templiers*, Editions de la Maison du Boulanger, p.37

52   Robinson, John, *Dungeon, Fire and Sword*, p.36

53   Gardner, Laurence, *The Bloodline of the Holy Grail*, p.256

54   Albany, HRH Prince Michael of & Salhab, Walid Amine *The Knights Templar of the Middle East*, p.66

55   *Ibid*, p.66

56   Seward, Desmond, *The Monks of War*, p.14

57   William of Tyre, *Historia rerum in partibus transmarinus gestarum*, bk.19, Ch.VII also de Vitry, Jacques *Histori orientalis seu Hieroslymitana* which details the gifts to the Templars.

58   Martin, Sean, *The Knights Templar: The History and Myths of the Legendary Military Order*, p.15

59 St Bertin, Simon de '*Gesta abbatum Sancti Bertini Sithensiu*' vol.13, p.649

60 Nicholson, Helen, *The Knights Templar, a New History*, pp.23–4

61 *Ibid*, p.27

62 *Ibid*, p.29

63 Ivo, Bishop of Chartres, Epistolae no.245 in Pl vol.162, cols 251–3

64 Albany, HRH Prince Michael of & Salhab, Walid Amine, *The Knights Templar of the Middle East*, p.66

65 Baigent, Leigh & Lincoln, *The Holy Blood and the Holy Grail*

66 Leroy, Thierry, *Hughues de Payns, Chevalier Champenois, Fondateur de L'Ordre des Templiers*, Editions de la Maison du Boulanger, pp.107–8

67 Brublee, *Histoire de l'abbaye de Sainte-Colombe*

68 Hopkins, Simmans & Wallace-Murphy, *Rex Deus*, p.112

69 *Ibid*,

70 Albany, HRH Prince Michael of & Salhab, Walid Amine, *The Knights Templar of the Middle East*, p.67

71 Hopkins, Simmans & Wallace-Murphy, *Rex Deus*, p.113

72 *Ibid*, p.114

73 Robinson, John, J, *Dungeon Fire and Sword*, p.31

74 Addison, Charles, G, *The Knights Templar*, p.5

75 Knight, C & Lomas R, *The Second Messiah*, p.73

76 Lamy, Michel, *Les Templiers:Ces Grand Seigneurs aux Blanc Manteaux*, Bordeux 1997, p.26

77 Nicholson, *The Knights Templar*, p.22

78 Anon., *Secret Societies of the Middle Ages*, p.190 & Nicholson, *The Knights Templar*, p.26

Chapter 6 **The Early Years & the Council of Troyes**

1 Hancock, Graham, *The Sign and the Seal*, pp.94 & 99 see also Ravenscroft & Wallace-Murphy, *The Mark of the Beast*, p.52

2 Hancock, Graham, *The Sign and the Seal* pp.49–51

3 Ravenscroft & Wallace-Murphy, *The Mark of the Beast*, p.52

4 Robinson, John, J, *Dungeon, Fire and Sword*, p.37

5 *Ibid*, p.38

6 *Ibid*, p.37
7 Cited by Malcolm Barber in *The New Knighthood, A History of the Order of the Temple*, CUP 1994, p.13
8 Bordonove, Georges, *La vie quotidienne des Templiers*, p.29
9 Anon., *Secret Societies of the Middle Ages*, p.195
10 Martin, Sean, *The Knights Templar, the History and Myths of the Legendary Military Order*, p.16
11 Nicholson, *Opus cit.* p.96
12 Anon. *Secret Societies of the Middle Ages*, p.199
13 Lees, B A, *Records of the Templars in England in the Twelfth Century*, London, 1935
14 Seward, Desmond, *The Monks of War*, p.16
15 Bernard of Clairvaux, *De Laude Novae Militiae*, c.1128
16 *Ibid*
17 *Ibid*
18 Seward, Desmond, *The Monks of War*, p.15

Chapter 7 – **The Order's Commercial Activities**

1 Melville, M, *Les Débuts de l'ordre du Temple*, p.26
2 Selwood, Dominic, *Knights of the Cloister*, p.61
3 *Ibid*, p.62
4 Nicholson, Helen, *The Knights Templar, A New History*, p.185
5 Read, Piers Paul, *The Templars*, p.182
6 Nicholson, Helen, *The Knights Templar, A New History*, pp.181–3
7 Lees, B A, *Records of the Templars*, pp.67–8
8 Nicholson, Helen, *The Knights Templar, A New History*, p.190
9 Holt, *Mills*, p.73
10 Pringle, *Secular Buildings*
11 *Ibid*
12 Bruno, S T, *Templar Organization*, (Privately published) p.65
13 *Ibid*, p.165
14 Read, Piers Paul, *The Templars*, 181
15 The original document, the Codex Calaxtinus, otherwise known as the *Liber Sancto Jacobi*, can be found in the archives of St Jaques de Compostela.

16 Wallace-Murphy, Tim, *The Templar Legacy and the Masonic Inheritance within Rosslyn Chapel*

17 Nicholson, Helen, *The Knights Templar, A New History*, p.192

18 *Ibid*

19 Barber, Malcolm, *Supplying the Crusader States*, p.324. Article reprinted in Malcolm Barber, ed., *Crusaders and Heretics, Twelfth to Fourteenth Centuries* (Variorum, 1995)

20 Nicholson, Helen, *The Knights Templar, A New History*, p.194 & Barber, Malcolm, *Supplying the Crusader States*, pp.324–6

21 Jay, Peter, *Road to Riches*, p.118

22 Nicholson, Helen, *The Knights Templar, A New History*, p.188

23 *Ibid*, pp.191–2

24 Martin, Sean, *The Knights Templar: The History and Myths of the Legendary Military Order*, p.47

25 Foray, *The Templars in the Corona of Aragon*, p.349

26 Martin, Sean, *The Knights Templar: The History and Myths of the Legendary Military Order*, p.48

27 *Ibid*

28 *Ibid*, p.50

29 *Ibid*, p.49

Chapter 8 – **Military Activities in Europe**

1 Bull, Marcus, *Knightly Piety and the Lay Response to the First Crusade*, OUP 1993, pp.72–8

2 Nicholson, Helen, *The Knights Templar, A New History*, p.91

3 Fletcher, Richard, *The Cross and the Crescent*, p.112

4 Fossier, Robert, ed, *The Cambridge Illustrated History of the Middle Ages*, vol.III, pp.65–6

5 Read, Piers Paul, *The Templars*, p.108

6 Nicholson, Helen, *The Templars, A New History*, pp.95–6

7 Forey, *The Templars in the Corona of Aragon*, p.22

8 *Ibid*, pp.21–3

9 Lomax, D W, *La Orden de Santiago 1170–1275*

10 Nicholson, Helen, *The Templars a New History*, p.105

11 Jackson, Peter, 'The Crusade against the Mongols', *Journal of Ecclesiastical History*, 42 (1991) pp.1–18

12 Aué, Michèle, *The Cathars*, p.3
13 Stoyanov, Yuri, *The Hidden Tradition in Europe*, p.159
14 Costen, Michael, *The Cathars and the Albigensian Crusade*, pp.32–4
15 *Ibid*, pp.37–9
16 *Ibid*, p.59
17 de Vries, Simon, *Cathars, Country Customs and Castles*, p.2
18 Aué, Michèle, *The Cathars*, p.13 & Guirdham, Arthur, *The Great Heresy*, p.15
19 Guirdham, Arthur, *The Great Heresy*, p.16
20 Aué, Michèle, *The Cathars*, p.3
21 Stoyanov, Yuri, *The Hidden Tradition in Europe*, p.158
22 *Ibid*, p.164
23 Guirdham, Arthur, *The Great Heresy*, p.18
24 Stoyanov, Yuri, *The Hidden Tradition in Europe*, p.156
25 Bernard of Clairvaux's letter cited in Wakefield & Evans, *Heresies of the Middle Ages*, pp.122–4
26 Stoyanov, Yuri, *The Hidden Tradition in Europe*, p.156
27 Costen, Michael, *The Cathars and the Albigensian Crusade*, p.58
28 de Vries, Simon, *Cathars, Country Customs and Castles*, p.2
29 Costen, Michael, *The Cathars and the Albigensian Crusade*, pp.112–14
30 Serrus, Georges, *The Land of the Cathars*, p.15
31 Aué, Michèle, *The Cathars*, p.15
32 Costen, Michael, *The Cathars and the Albigensian Crusade*, p.123
33 Caesarius of Heisterbach, vol. II, pp.296–8
34 Guébin et Moisoineuve, *Histoire Albigeoise de Pierre des Vaux Cernay*
35 Costen, Michael, *The Cathars and the Albigensian Crusade*, p.125
36 Guirdham, Arthur, *The Great Heresy*, p.63
37 Costen, Michael, *The Cathars and the Albigensian Crusade*, p.132
38 Aué, Michèle, *The Cathars*, p.12
39 Serrus, Georges, *The Land of the Cathars*, p.26
40 Costen, Michael, *The Cathars and the Albigensian Crusade*, p.151
41 Guirdham, Arthur, *The Great Heresy*, p.69
42 Costen, Michael, *The Cathars and the Albigensian Crusade*, p.160
43 Stoyanov, Yuri, *The Hidden Tradition in Europe*, p.173

44 Reznikov, Raymonde, *Cathars et Templiers*
45 Information supplied by Nicole Dawe of the Abraxus Templar Research Group.
46 Picknett & Prince, *The Templar Revelation*, p.104

Chapter 9 **The Templars in the Holy Land**

1 Hopkins, Marilyn, *The Enigma of the Templars*
2 Forey, Alan, *Military Orders and the Crusades*, Aldershot, Variorum, 1994
3 Bridge, Anthony, *The Crusades*, p.127
4 *Ibid*, p.125
5 *Ibid*, p.131
6 Fletcher, Richard, *The Cross and the Crescent*, p.86
7 *Ibid*, p.87
8 Cited by Francesco Gabrielli, *Arab Historians of the Crusades*, p.73
9 Fletcher, Richard, *The Cross and the Crescent*, p.91
10 Runciman, Stephen, *A History of the Crusades*, vol II p.319
11 Fletcher, Richard, *The Cross and the Crescent*, p.85
12 Runciman, Stephen, *A History of the Crusades*, vol.II, p.318
13 *Ibid*, p.320
14 Cited by Malouf in *The Crusades through Arab Eyes*, p.129
15 Cited by Malcolm Barber in *The New Knighthood*, p.93
16 Read, Piers Paul, *The Templars*, p.133
17 Prawer, Joshua, *The Latin Kingdom of Jerusalem*
18 Hopkins, Marilyn, *The Enigma of the Templars*
19 *Ibid*
20 Nicholson, Helen, *The Knights Templar, A New History*, p.54
21 Hopkins, Marilyn, *The Enigma of the Templars*
22 Nicholson, Helen, ed., *The Military Orders*, Vol.2, pp.89–109
23 William of Tyre, Chronique, Huygens, R B, ed., Turnholt, Brepols, 1986
24 Riley-Smith, Jonathan, 'The Templars and the Castle of Tortosa in Syria; an unknown document concerning the acquisition of the fortress', *English Historical Review*, 84 (1969)
25 Hopkins, Marilyn, *The Enigma of the Templars*

26 Mayer, Hans Eberhard, *The Crusades*, John Gillingham trans.
     OUP, 1988, pp.278–9
27 Nicholson, Helen, *The Knights Templar, A New History*, p.54
28 Hopkins, Marilyn, *The Enigma of the Templar*.
29 Seward, Desmond, *The Monks of War*, p.24
30 *Ibid*
31 Hopkins Marilyn, *The Enigma of the Templars*
32 *Ibid*
33 *Monumenta Germaniae Historia Scriptores*, Vol.6, p.401
34 Hopkins, Marilyn, *The Enigma of the Templars*

Chapter 10 **Saladin & the Decline of the Crusader States**

 1 Robinson, John, J, *Dungeon, Fire and Sword*, pp.323–4
 2 Bridge, Anthony, *The Crusades*, p.170
 3 *Ibid* pp.174–5
 4 *Ibid*, pp.179–80
 5 *Ibid*, p.181
 6 Seward, Desmond, *Monks of War*, pp.31–2
 7 The *Chronicles of the Crusades*, p.152
 8 *Estoire d'Eracles Historiens Orientaux*, vol. II, p.34
 9 Runciman, Stephen, *A History of the Crusades*, vol.II, pp.454–6
10 Read, Piers Paul, *The Templars*, p.159
11 Fletcher, Richard, *The Cross and the Crescent*, p.88
12 Cited by Regan, Geoffrey, *Lionhearts: Saladin and Richard I*, p.91
13 *Gesta Francorum et aliorum Hierosolimitanorum*, trans. Hill,
     Rosalind, Edinburgh, 1962, p.21
14 de Joinville, *Life of St Louis*, p.245
15 Bridge, Anthony, *The Crusades*, p.202–3
16 Runciman, Stephen, *A History of the Crusades*, vol.II p.466
17 *Ibid*, p.467
18 Hopkins, Marilyn, *The Enigma of the Templars*
19 Read, Piers Paul *The Templars*, p.162
20 Barber, Malcolm, *The New Knighthood*, p.117
21 Smail, R C, *Crusading Warfare*, p.38
22 Regan, Geoffrey, *Lionhearts: Saladin and Richard I*, pp.155–6
23 Runciman, Stephen *A History of the Crusades*, Vol.3, p.54

24 Bridge, Anthony, *The Crusades*, p.226
25 Hopkins, Marilyn, *The Enigma of the Templars*
26 Regan, Geoffrey, *Lionhearts: Saladin and Richard I*, p.218
27 Bridge, Anthony, *The Crusades*, p.202–3
28 Nicholson, Helen, *The Knights Templar, A New History*, p.68
29 Read, Piers Paul, *The Templars*, p.198
30 Cited by Malcolm Barber in *The New Knighthood*, p.130
31 Read, Piers Paul, *The Templars*, p.204
32 *Ibid*, p.206
33 Hopkins, Marilyn, *The Enigma of the Templars*
34 Read, Piers Paul, *The Templars*, p.208
35 Nicholson, Helen, *The Knights Templar, A New History*, p.82
36 Read, Piers Paul, *The Templars*, p.219

Chapter 11 **The Templars Lose Their** *Raison d'etre*

1   Nicholson, Helen, *The Knights Templar, A New History*, p.85
2   Read, Piers Paul, *The Templars*, p.240
3   *Ibid*, p.241
4   Nicholson, Helen, *Templars, Hospitallers*, p.127
5   Runciman, Stephen, *A History of the Crusades*, vol.3, p.420
6   Cronica, S, Petri Erfordiensis moderna, O Holder-Eggar ed. *Monumenta Germaniae Historica Scriptores*, Vol. 30, pp.424–5
7   Read, Piers Paul, *The Templars*, p.242
8   Nicholson, Helen, *The Knights Templar, A New History*, p.87
9   Schein, Silvia, *Fideles Crucis, The Papacy, the West and the Recovery of the Holy Land 1274–1314*, OUP, 1991, pp.74–6 & 114–28
10 Nicholson, Helen, *The Knights Templar, A New History*, p.52
11 Description Terrae Sanctae in Patrologia Latina; *Patrologus Cursus Completeus, Series Latina*, Vol.155, col.1087
12 Martin, Sean, *The Knights Templar: The History and Myths of the Legendary Military Order*, pp.46–7
13 Nicholson, Helen, *The Knights Templar, A New History*, p.63
14 *Ibid*, pp.63–4
15 Rodger of Howden, *Chronica*, Vol.3, p.183
16 Matthew Paris, *Chronica majora*
17 Smail, R C, *Crusading Warfare*, CUP, 1995, p.43

18 Martin, Sean, *The Knights Templar: The History and Myths of the Legendary Military Order*, p.59
19 Read, Piers Paul, *The Templars*, p.147
20 *Ibid*
21 Partner, Peter, *The Murdered Magicians, The Templars and their Myth*, OUP, 1982, p.30
22 Nicholson, Helen, *The Knights Templar, A New History*, p.161
23 Burns, R I, *The Crusader Kingdom of Valencia, Reconstruction on a Thirteenth Century Frontier*, 2 vols, Harvard UP, Vol.I, p.194
24 Nicholson, Helen, *The Knights Templar, A New History*, p.163
25 Barber, Malcolm, *The New Knighthood*, pp.296–7
26 Nicholson, Helen, *The Knights Templar, A New History*, pp.168–9
27 Barber, Malcolm, *The Trial of the Templars*, p.11

Chapter 12 **Philippe le Bel, the Templars & the Inquisition**

1 Robinson, John J, *Dungeon, Fire and Sword*, p.405
2 Barber, Malcolm, *The Trial of the Templars*, p.24
3 de Serres, L L, Borelli, *Les Variations monétaires sous Philippe le Bel*, 1902, pp.293–4
4 Ravenscroft & Wallace-Murphy, *The Mark of the Beast*, p.52
5 Barber, Malcolm, *The Trial of the Templars*, p.40
6 Beinhart, Haim, *Atlas of Medieval Jewish History*, p.59
7 Knight & Lomas, *The Second Messiah*, pp.127–8
8 *Ibid*, p.133
9 Currer-Brigs, Noel, *The Shroud and the Grail*, p.95
10 Bussel, F W, *Religious Thought and Heresy in the Middle Ages*
11 Currer-Brigs, *opus cit*, p.96
12 Barber, Malcolm, *The Trial of the Templars*, p.47
13 *Ibid*, p.45
14 Baigent, Leigh & Lincoln, *The Holy Blood and the Holy Grail*, p.46
15 Lizerand, *Le Dossier de l'Affaire des Templiers*, p.16
16 Barber, *The Trial of the Templars*, p.45
17 *Ibid*, p.47
18 *Ibid*, pp.47–8
19 Papal Bull of Innocent IV 1252 *Ad extirpanda*

20 Burman, Edward, *The Inquisition: The Hammer of Heresy*, p.62
21 Baigent and Leigh, *The Inquisition*, pp.27–8
22 Johnson, Paul, *A History of Christianity*, p.254
23 Cited by Peter de Rosa in *Vicars of Christ*, p.228
24 Johnson, Paul, *A History of Christianity*, pp.253–5
25 Lea, H C, *The Inquisition in the Middle Ages*, NY, 1955
26 de Rosa, Peter, *Vicars of Christ*, p.249
27 Baigent and Leigh, *The Inquisition*, pp.20–1
28 Stoyanov, Yuri, *The Hidden Tradition in Europe*, p.178
29 Burman, Edward, *The Inquisition: The Hammer of Heresy*, p.39
30 Papal Bull of Pope Innocent IV, *Super Extirpatione*
31 Burman, Edward, *The Inquisition: The Hammer of Heresy*, pp.42–3
32 Lea, H C, *The Inquisition in the Middle Ages*, NY, 1955
33 Johnson, Paul *A History of Christianity*, p.253
34 Lockhart, Douglas, *The Dark Side of God*, p.73
35 Burman, Edward, *The Inquisition: The Hammer of Heresy*, pp.62–5
36 Baigent and Leigh, *The Inquisition*, pp.34–6
37 *Ibid*, pp.31-2
38 *Ibid*, pp.34-6
39 *Ibid*
40 Ahmed, Rollo, *The Black Art*, 1971
41 Baigent and Leigh, *The Inquisition*, p.xvii
42 cited in Lockhart, Douglas, *The Dark Side of God,* p.75 from de
    Luc, Marianus, *Institutions of Public and Eccclesiastical Law*

Chapter 13 **Torture & Suppression**

1 Hopkins, Simmans & Wallace-Murphy, *Rex Deus*, p.170
2 Barber, Malcolm, *The Trial of the Templars*, p.56
3 Nicholson, *The Knights Templar A New History*, p.217
4 Barber, Malcolm, *The Trial of the Templars*, p.57
5 Summarized from Barber, Malcolm *The Trial of the Templars*, CUP
   1978, pp.248–52
6 Charpentier, Louis, *The Mysteries of Chartres Cathedral*
7 Article *Les Templiers dans les Alpes Maritimes*, published in *Nice
   Historique*, Jan/Feb 1938
8 Currer-Briggs, Noel, *The Shroud and the Grail*

9 Garza-Valdez, Leonicio, *The DNA of God*

10 Lea, Henry Charles, *A History of the Inquisition in the Middle Ages*, 3 vols McMillan, NY 1887–89, vol. 3 p.334

11 Nicholson, Helen, *The Knights Templar, A New History*, p.207

12 Cohen, *Europe's Inner Demons*, pp.123–30

13 Papal Bull of Clement V, *Pastoralis Praeminentiae*

14 Barber, *The Trial of the Templars*, pp.193–5

15 *Ibid*, p.200

16 Wallace-Murphy, Tim, *The Templar Legacy and the Masonic Inheritance within Rosslyn Chapel*, p.22

17 Wallace-Murphy, Tim, *The Templar Legacy and the Masonic Inheritance within Rosslyn Chapel*, p.22

18 Partner, Peter, *The Knights Templar and their Myth*, p.82

19 Hopkins, Simmans & Wallace-Murphy, *Rex Deus*, p.172

20 Partner, Peter, *The Knights Templar and their Myth*, p.83

21 Ravenscroft & Wallace-Murphy, *The Mark of the Beast*, p.53

22 Nicholson, Helen, *The Knights Templar, A New History*, p.221

23 Papal Bull of Clement V, *Vox in excelso*.

24 Baigent, Michael, & Leigh, Richard, *The Temple and the Lodge*, p.84

25 Dafoe, Stephen & Butler, Alan, *The Warriors and the Bankers*

26 Seward, Desmond, *The Monks of War*, p.222 see also *Rosslyn: Guardian of the Secrets of the Holy Grail*; *Rex Deus* & *Custodians of Truth* by Tim Wallace-Murphy et al.

27 Wallace-Murphy & Hopkins, *Rosslyn: Guardian of the Secrets of the Holy Grail*, p.106

28 Robinson, John J, *Born in Blood*, pp.164–6

29 Albany, HRH Prince Michael of, *The Forgotten Monarchy of Scotland*, pp.65 & 150

30 Wallace-Murphy, Tim, *The Templar Legacy and the Masonic Inheritance within Rosslyn Chapel*, p.22

31 Hay, Fr., *The Genealogie of the St Clairs of Roslin*

Chapter 14 **Did the Order Survive?**

1 Barber, *The Trial of the Templars*, p.46

2 Baigent, Michael, & Leigh, Richard, *The Temple and the Lodge*, p. 35

3 *Ibid*, p.148

4 *Ibid*, p.149

5 *Ibid*, pp.149–50

6 *Ibid*, p.150

7 *Ibid*, p.152

8 *Ibid*, p.155

9 Wallace-Murphy & Hopkins, *Rosslyn Guardian of the Secrets of the Holy Grail*, p.7

10 Albany, HRH Prince Michael of, *The Forgotten Monarchy of Scotland* p.102

11 Foss, Michael, *Chivalry*, p.189

12 Gardner, Laurence, *Genesis of the Grail Kings*, p.225

13 Baigent, Leigh and Lincoln, *The Holy Blood and the Holy Grail*, p.106

14 Baigent & Leigh, *The Temple and the Lodge*, p.263

15 Albany, HRH Prince Michael of and Salhab, Walid Amine, *The Knights Templar of the Middle East*, p.135

16 Wallace-Murphy, Hopkins & Simmans, *Rex Deus*, p.253

17 Albany, HRH Prince Michael of, *The Forgotten Monarchy of Scotland*, p.156

Section 3 The Worldwide Propagation of Rex Deus & Templar Beliefs

1 Runciman, Steven, *A History of the Crusades*, Vol. III pp.435–6

Chapter 15 The Beliefs of Rex Deus

1 Lévi, Magnus Eliphas, *Histoire de la Magie*, A E Waite trans.

2 Begg, Ean, *The Cult of the Black Madonna*

3 The Acts of the Apostles, Ch.2, v.46

4 Wallace-Murphy, Hopkins & Simmans, *Rex Deus*, p.201

5 Revelation, Ch.6, vs.5, 7, 9, & 12; Ch.7, v.2; Ch.8, v.1; Ch.9, v.4; Ch.20, v.3

6 Genesis, Ch.14, vs.18–20

7 *Epiphanus-haeres*, lxxxviii

8 Baigent, Leigh and Lincoln, *The Holy Blood and the Holy Grail*, p.52

9   Osman, Ahmed, *Moses Pharaoh of Egypt*
10 The Gospel according to Matthew, Ch.22, vs.36–40
11 Ranke-Heinemann, Ute, *Putting Away Childish Things*, p.17
12 Charpentier, Louis, *The Mysteries of Chartres Cathedral*

Chapter 16 **An Indelible Mark on the Landscape**

1   Gettings, Fred, *The Secret Zodiac*
2   Wallace-Murphy, Tim, *The Templar Legacy and the Masonic Inheritance within Rosslyn Chapel*
3   Colfs, J, F, *La filiation généalogique de toutes les Écoles Gothiques*
4   Anderson, William, *The Rise of the Gothic*, p.39 & Boney, Jean, *French Gothic Architecture of the 12th & 13th Centuries*, p.17
5   Strachan, Gordon, *Chartres*, p.14
6   Shah, I, *The Sufis*, pp.166–93
7   Strachan, Gordon, *Chartres*, p.29
8   Ouspensky, P. D, *A New Model of the Universe*, p.345
9   Fulcanelli, *Le Mystère des Cathédrals*, p.36
10 *Ibid*, pp.39–41
11 Charpentier, Louis, *The Mysteries of Chartres Cathedral*, p.145
12 *Ibid*, p.86
13 Dunlop, Ian, *The Cathedrals Crusade*, p.6
14 Information supplied by the Provencal Templar scholar, the late Guy Jourdan,
15 *La Régle de St Devoir de Dieu et de la Croissade*
16 Charpentier, Louis, *The Mysteries of Chartres Cathedral*, p.81
17 *Ibid*, p.165
18 *Ibid*, p.81
19 *Ibid*, p.139
20 Mertz, Blanche, *Points of Cosmic Energy*, p.105
21 Delaporte, Y, *Les Trois Notre Dames de Chartres*, p.11
22 Guidebook to The Cathedral of Amiens, p.5
23 Fulcanelli, *Le Mystère des Cathédrales*, p.123
24 Wallace-Murphy & Hopkins, *Rosslyn Guardian of the Secrets of the Holy Grail*, p.176
25 Cited in the Gospel of Thomas in the *Nag Hammadi Library*, ed J Robinson

Chapter 17 – **Tracing the Beliefs of the Knights Templar**

1　Begg, Ean, *The Cult of the Black Madonna*, p.103
2　Wallace-Murphy & Hopkins, *Rosslyn: Guardian of the Secrets of the Holy Grail*, p.105
3　*Ibid*
4　*Ibid*, p.62
5　*Ibid*, pp.181–2
6　Hopkins, Simmans & Wallace-Murphy, *opus cit*, p.148
7　Godwin, Malcolm, *The Holy Grail*, p.234
8　Starbird, Margaret, *The Tarot Trumps and the Holy Grail*, p.x
9　Cavendish, Richard, *The Tarot*, p.17
10　Hopkins, Simmans & Wallace-Murphy, *Rex Deus*, p.148
11　Starbird, Margaret, *The Tarot Trumps and the Holy Grail*, p.x
12　*Ibid*, p.3
13　*Ibid*, p.5
14　Godwin, Malcolm, *The Holy Grail* p.236
15　*Ibid,* p.338
16　Baigent, Leigh & Lincoln, *The Holy Blood and the Holy Grail*, p.163
17　*Ibid*
18　Cited by Fritjof Capra in *The Turning Point*, p.410
19　Cited by Ted Roszak in *Where the Wasteland Ends*, p.154
20　Godwin, Malcolm, *The Holy Grail*, p.14
21　*Ibid*, p.16
22　Mâle, Émile, *Notre Dame de Chartres*, p.141
23　Godwin, Malcolm, *opus cit* p.12
24　*Ibid*, p.18
25　Ravenscroft & Wallace-Murphy, *The Mark of the Beast*, p.52
26　Sinclair, Andrew, *The Discovery of the Grail*, p.27
27　*Ibid*, pp.27–8
28　Godwin, Malcolm, *opus cit*, p.6
29　Campbell Joseph & Moyers, Bill, *The Power of Myth*, pp.197–200
30　Baigent, Leigh & Lincoln, *The Holy Blood and the Holy Grail*, pp.262–8
31　Published by Red Wheel Weiser in Boston, MA, USA
32　The Gospel of Thomas, from the *Nag Hammadi Library*, edited by John Robinson.
33　Campbell, Joseph & Moyers, Bill, *The Power of Myth* pp.197–200

Chapter 18 **Rosslyn Chapel & Earl William St Clair**

1 Wallace-Murphy, Tim, *The Templar Legacy and the Masonic Inheritance within Rosslyn Chapel*, p.25
2 de St Clair, L-A *Histoire Généalogique de la Famille de St Clair*
3 *Ibid*
4 Ravenscoft & Wallace-Murphy, *The Mark of the Beast*, p.64
5 Wallace-Murphy, T, *An Illustrated Guidebook to Rosslyn Chapel*, p.3
6 *Ibid*, p.3
7 Hay, Fr Augustine, *The Genealogy of the Saint Claires of Roslin*, Maidement, Scotland, 1865
8 Cited by Knight & Lomas in *The Second Messiah*, p.32
9 Wallace-Murphy, Tim, *An Illustrated Guidebook to Rosslyn Chapel*, p.6
10 Article in *Interiors* magazine, 1982
11 Article entitled, *Les Templiers dans Les-Alpes Maritime*, J-A Durbec; *Nice Historique* Jan/Feb 1938, pp.4–6
12 *Ibid*
13 Wallace-Murphy, & Hopkins, *Rosslyn: Guardian of the Secrets of the Holy Grail*, p.121
14 Masonic archives in Freemasons Hall, Edinburgh.
15 Knight and Lomas, *The Second Messiah*, p.53
16 Roszak, Theodore, *The Unfinished Animal*, p.9
17 Wallace-Murphy & Hopkins, *Rosslyn Guardian of the Secrets of the Holy Grail*, Section 3

Chapter 19 **The Craft of Freemasonry**

1 Robert Graves' Introduction to the first edition of *The Sufis* by Idris Shah
2 *Ibid*
3 Bauval, Robert & Hancock, Graham, *Keeper of Genesis*, William Heineman, London, 1996, p.203
4 *Ibid*, p.193
5 Wallace-Murphy, Tim, *An Illustrated Guidebook to Rosslyn Chapel*
6 Geddricke, 18th-century historian of Freemasonry
7 Ward, J S M, *Freemasonry and the Ancient Gods*
8 Knight and Lomas, *The Second Messiah*, p.203
9 *Ibid*, p.204

SUGGESTED FURTHER READING

A

Addison, Charles G, *The History of the Knights Templars*, Black Books, 1995

Ahmed, Rollo, *The Black Art,* Senate Books, Taiwan, 1971

Albany, HRH Prince Michael of, & Akbar, S W Ahmed, *Discovering Islam*, Routledge, London, 2002

Albany, HRH Prince Michael of, *The Forgotten Monarchy of Scotland*, Element Books, 1998

Albany, HRH Prince Michael of, & Salhab, Walid Amine, *The Knights Templar of the Middle East*, RedWheel/Weiser, 2006

Allegro, J M, *The Dead Sea Scrolls and the Christian Myth*, Abacus, London, 1981

Allegro, John, *The Dead Sea Scrolls*, Penguin, 1964

Allen, Grant, *The Evolution of the Idea of God*, Watts, 1931

Ambelain, Robert, *Jesus ou le Mortel Sécret des Templiers*, Robert Lafont, 1970

Anon., *Secret Societies of the Middle Ages*, R A Kessinger publishing Co, 2003

Anderson, William, *The Rise of the Gothic*, Hutchinson, London, 1985

Armstrong, Karen, *A History of God*, Mandarin, London, 1994

Armstrong, Karen, *A History of Jerusalem*, HarperCollins, 1996

Armstrong, Karen, *Muhammad*, HarperCollins, San Francisco, 1993

Aué, Michèle, *Cathar Country*, MSM, 1995

B

Baigent, Michael, & Leigh, Richard, *The Dead Sea Scrolls Deception*, Corgi, 1992

Baigent, Michael, & Leigh, Richard, *The Inquisition*, Penguin, 1999

Baigent, Michael, & Leigh, Richard, *The Temple and the Lodge*, Corgi, 1992

Baigent, Leigh & Lincoln, *The Holy Blood and the Grail*, Jonathan Cape, 1982

Barber, Malcolm, *The Cathars*, Pearson Education Ltd, 2000

Barber, Malcolm, *The New Knighthood*, CUP, 1994

Barber, Malcolm, 'Supplying the Crusader States', Article reprinted in *Crusaders and Heretics, Twelfth to Fourteenth centuries,* Malcolm Barber, ed., (Variorum, 1995)

Barber, Malcolm, *The Trial of the Templars,* CUP, 1994

Barnavi, Levi, *A Historical Atlas of the Jewish People,* Hutchinson, 1992

Bauval, Robert, & Gilbert, Adrian, *The Orion Mystery,* Heinemann, 1994

Bauval, R, & Hancock, G, *Keeper of Genesis,* William Heinemann, London, 1996

Bede, *A History of the English Church and People,* Penguin, 1978

Begg, Ean, *The Cult Of The Black Virgin,* Arkana, 1985

Beinhart, Haim, *Atlas of Medieval Jewish History,* Robert Lafont, 1970

Birks, Norman, & Gilbert, R A, *The Treasure of Montségur,* The Aquarian Press, 1990

Bordonove, Georges, *La vie quotidienne des Templiers,* Hachette, 1975

Bridge, Anthony, *The Crusades,* Granada, London, 1980

Bright, Simon, *In Search of the Knights Templar,* Weidenfeld & Nicolson, London, 2006

Bruno, S T, *Templar Organization,* (Privately published)

Bull, Marcus, *Knightly Piety and the Lay Response to the First Crusade,* OUP, 1993

Burman, Edward, *The Inquisition: The Hammer of Heresy,* Aquarian Press, 1984

Burman, Edward, *The Templars, Knights of God,* Destiny Books, Rochester VT, 1990

Bussel, F W, *Religious Thought and Heresy in the Middle Ages,* Robert Scott, London, 1918

C

Campbell, Joseph, & Moyers, Bill, *The Power of Myth,* Doubleday, 1990

Cannon, Dolores, *Jesus and the Essenes,* Gateway Books, 1992

Cantor, N, *The Sacred Chain – A History of the Jews,* Fontana, London, 1996

Cavendish, Richard, *The Tarot,* Bounty Books, 1986

Charpentier, Louis, *The Mysteries of Chartres Cathedral,* RILKO, 1993

Charpentier, Louis, *Les Mystères Templiers,* Lafont, 1993

Christie-Murray, David, *A History of Heresy*, OUP, 1989

Cohen, *Europe's Inner Demons*, Pimlico, 1993

Colfs, J F, *La filiation généalogique de toutes les Ecoles Gothiques*, Baudry, 1884

Costen, Michael, *The Cathars and the Albigensian Crusade*, Manchester University Press, 1997

Crossan, John Dominic, *Jesus – a Revolutionary Biography*, Harper Collins, 1994

Currer-Briggs, Noel, *The Shroud and the Grail*, Weidenfeld and Nicholson, 1987

D

Dafoe, Stephen, & Butler, Alan, *The Warriors and the Bankers*, Templar Books, Canada, 1998

De la Croix, Arnaud, *Les Templiers*, Editions du Rocher, Monaco, 2002

Delange, Nicholas, *Atlas of the Jewish World*, Guild Publishing, London, 1984

Delaporte, Y, *Les Trois Notre Dames de Chartres*, E Houvet, Chartres, 1996

Delclos, Marie, & Caradeau, Jean-Luc, *L'Ordre du Temple*, Trajectionne, Paris, 2005

de Lubicz, Rene Schwaller, *Sacred Science*, Inner Traditions International, 1988

de Rosa, Peter, *Vicars of Christ*, Corgi, 1989

de Serres, L L Borelli, *Les Variations monétaires sous Philippe le Bel*, Chalon-sur-Saône, 1902

Desgris, Alain, *L'Ordre de Templiers et la Chevalerie Macconique Templière*, Guy Trédaniel, 1995

de Vries, Simon, *Cathars, Country, Customs and Castles*, Comtal Press, 1993

Doresse, Jean, *Les Livres Secrets des Gnostiques d'Egypte*, Librairie Plon, Paris, 1958

Dowley, Tim, (ed), *The History of Christianity*, Lion Publishing, Herts, 1977

Dubos, Rene, *A God Within*, Abacus/Sphere, 1976

Dunford, Barry, *The Holy Land of Scotland*, Sacred Connections, 1982

Dunlop, Ian, *The Cathedrals Crusade*, Hamish-Hamilton, 1982

E

Eisenman, Robert, *The Dead Sea Scrolls and the First Christians*, Element, 1996

Eisenman, Robert, *James the Brother of Jesus*, Faber and Faber, 1997

Eisenman, Robert, *Maccabbis, Zadokites, Christians and Qumraan*, E J Brill, 1983

Eisenman, Robert, & Wise, Michael, *The Dead Sea Scrolls Uncovered*, Element, 1992

Elder, Isabel Hill, *Celt, Druid & Culdee*, Covenant Publishing Co. Ltd, 1994

Elkington, David, *In the Name of the Gods*, Green Man Press, 2001

Eusebius, *Ecclesiastical History*

Epstein, Isadore, *Judaism*, Penguin, 1964

F

Faulkner, Neil, *Apocalypse – the Great Jewish Revolt against Rome, AD 66–73*, Tempus Publishing Ltd, 2002

Faulkner, R, *The Ancient Egyptian Book of the Dead*, British Museum Press, London, 1972

Feather, R, *The Copper Scroll Decoded*, Thorsons, London, 1999

Fisher, H A L, *A History of Europe*, Edward Arnold & Co, 1936

Fletcher, Richard, *The Cross and the Crescent*, Allen Lane, Penguin, London, 2003

Forbes-Leith, *The Scots Men-at-Arms and Life Guards in France*, Edinburgh, 1882

Foss, Michael, *Chivalry*, Michael Joseph, 1975

Fossier, Robert (ed), *The Middle Ages*, 3 Vols., CUP, 1989

Fox, Robin Lane, *Pagans and Christians*, Penguin, 1988

Fox, Robin Lane, *The Unauthorised Version: Truth and Fiction in the Bible*, Penguin, 1991

Franke & Cawthorne, *The Tree of Life and the Holy Grail*, T Lodge, 1996

Frazer, James, *The Golden Bough*, Wordsworth Editions, 1993

Freud, S, *Moses and Monotheism*, London 1939

Fulcanelli, *Le Mystère des Cathédrales*, Neville Spearman, 1977

G

Gardner, Laurence, *Bloodline of the Holy Grail*, Element Books, 1995

Gardner, Laurence, *Genesis of the Grail Kings*, Bantam, 1999

Garza-Valdes, Leonicio, *The DNA of God?* Hodder & Stoughton, 1998

Gettings, Fred, *The Secret Zodiac*, Routledge, Keegan & Paul, London 1987

Gibbon, Edward, *The Decline and Fall of the Roman Empire*, 8 Vols, The Folio Society, 2001

Gimpell, Jean, *The Cathedral Builders*, Cresset, 1988

Glover, T R, *The Conflict of Religions in the Early Roman Empire*, R A Kessinger, 2003

Godwin, Malcolm, *The Holy Grail*, Bloomsbury, 1994

Golb, Norman, *Who Wrote the Dead Sea Scrolls?* Simon & Schuster, 1996

Goodwin, Godfrey, *Islamic Spain*, Chronicle Books, 2000

Graffin, Robert, *L'Art Templier des Cathédrales*, Garnier, 1993

Gruber, Elmer R, & Kersten, Holger, *The Original Jesus*, Element, 1995

Guébin & Moisoineuve, *Histoire Albigeoise de Pierre des Vaux-de-Cernay*, Paris, 1951

Guillaume, Alfred, *Islam*, Penguin, London, 1956

Guirdham, Arthur, *The Great Heresy*, C W Daniel, Saffron Walden, 1993

H

Halam, Elizabeth (ed.), *The Chronicles of the Crusades*, Bramley Books, 1997

Hamill, John & Gilbert, *World Freemasonry*, Aquarian Press, 1991

Hamilton, B, *The Albigensian Crusade*, The Historical Association, London, 1974

Hancock, Graham, *The Sign and the Seal*, Mandarin Paperbacks, 1993

Hassnain, Prof. Fida, *A Search for the Historical Jesus*, Gateway Books, 1994

Hattstein, Marcus, & Delius, Peter (eds) *Islam Art & Architecture*, Könemann, Cologne, 2000

Hay, Fr., *The Genealogie of the St Clairs of Roslin*, Maidement, Edinburgh, 1835

Hodgekin, T, *The Barbarian Invasion of the Roman Empire*, 3 Vols, The Folio Society, 2001

Holmes, George (ed.), *The Oxford Illustrated History of Medieval Europe*, OUP, 1988

Hopkins, Marilyn, *The Enigma of the Templars*, Disinformation, 2007

I

Ibn al Qalnis, *Continuation of the Chronicle of Damascus: the Damascus Chronicle of the Crusades*, H A R Gibb trans., London, 1932

J

Jackson, J, *The Chivalry of Scotland in the Days of Robert the Bruce*,

Jackson, Keith B, *Beyond the Craft*, Lewis Masonic, 1982

James, Bruno S, *St Bernard of Clairvaux*, Hodder and Stoughton, London, 1957

Jedin, Hubert (ed.), *The History of the Church*, Vol 1. Burns and Oats, 1989

Jennings, Hargrave, *The Rosicrucians – Their Rites and Mysteries*, Chatto & Windus, London, 1879

Johnson, Paul, *A History of Christianity*, Weidenfeld and Nicolson, London, 1978

Johnson, Kenneth Rayner, *The Fulcanelli Phenomenon*, Neville Spearman, London, 1980

Josephus, *The Antiquities of the Jews* and *The Wars of the Jews*, Nimmo, 1869

K

Kersten, H, & Gruber, E R, *The Jesus Conspiracy*, Element, 1994

Knight, Chris, & Lomas, Robert, *The Hiram Key*, Century, 1996

Knight, Chris, & Lomas, Robert, *The Second Messiah*, Century, 1997

Knoup, James, *The Genesis of Freemasonry*, Manchester University Press, 1947

Knowles, D, *Christian Monasticism*, Weidenfeld & Nicolson, 1969

L

Lacroix, P, *Military and Religious Life in the Middle Ages,* Chapman & Hall, 1874

Lamy, Michel, *Les Templiers:Ces Grand Seigneurs aux Blanc Manteaux,* Bordeux 1997

Lea, H C, *The Inquisition in the Middle Ages*, NY, 1955

Lees, B A, *Records of the Templars in England in the Twelfth Century,* OUP, 1935

Leroy, Thierry, *Hugues de Payns, Chevalier Champenois, Fondateur de L'Ordre des Templiers*, Editions de la Maison du Boulanger, 2003

Lévi, Eliphas, *The Key of The Mysteries*, Rider & Co., 1969

Lizerand, *Le Dossier de l'Affaire des Templiers*, Axiom, 1980

Lockhart, Douglas, *The Dark Side of God*, Element, 1999

Lockhart, Douglas, *Jesus the Heretic*, Element, 2000

Lost Books of the Bible, The, Gramercy Books, 1980

M

Mack, Burton L, *The Lost Gospel*, Element, 1993

Macintosh, Christopher, *The Rosicrucians*, Crucible, Thorensons, 1987

Mackenzie, Kenneth, *The Royal Masonic Cyclopedia*, Aquarian Press, 1987

Mâle, Emile, *Notre Dame de Chartres*, Flammarion, 1983

Malmes, *History of the Kings,* J Sharp trans., George Bell and Sons, London, 1904

Martin, Sean, *The Knights Templar, The History and Myths of the Legendary Military Order*, Pocket Essentials, 2004

Mathews, John, *The Grail Tradition*, Element Books, 1990

Matrasso, Pauline (trans.), *The Quest of the Holy Grail*, Penguin Classics, 1977

McManners, John (ed.), *The Oxford History of Christianity*, OUP, 1993

Mertz, Blanche, *Points of Cosmic Energy*, C W Daniel, 1995

Miller, Malcolm, *Chartres Cathedral*, Pitkin Pictorials, 1992

Moore, L David, *The Christian Conspiracy*, Pendulum Press, 1983

Moore, R I, *The Formation of a Persecuting Society*, Basil Blackwell & Co., Oxford, 1990

Murray, David Christie, *The History of Heresy*, OUP, 1976

N

Nicholson, Helen, *The Knights Templar, a New History*, Sutton Publishing, 2004

Nicholson, Helen, & Nicolle, David, *Gods' Warriors*, Osprey Publishing, Oxford, 2005

O

Oldenbourg, Zoé, *Massacre at Montségur*, Phoenix, 1999

Orton, Previte, *Outlines of Medieval History*, Biblo and Tannen Booksellers and Publishers, 1904

O'Shea, Stephen, *The Perfect Heresy*, Profile Books Ltd, 2000

Osman, Ahmed, *Moses Pharaoh of Egypt*, Paladin, 1991

Ouspensky, P D, *A New Model of The Universe*, London, 1931

P

Parfitt, Will, *The Living Quaballah*, Element Books, 1988

Partner, Peter, *The Knights Templar and their Myth*, Destiny Books, 1990

Philips, Graham, *The Moses Legacy*, Sidgewick & Jackson, London, 2002

Picknett & Prince, *The Templar Revelation*, Bantam, 1997

Picknet & Prince, *Turin Shroud: In Whose Image?*, Bloomsbury, 1994

Powell, Mark Allen, *The Jesus Debate*, Lion Publishing, 1998

Prawer, Joshua, *The Latin Kingdom of Jerusalem*, Weidenfeld & Nicolson, 1972

Q

Querido, René, *The Golden Age of Chartres*, Floris Books, Edinburgh, 1987

Querido, René, *The Masters of Chartres*, Floris Books, Edinburgh, 1987

Querido, René, *The Mystery of the Holy Grail*, Rudolf Steiner College, 1991

R

Ranke-Heninemann, Ute, *Putting Away Childish Things*, HarperCollins, 1995

Ravenscroft, Trevor, *The Cup of Destiny*, Samuel Weiser, 1982

Ravenscroft, Trevor, *The Spear of Destiny*, Samuel Weiser, 1982

Ravenscroft, Trevor, & Wallace-Murphy, Tim, *The Mark of The Beast*, Sphere Books, London, 1990

Read, Piers Paul, *The Templars*, Wiedenfeld & Nicholson, 1999

Regan, Geoffrey, *Lionhearts: Saladin and Richard I*, Constable, London, 1998

Regne, J, *Etudes sur la Condition des Juifs de Narbonn*, Lafitte Reprints, Marseilles, 1981

Reznikov, Raymonde, *Cathars et Templiers*, Editions Loubatières, 1993

Richardson, Peter, *Herod, King of the Jews and Friend of the Romans*, University of South Carolina Press, 1996

Riley-Smith, Jonathan, *The First Crusade and the Idea of Crusading*, London, Athlone Press, 1986

Robinson, James M, (ed.), *The Nag-Hammadi Library*, HarperCollins, 1990

Robinson, John J, *Born in Blood*, Arrow Books, 1993

Robinson, John J, *Dungeon, Fire and Sword*, Brock Hampton Press, 1999

Roth, Cecil, *A Short History of the Jewish People*, East West Library, London, 1953

Runciman, Stephen, *A History of the Crusades*, 3 vols, Pelican, 1971

S

Saige, G, *Les Juifs du Languedoc*, Greg International, Farnborough, 1991

Schein, Silvia, *Fideles Crucis, The Papacy, the West and the Recovery of the Holy Land 1274–1314*, OUP, 1991

Schonfield, Hugh, *The Essene Odyssey*, Element, 1985

Schonfield, Hugh, *The Pentecost Revolution*, Element, 1985

Schonfield, Hugh, *The Passover Plot*, Element, 1985

Serrus, Georges, *The Land of the Cathars*, Editions Loubatières, 1990

Seward, Desmond, *The Monks of War*, The Folio Society, 1991

Shah, Idries, *The Sufis,* Jonathan Cape & Co., 1969

Sinclair, Andrew, *The Discovery of the Grail*, Century, 1998

Sizekely, E B, *Essene Teaching from Enoch to the Dead Sea Scrolls*, C W Daniel, 1978

Smail, R C, *Crusading Warfare 1097–1193*, CUP, 1956

Smith, Morton, *The Secret Gospel*, Aquarian Press, 1985

St Clair, L-A de, *Histoire Genealogique de la Famille de St Clair*, Paris, 1905

Starbird, Margaret, *The Tarot Trumps and the Holy Grail*, WovenWord Press, 2000

Starbird, Margaret, *The Woman with the Alabaster Jar*, Bear & Co., 1993

Stevenson, David, *The First Freemasons*, Aberdeen University Press, 1989

Stourm, *Notre Dame d'Amiens*, Hachette, 1960

Stoyanov, Yuri, *The Hidden Tradition in Europe*, Arkana, 1994

Strachan, Gordon, *Chartres*, Floris Books, 2003

T

Taylor, Joan E, *The Immerser, John the Baptist in Second Temple Judaism*, Wm B Eerdmans Publishing Co., 1997

Thiering, Barbara, *Jesus the Man*, Corgi, 1992

Thurston, Herbert (trans.), *Memorandum of P. D'Arcis*, the original document is in the Bibliotheque Nationale in Paris among the Collection de Champagne, vol. 154, Folio 138.

Trevor-Roper, Hugh, *The Rise of Christian Europe*, Thames and Hudson, 1965

U

Upton-Ward, J M, *The Rule of The Templars*, Boydell Press, 1992

V

VandenBroeck, Andre; *Al-Kemi*, Lindisfarne Press, 1987

Vermes, Geza, *Jesus the Jew*, Augsburg Fortress Publishing, 1981

W

Waite, A E, *The Holy Kabbalah*, Oracle, 1996

Wakefield, Walter, & Evans, Austin P, *Heresies of Middle Ages*, Columbia University Press, 1991

Wallace-Murphy, Tim, *Cracking the Symbol Code*, Watkins, 2005

Wallace-Murphy, Tim, *The Enigma of the Freemasons*, Disinformation co., 2006

Wallace-Murphy, Tim, *An Illustrated Guide Book To Rosslyn Chapel*, The Friends of Rosslyn, 1993

Wallace-Murphy, Tim, *The Templar Legacy and the Masonic Inheritance Within Rosslyn Chapel*, The Friends of Rosslyn, 1994

Wallace-Murphy, Tim, *What Islam Did For Us*, Watkins, 2006

Wallace-Murphy, Tim, & Hopkins, Marilyn, *Custodians of Truth*, RedWheel/Wesieser, 2004

Wallace-Murphy, Tim, & Hopkins, Marilyn, *Rosslyn Guardian of the Secrets of the Holy Grail*, Element Books, 1999

Wallace-Murphy, Tim, Hopkins, Marilyn, & Simmans, G, *Rex Deus*, Element Books, 2000

Wakefield & Evans, *Heresies of the Middle Ages*, Columbia University Press, 1991

Ward, Colin, *Chartres: The Making of a Miracle*, Folio Society, 1986

Ward, J S M, *Freemasonry and the Ancient Gods*, R A Kessinger and Co, 1996

Welburn, Andrew, *The Beginnings of Christianity*, Floris, 1991

Wilson, A N, *Jesus*, HarperCollins, 1993

Wilson, A N, *Paul, the Mind of the Apostle*, Pimlico, 1998

Wilson, Colin (Ed.), *Men of Mystery*, W H Allen, London, 1977

Wilson, Colin, *The Occult*, Grafton Books, 1979

Woods, Richard, *Understanding Mysticism*, Doubleday/Image, 1980

Wright, Esmond, *The Medieval and Renaissance World*, Hamlyn, 1979

Z

Zuckerman, A J, *A Jewish princedom in Feudal France 768–900*, Columbia University Press, 1972

INDEX

PICTURE CREDITS

Pictures 5–7, 9–10, 12–14, 23–34 All courtesy of Tim Wallace-Murphy

1 Departing for the Crusades. Illustration from *Histoire de France* by Jules Michelet (1798-1874) c.1900 (colour litho), Bombled, Louis (1862-1927)/Private Collection, Archives Charmet/The Bridgeman Art Library.

2 St Bernard of Clairvaux (c.1090-1153) from the Crypt of St. Peter (mosaic) (detail), Italian School, (15th century)/St Peter's, Vatican, Rome, Italy/The Bridgeman Art Library.

3 Institution of the Order of the Templars in 1128, 1840 (oil on canvas), Granet, Francois-Marius (1775-1849)/Chateau de Versailles, France, Lauros/Giraudon/ The Bridgeman Art Library.

4 Courtesy of Arqua.

8 Pilgrims under escort of Knights Templar in front of Jerusalem in the 12th century (engraving), English School, (19th century)/Private Collection, Ken Welsh/ The Bridgeman Art Library.

11 Courtesy of Richard Buades.

15 Saladin's army surround the crusaders. Illustration from *Bibliothèque des Croisades* by J-F. Michaud, 1877 (litho) by Dore, Gustave(1832-83)© Private Collection/ Ken Welsh/The Bridgeman Art Library.

16 Saladin in Jerusalem. c.1830-50 (oil on canvas) by Fragonard, Alexandre Evariste (1780-1850) © Musée des Beaux-Arts, Quimper, France/Giraudon/ The Bridgeman Art Library.

17 Decorated tile with roundels of Richard I (1151-99) and Saladin (1137-93), from the Benedictine Abbey at Chertsey, Surrey, 13th century (ceramic) © British Museum, London, UK/The Bridgeman Art Library.

18 Guillaume de Clermont defending Ptolemais (Acre) in 1291. Oil on canvas by Papety, Dominique Louis (1815-49) © Chateau de Versailles, France/Lauros/ Giraudon/The Bridgeman Art Library.

19 Jacques de Molay (c.1243-1314) Master of the Knights Templars (engraving) (b/w photo) by French School © Bibliothèque Nationale, Paris, France/Giraudon/ The Bridgeman Art Library.

20 Burning of the Templar leaders. Illustration from *L'Histoire de France* by Jules Michelet (1798-1874) (engraving) (b/w photo) by Vierge, Daniel Urrabieta (1851-1904) © Bibliothèque Nationale, Paris, France/Lauros/Giraudon/ The Bridgeman Art Library.

21 Templars before Philippe le Bel and Clement V. From The Chronicles of France (vellum) by Boucicaut Master, (fl.1390-1430) (and workshop) © British Library, London, UK/The Bridgeman Art Library.

22 The Black Madonna. © Musée Crozatier, Le Puy-en-Velay, France/Giraudon/ The Bridgeman Art Library.